For a Significant Social Psychology

For a Significant Social Psychology

The Collected Writings of M. Brewster Smith

M. Brewster Smith

FOREWORD BY GEOFFREY MARUYAMA

New York University Press

NEW YORK AND LONDON

NEW YORK UNIVERSITY PRESS
New York and London
www.nyupress.org

Library of Congress Cataloging-in-Publication Data
Smith, M. Brewster (Mahlon Brewster), 1919–
For a significant social psychology :
the collected writings of M. Brewster Smith.
p. cm.
Includes bibliographical references and index.
ISBN 0-8147-9822-5 (cloth : alk. paper) —
ISBN 0-8147-9823-3 (pbk. : alk. paper)
1. Social psychology. 2. Personality and culture. I. Title.

HM1033.S62 2003
302—dc21   2003053995

New York University Press books are printed on acid-free paper,
and their binding materials are chosen for strength and durability.

Manufactured in the United States of America

10 9 8 7 6 5 4 3 2 1

Contents

Acknowledgments

The chapters originally appeared in the following books or journals. In each case, permission to reprint my copyrighted material is gratefully acknowledged.

Chapter 1: "The shaping of American social psychology: A personal perspective from the periphery," *Personality and Social Psychology Bulletin*, (1983), 9 (3), 165–180. Copyright © 1983 by Sage Publications, Inc. Reprinted by permission of Sage Publications, Inc.

Chapter 2: "Quest for power," review of E. Herman, *The romance of American psychology: Political culture in the age of experts*, (1995), Berkeley: University of California Press, in *Readings: A Journal of Reviews and Commentary in Mental Health*, (1996), 11 (2), 4–7. Copyright © 1996 by American Orthopsychiatry Association, Inc. Reprinted with permission.

Chapter 3: "*The American Soldier* and its critics: What survives the attack on positivism?", *Social Psychology Quarterly*, (1984), 47 (2), 192–198. Copyright © 1984 by M. Brewster Smith.

Chapter 4: "A forgotten classic: Murphy's Integrative view of personality," review of G. Murphy, *Personality: A biosocial approach to origins and structure*, (1947), *Contemporary Psychology*, (1995), 40, 631–633. Copyright © 1995 by the American Psychological Association. Reprinted with permission.

Chapter 5: "Personology Launched," review of H. A. Murray et al., *Explorations in personality*, (1938), New York: Oxford University Press, in *Contemporary Psychology*, (1990), 35, 537–539. Copyright © 1996 by the American Psychological Association. Reprinted with permission.

Chapter 6: "Beyond Aristotle and Galileo: Toward a contextualized psychology of persons," *Theoretical and Philosophical Psychology* 8 (2) (1988), 2–15. Copyright © 1988 by Division 24, Theoretical and Philosophical Psychology, American Psychological Association. Reprinted with permission.

(1979), *Political Psychology*, 1 (2), 82–86. Copyright © 1979 by the International Society of Political Psychology. Reprinted by permission of Blackwell Publishing.

Chapter 19: "Psychology and truth: Human science and the postmodern challenge," *Interamerican Journal of Psychology*, 30 (2), (1996). 145–158. Copyright © 1996 by the InterAmerican Society of Psychology. Reprinted by permission.

Foreword

Imagine that you had the opportunity to participate at the forefront of the field of psychology generally and social psychology in particular for more than 60 years, and that at the end of that time you decided to look back at those 60 years and reflect upon them and the accomplishments and changes that had occurred. And imagine that the product of those reflections was a book, made up primarily of your previous writings, but linked to present events in the world as well as to current trends in the discipline of social psychology. And that you threaded through that book your critiques of the field and its directions, along with your analysis of the prominent accomplishments, plus your hopes for the future of social psychology. What a great resource you would leave for colleagues!

And yet, what are the chances that at the beginning of the twenty-first century a prominent social psychologist would remain engaged enough to provide such a perspective, and ambitious enough to undertake the writing of a book? Particularly one whose personal history goes back to before World War II and includes being a student of Gordon Allport and being influenced heavily by people like Henry Murray, Gardner Murphy, Kurt Lewin, Otto Klineberg, and Muzafer Sherif. One who was editor of the *Journal of Abnormal and Social Psychology* *before* it split into the *Journal of Abnormal Psychology* and the *Journal of Personality and Social Psychology*. And one whose academic history includes stops at Harvard, Vassar, NYU, UC Berkeley, the University of Chicago, and UC Santa Cruz. And whose work experiences included research during World War II that resulted in co-authorship of *The American Soldier* and that included stints working for the Social Science Research Council. And who just happened to spend five terms on the American Psychological Association Board of Directors, as well as being its president, not to mention being president of APA Divisions 24 (Philosophical and Theoretical Psychology) and 32 (Humanistic Psychology), of the Western Psychological Association, and of Psychologists for Social Responsibility. Oh, and, by the way, an individual who spent five years as vice chancellor for social sciences at UC Santa Cruz. Well, at this point the universe of possible answers has been narrowed down to one individual, M. Brewster Smith.

As probably is obvious by now, the answer is that it has happened, and the book described in this foreword is the book that provides that perspective. Before I describe the contents of the book in more detail, I should note that I left out one additional piece of history that I, as immediate past-president of the Society for the Psychological Study of Social Issues (SPSSI), view as particularly important. That is that throughout his career, Brewster has been actively involved in SPSSI and its issues, an involvement that he describes as manifesting "the Lewinian integration of social science and social action that it represents."

Brewster's involvement in SPSSI issues includes being a signatory of the 1952 social science statement that was an amicus brief for the *Brown v. Board of Education* landmark school desegregation decision. That brief, cited by the Court in its decision, marks the first occasion where social science research was used to influence federal judicial policy. Prior to that time, he gave expert witness testimony in the Richmond, Virginia, federal desegregation court case; the case was one of five cases that were combined into *Brown v. Board of Education*. As a result of such activities, Brewster, along with many other early SPSSI members, was a target of McCarthyism (see chapter 11).

Brewster's formal SPSSI service included being editor of the *Journal of Social Issues* in the early 1950s, president in 1958–1959; SPSSI representative to APA Council in the early 1990s, and serving as SPSSI's historian from 1996 to 1999. It was through his involvement with SPSSI in the 1990s that I got to know Brewster and more fully appreciate the wealth of knowledge that he possesses. His knowledge is coupled with a common-sense approach that is reflected in the book. On SPSSI Council, he was a voice of reason.

It is a great privilege to be asked to write a foreword to this book, for I greatly admire Brewster's work and accomplishments. But even more important, this book is just plain interesting. In an engaging way, it articulates the view that it is time to reexamine social psychology as it has evolved, and to move back to a more general orientation that addresses meaningful issues. I imagine that it will provide fodder for exciting and perhaps even healthily contentious proseminars.

Briefly, the book has four parts. Each one includes past writings by Brewster plus new reflections that provide a current context for the writings. The first looks at the field(s) of personality and social psychology, in part focusing on the fragmentation of the field into subspecialties that he argues has lessened the broad knowledge that has come from the field. The second focuses on self-awareness as it has been viewed in both personality and social psychology. The third examines the tension between providing knowledge that is practically useful with that which is conceptually important. The fourth looks at the effects of postmodernism on psychology and on the significance of its contributions.

Ironically, Brewster describes himself as out of tune with mainstream social psychology. That sentiment almost certainly resonates with many colleagues, as it does with me, and encourages us to persist in the hope that we might someday have an impact that approaches his. He attributes his being out of step with the mainstream to his being instilled with an enduring regard for interdisciplinary approaches plus a strong appreciation for ideas like Lewin's on action research. Those perspectives kept him reflective and critical in constructive ways. For example, his "significant" social psychology is inherently interdisciplinary, scientific in its respect for empirical evidence, innovative in its capacity to construct facts and knowledge from phenomena that are not observable, socially relevant, and humanistic.

Readings in Part I give readers the flavor of social psychology and personality at the middle of the twentieth century. For example, it includes a look at early work under the leadership of Carl Hovland on persuasive communication research. That work has blossomed and shaped the thinking of those who study topics like marketing and consumer behavior, not to mention its role in international relations. The section wraps back into an agenda for personality theory.

Part II, focused on the self, exposes Brewster's qualitative work in personality. The work reflects the breadth of his interests and methods, as well as the stronger links that occurred across subareas of psychology back then. It includes his early exemplification of idiographic psychodynamics and his later focus on the centrality of self-conscious reflexiveness and accommodation to the emerging salience of the narrativist approach (personal stories as the essence of identity). These perspectives attend to historical, cultural, and situational contexts. For me, his attention to hopelessness gets to the core of challenges we face today. How can individuals feel secure and in control of their lives when random, unpredictable events can befall anyone? How does living in today's world shape the dispositions of individuals?

Hopelessness provides a nice transition into Part III, which focuses on the role of social scientists in helping to bring about positive social change. No social issues are more important now than the "three Ps" he discusses, Poverty, Prejudice, and Peace. It seems to me that those issues today are closely knit; extreme Poverty is likely an antecedent of hopelessness, which in turn makes individuals more susceptible to influence by groups that harbor strong Prejudices against others. Those groups are more likely to act out their prejudices in acts of violence against outgroups. If such processes occur, Poverty and Prejudice are major obstacles to Peace. Because Peace has been a major focus of Brewster's, he examines wars from World War II to the "War on Terrorism." As part of his latter analyses, he notes the struggles faced by dissenters when they try to articulate positions that go "against" patriotism. In this section Brewster also touches in two chapters on a thorny issue facing diverse societies: Are different values really equally acceptable and valued, and can individuals truly respect others who hold values that they don't accept or even respect? His writings illustrate the types of value conflicts that can occur. In addition, in Part III he notes the field's progress in studying prejudice and discrimination and its impact on *Brown v. Board of Education.*

Part IV is Brewster's "look back," his chance to focus on major movements in psychology—behaviorism, positivism, humanism—that shaped psychology, and to tease them apart in instances where they have been intertwined. He also takes on postmodernism, which he views as undermining inquiry and practice. Finally, in closing, he returns to issues of a significant social psychology, which deals critically and respectfully with empirical evidence, is relevant to current realities, and is sensitive to criticisms without losing hope about our science. I hope readers agree with me that the issues are the big ones, the approaches well thought out and defended, and the reflections valuable if controversial. If nothing else, it should challenge us to be sure that we are continuing to create the significant social psychology that Brewster knows we are capable of creating.

GEOFFREY MARUYAMA
Professor, Educational Psychology, University of Minnesota; President 2001–2002, Society for the Psychological Study of Social Issues.

Introduction

In my ninth decade, I have the advantage of wide participant observation in psychology over a span of more than a half century. Mine was a fortunate cohort, since I could get sufficiently launched in psychology before World War II to function as a psychologist during the war, and then emerge equipped to ride the postwar surge of academic expansion. Early on, I became committed to the juncture of "personality and social psychology" as exemplified by Gordon Allport, Gardner Murphy, and Kurt Lewin before midcentury. Like them, I wanted psychology not only to yield scientific understanding but also to apply to the amelioration of social problems and the improvement of human life. I joined the Society for the Psychological Study of Social Issues (SPSSI) at my earliest opportunity, and continue to identify with the Lewinian integration of social science and social action that it represents.

Involvement as graduate student and then junior faculty in Harvard's short-lived interdisciplinary Department of Social Relations just after World War II, and service as staff at the Social Science Research Council not long thereafter instilled in me a lasting regard for interdisciplinary approaches, at least as they extend to psychology, sociology, anthropology, and political science, which occupy substantially overlapping territories. And as the son of an English professor, I have felt open to the humanistic tradition of literature and history, and wanted psychology to join in the deepening of our reflective appreciation of human experience.

So I have aspired to an interdisciplinary social psychology that is scientific in its respect for empirical evidence and its use of ingenious tactics to construct facts and interpretations that are substantially constrained by things as they are in human relations and experience. I have wanted to contribute to a discipline that can be applied to social issues in our time, an era that has seemed to me continuously and increasingly critical for the survival and welfare of humankind and its natural environment. I have wanted it also to be humanistic in its concern for human experience and for the precarious standing of human values.

In these respects I have been out of tune with principal trends in American social psychology during the half century of my participation. Although social psychology and personality remain formally linked in the Society for Personality and Social Psychology (Division 8 of the American Psychological Association), their association has long been tenuous and strained. My social psychological colleagues at the University of California at Santa Cruz tend to regard any reference to personality traits and dispositions as inherently tainted by Lee Ross's (1977) "fundamental attribution error." In my institutional setting, faculty interested in personality are more comfortably at home with the developmental psychologists.

Interdisciplinary concerns have withered in the general tide of increased specialization, so that even though a parallel subfield of social psychology thrives in sociology, psychological social psychologists have little intellectual contact with it. As a specialized area, social psychological science has made considerable progress in its research methods and in the clarification of selected problems, but, as has been frequently noted (recently by Just & Kruglanski, 2002), its focus on narrow issues has yielded less overall progress than might have resulted if there had been more investment in attempts at broader integration. The prevailing academic culture that has involved competition for research grants and for tenure, based heavily on the number of refereed publications, continues to accentuate this problem.

Humanistic psychology as an ideological movement that still bears marks of its origins in the "hippie" '60s remains isolated from academic psychology, even though strong parallels can be found between the recent handbooks of humanistic psychology (Schneider et al., 2001) and "positive psychology" (Snyder & Lopez, 2002), the latter firmly anchored in the mainstream, though it is a divergent, protesting current. But the conflictual polarity between the psychological approaches of interpretative, historical humanism and explanatory, empirical science—long ago tagged by Dilthey (1976) as *Geisteswissenschaften* vs. *Naturwissenschaften*—seems to have been only exacerbated by the impact of "postmodern" constructionism in its more antiscientific variants (e.g., Gergen, 1992). Dissidents within social psychology have found themselves more akin to the humanities than to the hard sciences and the social sciences that they identify with a now rejected positivism. To be scientific and humanistic requires bucking the current tide. I am encouraged by recent attempts to bridge or transcend the gap: Just and Kruglanski's (2002) venture from the stronghold of experimental social psychology and Fishman's (1999) pragmatic psychology from the standpoint of clinical and educational practice. But these have yet to turn the tide.

The application of scientific psychology to social issues, in the style of SPSSI, has fared better in recent years, maybe in part because of the increasing presence of women in psychology and therefore in SPSSI leadership. All the same, it remains marginal to the scientifically focused mainstream.

All told, my relation to social psychology as I have witnessed it and participated in it has not only been marginal but contrary to its main currents. Because I continue to aspire to a "personality and social psychology" that is interdisciplinary, scientific, humanistic, and socially relevant, I am republishing writings here that seem to me still to be useful in advancing such a conception. They include recent papers written in a retrospective vein since the publication of my previous collections (Smith, 1969, 1974, 1991), some earlier ones not previously republished that seem to me still relevant, and only three from my earlier collections that seem to me to belong here to complement more recent writings. Together they advocate and, I hope, exemplify to a limited degree what I call in my title "a significant social psychology."

That title makes an implicit reference to Sigmund Koch's (2000) derogation of much contemporary psychology as "ameaningful"—as deliberately excluding the employment of human intelligence in the scientific enterprise of human self-understanding. Koch delighted in overstating his case, but it applied to experimental social psychology as much as it did to the rest of the academic discipline. We ought to do better, and we can.

The book is divided into four parts, and I provide context for each in introductory comments. The first, " 'Personality and Social Psychology': Midcentury Roots and Present Perspectives," consists of essays that examine the origins of "personality and social psychology" near midcentury in relation to more contemporary perspectives. An understanding of our past is surely relevant to the critical reappraisal of our present. "Toward an Understanding of Selfhood," which follows, includes products of my long-term preoccupation with the distinctively human feature of reflexive self-awareness. I came to the conviction that any adequate psychological treatment of selfhood requires an integration of causal/explanatory and interpretative approaches. Part III, "Toward an

Emancipatory Human Science," includes an account of my own involvement in the historical episode of McCarthyism (which also informs the reader of personal background that is relevant to my enduring political perspective), and discussions of the psychology of prejudice, racism, and war/peace, which have been enduring concerns of the politically involved psychology represented by SPSSI. In Part IV, "Reappraising Our Foundation," I address the question, Can a significant psychology make sense?—the question raised by the postmodern assault on the scientific aspirations of psychology. This book is obviously a by-product of the life-review that is a characteristic agenda at my age. I hope that it provides materials for some intergenerational communication and exchange, to the benefit of the discipline as well as to my authorial ego.

References

Dilthey, W. (1976). *Selected writings.* (H. P. Rickman, Tr. & Ed.) Cambridge: Cambridge University Press.

Fishman, D. B. (1999). *The case for pragmatic psychology.* New York: New York University Press.

Gergen, K. J. (1992). Toward a postmodern psychology. In S. Kvale (Ed.), *Psychology and postmodernism* (pp. 17–30), Newbury Park, CA: Sage.

Just, J. T., & Kruglanski, A. W. (2002). The estrangement of social constructionism and experimental social psychology: History of the rift and prospects for reconciliation. *Personality and Social Psychology Review, 6,* 168–187.

Koch, S. (2000). *Psychology in human context: Essays in dissidence and reconstruction.* (D. Finkelman & F. Kessel, Eds.). Chicago: University of Chicago Press.

Ross, L. (1977). The intuitive psychologist and his shortcomings. In L. Berkowitz, (Ed.), *Advances in experimental social psychology* (vol. 6, pp. 173–220), New York: Academic Press.

Schneider, K. T., Bugenthal, J.F.T., & Fraser, J. (Eds.) (2001). *The handbook of humanistic psychology.* Thousand Oaks, CA: Sage Publishers.

Smith, M. B. (1969). *Social psychology and human values: Selected essays.* Chicago: Aldine Publishing Company.

Smith, M. B. (1974). *Humanizing social psychology.* San Francisco: Jossey-Bass Publishers.

Smith, M. B. (1991). *Values, self, and society.* New Brunswick, NJ: Transaction Publishers.

Snyder, C. R., & Lopez, S. J. (Eds.). (2002). *Handbook of positive psychology.* New York: Oxford University Press.

Part I

"Personality and Social Psychology"
Midcentury Roots and Present Perspectives

Commentary

As I noted in the introduction, "personality and social psychology," as enshrined in the title of Division 8 of the American Psychological Association, represents a conjunction of interests that prevailed shortly before midcentury when I entered psychology. It was embodied in the *Journal of Abnormal and Social Psychology*, the rigorous journal of "soft psychology" long edited by my mentor, Gordon Allport, and that I too edited before it divided into the *Journal of Abnormal Psychology* and the *Journal of Personality and Social Psychology*. In spite of the continued eminence of the latter journal and the continuing linkage in Division 8, personality and social psychology has not fared well in the subsequent decades. When I came in, several great psychologists had given initial shape to a field that embraced concern with experience and behavior in the context of society and culture and with the personality of actors in that human arena. The ones I particularly admired, and continued to admire, were Gordon Allport, Henry Murray, Otto Klineberg, Gardner and Lois Murphy, Kurt Lewin, and (a bit later) Muzafer Sherif.

In social psychology proper, Allport (1935) had summarized the early stages of one of social psychology's central topics in his handbook chapter on attitudes. His textbook on personality (1937) essentially launched that academic specialty, and his work on prejudice (1954) brought social psychological and personological perspectives effectively to bear on a social problem. I pay passing attention to the last in chapter 13, but do not find in my earlier writings an adequate appreciation of his leadership in the psychology with which I was first acquainted, in which my own identity as a psychologist took shape. I therefore note here that he was the closest to a father figure that I had in psychology. I emulated him, I revolted from him, and in retrospect I find a good many of his features somehow embedded in my psychological self.

Gardner and Lois Murphy also spanned both social and personality psychology, and developmental psychology as well. Gardner and Lois wrote one of the major early textbooks (Murphy & Murphy, 1931), which, in spite of its title, *Experimental Social Psychology*, was focused primarily on socialization, a developmental topic. My contact with Gardner was entirely via the printed page, but I got to know Lois quite well in the later years of her productive career in developmental psychology. I appreciate Gardner's contribution to the psychology of personality in chapter 4. The Murphys were strong advocates and exemplars of a socially involved psychology.

Kurt Lewin is best known as the conceptual progenitor of the first generation of American social psychologists after World War II (cf. Lewin, 1951), but his first book in English was entitled *A Dynamic Theory of Personality* (1935). He also advocated and exemplified a psychology that linked research and theory with both laboratory and field, with ventures in social action.

The remaining figures were just as broad-gauged but did not happen to span both personality and social psychology. Otto Klineberg wrote an excellent textbook of social psychology (1940), one that was open to the interdisciplinary boundary with anthropology, and participated very effectively in correcting the egregious "scientific" racism characteristic of the previous generation in American psychology (e.g., Klineberg, 1935). I was deeply indebted to him personally for crucial help when he was serving in an administrative capacity for the Society for the Psychological Study of Social Issues. I had become editor of its *Journal of Social Issues* in 1950, and was initially stalled in a panic, unable to get started. Otto gave me psychologically and technically expert and compassionate couseling that got me over the hump—and thus laid the basis for an editorial career that has been a source of satisfaction for me. Near the end of his long and valuable life as a psychologist, I was fortunate to renew an admiring friendship.

Muzafer Sherif was an outstanding psychologist who initiated styles and trends in social psychology rather than following them. In retrospect, I no longer value his initial contribution, *The Psychology of Social Norms* (1936), as highly as I did at first. His laboratory demonstration of the formation of social norms in the context of the autokinetic phenomenon, an esoteric delight of experimental psychologists, was an effective piece of scientific rhetoric. It legitimized the well-established sociological concept of social norms for a laboratory-entranced psychology, but it did not produce important new knowledge. His later field experiment on the creation and reduction of intergroup conflict in a children's camp (Sherif et al., 1961) was also valuable more as an illustrative demonstration of social psychological processes than for testing theoretical hypotheses about them, but its importance to the development of the field is indubitable. Indeed, the influential classics of social psychological research seem to share this quality of vivid demonstration. I was pleased to have some direct contact with Sherif late in his career.

Henry Murray was the other great Harvard psychologist of personality. The fact that both Allport and Murray were at Harvard was a prime reason for my choosing Harvard over Yale when I had to compare fellowship offers from the two excellent programs after getting a Stanford master's degree in 1940. I had recently read Allport's text in a course in personality, taught by Lewis Terman (of IQ fame) in my senior year, and followed it by reading Murray's *Explorations in Personality* (1938) on my own. Murray's holistic dynamic psychology drew overtly on the psychoanalytic ideas of Freud and Jung, and covertly on the good ideas of the instinct theorist William McDougal, then and still in disrepute that he only partly deserved. I found it more exciting than Allport's more sedate scholarship. Chapter 5 is my retrospective appraisal.

The selections in this part evoke the midcentury scene in which "personality and social psychology" emerged, and offer my recent retrospective appraisals. Chapter 1, "The Shaping of American Social Psychology," gives both a brief account of my own induction into the field, and my personal version of what the field looked like during and shortly after World War II. Rereading my retrospective critical comments at the end of the chapter, I find that when I wrote them two decades ago, my views were much the same as they are today. Since then, there have been desirable developments along the lines of my critique, particularly in attention to affect and its relation to cognition, and in increasing recognition of the importance of social/cultural/historical context. But the revolt against positivism—the inappropriate application of natural science models—has taken some of its proponents (e.g., Gergen, 1992) to a "postmodern" extreme that I find incompatible with responsible science, practice, or policy development (see chapter 19).

The account in chapter 1 of how I became a psychologist, not just a student of psychology, during the war, could be matched by many other psychologists of my cohort. Psychologists did their best to contribute to the "war effort," and it was a formative experience for the individual psychologists as well as for their field. I was therefore upset by a well-researched book by a competent historian, Ellen Herman (1995), devoted to the thesis that American psychology, and more generally, the mental health professions, were mainly concerned during the war and thereafter with increasing their prestige and power. Chapter 2, my review essay, sought to preserve what I regard as a generally honorable chapter of our past from the cynicism that is so understandably prevalent since the Vietnam War, Watergate—and Enron.

As an enlisted man in World War II, I had experience in test development in Colonel John C. Flanagan's Aviation Psychology Program (Flanagan, 1948). My most challenging and formative experience, however, was as an officer with the Research Branch of the army's Morale Services Division (later designated Information and Education Division), where I worked under the leadership of the psychologist Carl Hovland on persuasive communication research and the sociologist Samuel Stouffer on opinion surveys. Immediately after my release from the army, I worked with Stouffer and others on the analysis of our survey findings, drafting chapters for a serious attempt to reap social scientific gains from the practically focused army work. Our product, *The American Soldier* (Stouffer et al., 1949), was hailed and condemned as a conspicuous example of quantitative empirical social science on a large scale. In chapter 3, I summarize the initial critical reaction, and appraise it from the perspective of some three decades later, which does not differ greatly from that of today: already the "positivist" faith in quantitative natural science models was waning. The discussion remains relevant to my current concern with retaining the value of evidential empiricism in spite of postmodernist attacks.

Chapters 4 and 5 are my retrospective reviews of two of the three great books that launched the study of personality in American psychology: Murphy's *Personality: A Biosocial Approach to Origins and Structure* (1947) and Murray's *Explorations in Personality* (1938). I regret that I have no such essay on Allport's *Personality: A Psychological Interpretation* (1937) to offer. The surprising thing is our differential historical memory for these three books, which I discuss in chapter 4. Although Murphy's version of a field theoretical approach stands up very well in present perspectives and he anticipated the wave of recent interest in the self, his work is virtually forgotten. Because I identify with Murphy's broad attempts at integration in a spirit of open reasonableness, I wince a little at seeing how such a contribution is absorbed by the field but not remembered.

Finally, in chapter 6, I pay tribute to Kurt Lewin's (1931) aspiration for Galilean rather than Aristotelian theory of personhood but note that our increasing recognition of the importance of social/cultural/historical context carries us beyond Lewin's too-physicalistic conceptions. At the same time, I object to the metatheoretical position of "contextualism" advocated by my friend and colleague Ted Sarbin (1976), part of a continuing debate that now extends to my admiration but criticism of the increasingly popular conception of "narrativism," which he had a substantial part in launching (cf. Sarbin, 1986.) The chapter ends with a brief account of my sense of agenda for personality theory—which makes as much sense to me today as it did a decade and a half ago.

References

Allport, G. W. (1935). Attitudes. In C. Murchison (Ed.), *A handbook of social psychology* (pp. 798–884). Worcester, MA: Clark University Press.

Allport, G. W. (1937). *Personality: A psychological interpretation.* New York: Holt.

Allport, G. W. (1954). *The nature of prejudice.* Cambridge, MA: Addison-Wesley.

Flanagan, J. C. (Ed.) (1948). *The aviation psychology program in the Army Air Forces.* Report No. 1. Washington, D.C.: U.S. Government Printing Office.

Gergen, K. J. (1992). Toward a postmodern psychology. In S. Kvale (Ed.), *Psychology and postmodernism* (pp. 17–30). Newbury Park, CA: Sage.

Herman, E. (1995). *The romance of American psychology: Political culture in the age of experts.* Berkeley: University of California Press.

Klineberg, O. (1935). *Negro intelligence and selective migration.* Westport, CT: Greenwood.

Klineberg, O. (1940). *Social psychology.* New York: Holt.

Lewin, K. (1931). The conflict between Aristotelian and Galilean modes of thought in contemporary psychology. *Journal of Genetic Psychology, 5,* 141–177.

Lewin, K. (1935). *A dynamic theory of personality.* New York: McGraw-Hill.

Lewin, K. (1951). *Field theory and social science.* New York: Harper.

Murphy, G. (1947). *Personality: A biosocial approach to origins and structure.* New York: Harper.

Murphy, G., & Murphy, L. B. (1931). *Experimental social psychology*. New York: Harper.

Murray, H. A., et al. (1938). *Explorations in personality*. New York: Oxford University Press.

Sarbin, T. R. (1976). Contextualism: A world view for modern psychology. In A. W. Landfield (Ed.), *Nebraska Symposium on Motivation*, 24. Lincoln: University of Nebraska Press.

Sarbin, T. R. (Ed.) (1986). *Narrative psychology: The storied nature of human conduct*. New York: Praeger.

Sherif, M. (1936). *The psychology of social norms*. New York: Harper.

Sherif, M., Harvey, O. J., White, B., Hood, W., & Sherif, C. (1961). *Intergroup conflict and cooperation: The robbers' cave experiment*. Norman: University of Oklahoma Press.

Stouffer, S. A., et al. (1949). *The American soldier* (2 vols.). Princeton: Princeton University Press.

_____

Chapter One

The Shaping of American Social Psychology
A Personal Perspective from the Periphery

In this article, I will primarily discuss the earlier years of social psychology—before, during, and just after World War II—when the field as we know it today was first taking form, since by longevity and good chance I was well located as a participant observer of these developments. I will end with some thoughts about the present situation of social psychology and the challenges to which it might respond as viewed from my currently peripheral perspective.

Where I Came In: Some Prehistory

Any psychologist, upon reading Proust, should be fascinated by the difficulty of reconstructing how we arrived at the "sophisticated" grasp of people, issues, and concepts that we presently take for granted. For this reason I do not trust implicitly my recollections about how I first became aware of social psychology. I know that as I was getting interested in psychology at Reed College in 1935–38, it was my student radicalism that made me think I ought to know about social psychology, but I do not think I really made head or tail of the systematic book by Brown (1936) that managed to be orthodox in both Marxist and Freudian theory and also to introduce the ideas of Kurt Lewin to American psychology. (I remember Monty Griffith, Reed's great Rabelaisian teacher, guffawing at the Lewinian term "hodological space.") I was more interested in Lasswell's (1927) work on propaganda analysis and in Floyd Allport's (1933) individualistic critique of what he regarded as the "group fallacy" in popular and social scientific thinking about social institutions. (How differently the latter issue appears today!)

When I transferred to Stanford for a final undergraduate year and a master's degree, the exciting ideas around were Hullian neo-behaviorism as mediated by Jack Hilgard (still newly from Yale), and Gordon Allport's and Henry Murray's new psychology of personality (their books were just out) as mediated by Lewis Terman and by Robert Ross. (But I learned the Stanford Binet and, against the infidels of Iowa, the stable and mostly inherited IQ; I did rat research with Calvin Stone, a reminiscence study of motor learning with Hilgard, and a master's thesis with Hilgard on Lewin's new topic of level of aspiration.) My first actual course in social psychology was a disaster, mistaught by an incompetent sociology instructor using the text by La Piere and Farnsworth (1936), a Stanford team consisting of a sociologist and a psychologist that was heavily dominated by the sociologist. That course might have soured me permanently against G. H. Meadian theory, but other reading assigned in the course did get me interested in Margaret Mead's popular works in culture and personality.

Meanwhile, before I went to the Harvard doctoral program in psychology in the fall of 1940, I had read Murphy, Murphy, and Newcomb's *Experimental Social Psychology* (1937) from cover to cover, as well as Woodworth's *Experimental Psychology* (1938). From today's perspective, it is surprising that the Murphys organized both editions of their text around the central concept of socialization, with the major treatment of attitudes by Newcomb being added in the 1937 edition. Encouraged by the Murphys' text I delved into Sherif's *Psychology of Social Norms* (1936), with its ingenious use of the autokinetic phenomenon to legitimize a standard sociological concept for psychologists. I was also reading Klineberg's (1940) classic interdisciplinary text, with its emphasis on common ground with anthropology and its attempt to salvage in the concept of "dependable motives" something from McDougall's instincts, a project more enduringly accomplished by Murray et al. (1938).

There was really no coherence of conception among the textbooks of social psychology to which I had exposed myself, or among the scattered array of social psychological topics with which I had become superficially acquainted. Because of its quantitative respectability, psychologists in social psychology invariably emphasized attitude measurement, but even though Gordon Allport (1935) had declared attitudes to be the central topic of social psychology, there was essentially no developed theory or research about attitude formation and change or about the effects of attitude on behavior.

Prewar Social Psychology at Harvard

In 1940–41, my first year of graduate study in psychology at Harvard was dominated by a frighteningly intensive-extensive proseminar chaired by E. G. Boring, followed by preliminary examinations in general psychology and special fields, which for me were personality and social psychology. At that time, students of social psychology at the dissertation level met irregularly with some junior faculty at Allport's apartment in an informal coffee klatch that called itself the Group Mind (facetiously echoing the McDougall tradition). As we beginning social psychologists drew together to promote our own education, we found ourselves labeled the "Junior G-Men" after a group of kids in the popular comic strip *Dick Tracy.*

Among my more vivid but scattered memories are reading Kurt Lewin's demanding monograph "The Conceptual Representation and Measurement of Psychological Forces" (1938) in an informal group that included Irvin Child, Jud Brown, and Silvan Tomkins; struggling through a course on mathematical logic with W. V. Quine; discovering the culture-and-personality approach of Kardiner (1939) in Irvin Child's sessions of the proseminar; working through the operational approach to measurement theory in a seminar with Smitty Stevens, whose positivism I somehow found no reason to quarrel with; and encountering Erich Fromm's brilliant integration of Marxist and neo-Freudian ideas in *Escape from Freedom* (1941), his account of the psychohistorical roots of Nazism and the perils of modern democracy.

Indeed. Nazism and the war in Europe loomed ominously and took an increasingly central place in the life of the Harvard Psychology Department. Allport played the central role in organizing a Morale Seminar that produced a number of mimeographed analyses of topics bearing on civilian morale. These were understood to have some circulation in Washington. A bit later, in the fall of 1941, Murray organized a series of evening sessions at the Psychological Clinic in which refugees in the Boston area were drawn upon to explore ideas that might help guide psychological warfare. For a couple of months that fall, I did library research for psychoanalyst Walter Langer on the national character of the Finns and the Portuguese (reading only sources in English), this somehow being relevant to the schemes of the organization that was predecessor to the office of Strategic Services, the office of the Coordinator of Information, then headed by Walter's brother, William Langer, the Harvard historian. (For doing this I received the unique civil service title of Junior Psychoanalyst—presumably a promotion from Junior G-Man!)

Then came Pearl Harbor—bursting on us, I remember, while several of us, including Fred Wyatt, a recent refugee who later became Director of the Psychology Clinic at Ann Arbor, were listening to the Sunday radio concert of the New York Philharmonic in Silvan Tomkin's office at the clinic. Almost immediately I was drafted—the first from the department to go.

A Wartime Education in Social Psychology

After basic training in the field artillery and experience while an enlisted man with Stuart Cook and Lloyd Humphreys in test development for aviation cadet classification in John Flanagan's program, Officer Candidate School provided me with a direct experience of the sort of intensive resocialization later labeled as "coercive persuasion" by Schein and his collaborators (1961) and provocatively analyzed by Sarbin and Adler (1970–71) as "self-reconstitution processes" (see my account in Stouffer et al., 1949a, pp. 389–390). My serious education in social psychology began, however, when after nearly a year of experience as a testing and classification personnel officer at Army induction and training sites, Carl Hovland (working for the Army as a civilian) had me called to the Pentagon to join his experimental section of Sam Stouffer's Research Branch of what was first labeled the Morale Services Division, then the Information and Education Division of the Army. Hovland, Stouffer, and Arnold Rose, all involved in the Research Branch, were my main mentors in becoming a working social psychologist, no longer just a curious student.

In Hovland's unit I participated in some of the experimental field research on mass communications that was reported after the war by Hovland, Lumsdaine, and Sheffield (1949) and that laid the foundation for the highly productive program on Communication and Persuasion at Yale (Hovland, Janis, & Kelley, 1953), one of the main initial thrusts of postwar social psychology. With his exceptional gift for Socratic questioning, Carl Hovland was in ideal research director and a spectacular teacher of research design and analysis, which I learned in work on the impact of the "Why We Fight" series of orientation films. The Army training camp provided nearly ideal circumstances for field experimentation with random assignment to experimental and control conditions. I also began to participate in the administration of opinion surveys under the direction of sociologist Sam Stouffer who, along with Paul Lazarsfeld (a consultant to the Research Branch), was a principal founder of modern survey research. In the Research Branch I got to know a number of people who later came to play leading roles in the behavioral sciences, including John Finan, Irving Janis, Art Lumsdaine, Nathan Maccoby (whom I had known since he was a T.A. at Reed), and Fred Sheffield in psychology, as well as John Clausen, Leonard Cottrell, Ward Goodenough, Shirley Star, and Robin Williams, to mention friends and colleagues with whom I have had continued contact. Because we were teamed together in North Africa and Italy for a year and a half, however, Arnold Rose had by far the greatest influence on me.

When we set out to join Fred Sheffield in Algiers, I was an officer and Arnold a newly drafted enlisted man—an incongruous state of affairs, since although we were then both "A.B.D.s," he had followed his Chicago sociology training with Stouffer, Blumer, and others by joining as a junior collaborator Myrdal's (1944) team that was researching and writing the classic study of Negro-white race relations, *An American Dilemma*, and I rightly regarded him as my professional senior. In the course of many evenings in Algiers, Caserta, and Florence (or in the field), I got quite a good education in Chicago sociology, especially symbolic interactionism, and also in race relations and Negro perspectives (the term "Black" came later). My education about race relations was considerably accelerated by one of our early assignments, a study of a representative sample of former members of the Negro Second Cavalry Division, the components of which, including some traditionally elite Negro regiments, had been broken up and reassigned to ignominious duties in labor battalions, with resulting turmoil in the Negro press sparked by Negro protest organizations. Our study was hot politically, and we did it with scrupulous care—finding, not surprisingly, that no matter how we worded the question in parallel forms, only a minority wanted to get into "front-line fighting in a combat outfit," but that even this minority was a great deal larger than the tiny proportion of white troops in comparable service organizations who said that they would prefer to get into the front lines.

Of course, we and our colleagues were also having varied experience in applied survey research, working on problems such as the excessive

AWOL rate in veteran combat troops and the high rate of venereal disease. In the latter study, in which we anticipated Kinsey but with representative samples, we exploded some prevailing racial myths: Black troops did indeed have higher VD rates, but they did not differ from whites in frequency of reported sexual contact or in knowledge of prophylactic practices and self-reported use of them. Where they did differ was in the fact that mostly only the lower-quality prostitutes were available to them and that they were much less likely to be "shacked up" in stable relationships. We also administered surveys originating centrally in Washington to Mediterranean Theater samples.

Immediately after I got out of the Army, I joined Stouffer, Irving Janis, Shirley Star, and a few others for a six-month stint in rented space at American University doing analyses of accumulated Research Branch data and drafting chapters for what eventually resulted in *The American Soldier* (Stouffer et al., 1949a and b). Our main resource was the still-quite-new IBM punch card and counter-sorter, which allowed a kind of direct involvement with the raw data in exploratory analysis that has only recently been regained (though not by me) in interactive byplay with modern computers. The chapters that Irving and I individually contributed were more descriptive than analytic, with relatively straightforward analyses; our drafts were retained in the published volumes essentially as we had written them. Stouffer, on his part, could not be satisfied with less than analytic perfection in the chapters dealing with adjustment to Army life, for which he assumed primary responsibility. He kept working on these night and day in every moment he could spare for another couple of years at Harvard before he could let go of them. His main strategy, which has echoes in contemporary meta-analysis, was the many-times-replicated demonstration of a given relationship in independent samples and subgroups.

After this egocentric account of social psychology in the war years, let me step aside briefly to note some general features of the scene. The intervening trauma of Vietnam makes it hard for younger generations to realize that while ostentatious patriotism was out of style, there was very strong social consensus in support of the Allied war effort against the Axis powers. The contribution of psychologists was desired in the war, and psychologists wanted to contribute. They did contribute in many practical and imaginative ways, and the degree of cooperative wartime effort undoubtedly had much to do with the postwar emergence of psychology as a science and profession on a scale previously undreamed of. Sometimes the major contributions were not psychological at all. Thus, Fred Sheffield set up a system of casualty statistics for the Fifth Army in Italy that provided a model for later use after the Normandy invasion. Psychologists in the war were not trying to prove how scientific they were; rather, they were trying to use all the science they knew— and everything else, too—to cope with urgent problems. As it happened, and I do not think it was accidental, this problem-focused applied effort was good for the science.

Modern social psychology was born out of efforts like those I have described, including Kurt Lewin's work on changing food habits, Dorwin Cartwright's on war bond sales, and Rensis Likert's and Angus Campbell's Bureau of Program Surveys of the U.S. Department of Agriculture, which provided the psychological counterpart to Stouffer's and Lazarsfeld's sociological tradition of survey research. As faculty and former graduate students returned from war duty to the campuses, academic social psychology was straining to burst forth.

Social Relations at Harvard After the War

After the intensive work on *The American Soldier*, I returned to Harvard with only a dissertation to complete—not for the Psychology Department but for the new Department of Social Relations, a coalition of social and clinical psychology, sociology, and cultural anthropology led respectively by Gordon Allport, Henry Murray, Talcott Parsons, and Clyde Kluckhohn, with Parsons as founding chair. The new venture was as much responsive to chronic political tensions in the old Psychology Department as it was to clearly articulated goals of interdisciplinary integration. I was an enthusiastically committed advocate, and so far as I know I was its first Ph.D., in 1947. Even then I did not regard the particular combination of disciplines in Social Relations as dictated by anything other than pragmatic and political reasons. There is a narrow practical limit on how many disciplines can be brought together in any single department, and there would be considerable gain in having different combinations tried at different institutions and at different times. I think of the more than two decades in which the department flourished at Harvard as a considerable success, not as a failure because it did not last longer.

While I was still with Stouffer at American University, I had been plotting with Jerry Bruner and Robert White the initial plans for a study of how people's opinions on public issues are embedded in the functioning of their personalities as a project with the new Laboratory of Social Relations that Stouffer was to head. One part was to follow the pattern of cooperative clinical investigation established at the Psychological Clinic by Harry Murray and continued by White—the well-known Diagnostic Council approach. Ideas emerging from the qualitative clinical study were to be tested in a small-scale interview survey in a convenient community. The focal topic was opinion about Soviet Russia (at the outset of the Cold War). I was to be Project Director and use the quantitative survey as the basis for my dissertation. All this came to pass, and led eventually (after some years of neurotic blockage on my part) to *Opinions and Personality* (Smith, Bruner, & White, 1956), which I shall not rehearse here. While this work played a part in the so-called "functional movement" in attitude theory, its larger life has been maintained by political scientists following the tradition of Harold Lasswell. After I got my degree, I stayed on at Harvard another two years. I was teaching, but not getting effectively launched in my own research. I discovered, however, that the best way to learn a subject is to teach it. Only by my second year of teaching the basic social psychology course did I begin to feel a sense of coherence, my own structuring of the field.

Harvard was an exciting place in those years. The senior faculty could not really bring off the interdisciplinary integration to which they sometimes aspired (for example, Parsons & Shils, 1951), but some of their juniors and many of the graduate students did struggle toward new multidisciplinary perspectives, with impressive results. In addition, in social psychology there was considerable interchange with the even more exciting cluster of young social psychologists around Kurt Lewin in the Research Center for Group Dynamics at MIT: Back, Cartwright, Festinger, French, Deutsch, Kelley, Lippitt, Schachter, and Zander.

An unanticipated consequence followed from the fact that social psychology was one of the four constitutive components of Social Relations. Since clinical psychology had a firm sense of subdisciplinary identity annealed in the course of many struggles at Harvard and elsewhere, and since there was no doubt about who was a sociologist or an anthropologist, any psychologist in Social Relations who was not a clinician tended to be defined residually as a social psychologist; one did not have to pursue specifically social topics to validate an identity as a social psychologist. Thus Richard Solomon engaged in research leading to his later distinguished career at Pennsylvania in experimental and physiological psychology, and Jerry Bruner moved progressively from his central involvement in social psychology through "new look" perceptual studies to his position at the forefront of cognitive and developmental research. There was nothing in the organizational structure to encourage the development of a social psychological identity. In this respect, the most relevant contrast to Harvard was social psychology at the University of Michigan over the next decade, a contrast that I often thought about.

Some Postwar Sources of the Stream of Social Psychology

At this point, I will drop my autobiographical approach. I was soon participating in the national scene of psychology as an active member of SPSSI and of Division 8 of the APA as a reviewer (for example, Smith, 1952) and editor and, after three years at Vassar, as a staff member of the Social Science Research Council for four years in the early 1950s.[1] I will organize my retrospective view of the postwar emergence of social psychology around a survey of developments in a relatively small number of key departments, all of which I had some direct contact with.

Consider the University of Michigan. When Donald Marquis arranged for Rensis Likert's and Angus Campbell's Bureau of Program Surveys to be brought to Ann Arbor in 1946, to be joined in 1948, after Lewin's death, by the Research Center for Group Dynamics, the two units composing the Institute for Social Research, Michigan attained the enduring distinction of harboring more psychological social psychologists than any other university. Under Ted Newcomb's leadership, however, its doctoral program in social psychology was explicitly interdisciplinary. Newcomb himself had valid credentials in both psychology and sociology and wrote the first introductory text (Newcomb, 1950) to fuse effectively the sociological traditions of symbolic interactionism and role theory with psychological research on attitudes and group processes. Structurally, students could enter the doctoral program with master's degrees in either psychology or sociology; entry to the program involved an explicit commitment to social psychology as an interdisciplinary field. It has seemed to me that this structural feature, while it lasted, helped the Michigan program to play a major role in defining social psychology, one that Harvard's program in social relations never did. Later on, when the joint program was abandoned the structural change surely facilitated slippage from concern with genuine group processes to the present individualistic focus on "social" cognition and allied topics (see Steiner, 1974).

At Yale, as I have already noted, Carl Hovland brought together a stellar group to continue the studies of persuasive communication that he had launched while doing Army research. Under his leadership, attitude change came to be a central topic in social psychology. The Yale group (Hovland et al., 1953) worked with a broad, theoretically neutral map of the empirical terrain—source, message, channel, and audience factors, as well as factors affecting attention to and comprehension, acceptance, and retention of the persuasive message—that could incorporate research inspired by theoretical assumptions as disparate as those of Hovland's own learning theory perspective, Janis's psychoanalytic interests, and Kelly's Lewinian origins. Sherif's social judgment theory could be accommodated. McGuire's (1969) monumental *Handbook* chapter summarizes the achievements of this line of work at a point when it had ceased to be a growing source of advancement.

What happened to the thrust of attitude change research along the lines of the Yale program? For one thing (no minor one) Carl Hovland died young in 1961. Substantively, work in the Yale tradition skimmed the cream of exploratory research without digging definitively into the underlying processes. That is, the Yale studies typically employed trivial beliefs and attitudes that could be manipulated in the laboratory by equally trivial communicative interventions. (Janis's subsequent work on fear appeals and on "hot" decision making is a clear exception.) There was also little attempt to link the research with the psychometrics of attitude measurement or with the implicit attitude theory growing out of survey research. But the main reason for loss of centrality was surely that when Festinger's (1957) theory of cognitive dissonance emerged as the first conspicuous theory truly indigenous to social psychology, research interest came to center on the theory itself so that the particular context of persuasive communication and attitude change no longer seemed so interesting to social psychologists.

In the case of Berkeley, the next entry in my roll call of major sources of input to postwar social psychology, the relevant focus is not the department or its social psychology program, though David Krech and Richard Crutchfield (1948) were indeed influential with their excellent Gestalt-oriented text, but rather the research project on the characterological roots of anti-Semitism and ethnocentrism carried out by Nevitt

Sanford, Else Frenkel-Brunswik, and their student, Daniel Levinson, during the war years (Adorno, Frenkel-Brunswik, Levinson, & Sanford, 1950). Influenced by the amalgam of psychoanalysis and Marxism characteristic of the Frankfurt school, one of whose members, Adorno, joined the project in midstream, the Berkeley study offered a potential model for large-scale, theoretically guided programmatic research using sophisticated empirical methods and bearing on an important social problem seen in its historical social context. The resulting volume, *The Authoritarian Personality*, did attract a great deal of attention from social psychologists for a full decade, but much critical methodological attention was focused on a single aspect of the many-faceted work: the "F-scale" of proto-Fascist dispositions. Indeed, the F-scale had many defects. By the 1960s, interest in research on authoritarianism had flagged, and cognitive dissonance again carried the day.

I had followed the Berkeley work with keen interest almost since its inception, so I was (and still am) deeply disappointed that the problem of authoritarianism—and more broadly, of the relation between character, social structure, and ideology—was dropped before the methodological problems that had beset the Berkeley research team had been adequately resolved, leaving the unquestionably important substantive issues hanging. This shocking failure may have helped to confirm subsequent experimental social psychology in its historical, narrowly natural-science-oriented ways. Perhaps the current availability of better measures (Altemeyer, 1981) will allow the topic to be revived.

The group of social psychologists assembled by Stuart Cook at New York University during the 1950s shared with the Berkeley investigators a strong commitment to bring social psychology to bear on social problems, in addition to a readiness to regard psychodynamics as relevant. Richard Christie provided a direct link with Berkeley. He, Isador Chein, Morton Deutsch, and Marie Jahoda were among the productive members of the group that I joined for a while in the latter part of the decade. Among the group's solid accomplishments were studies of the attitudinal impact of interracial housing (Deutsch & Collins, 1951; Wilner, Walkely, and Cook, 1955) and of juvenile heroin use in its social context (Chein, Gerard, Lee, & Rosenfeld, 1964). More than anyone besides Kenneth B. Clark, Cook was responsible for bringing social psychological knowledge to bear in the legal fight against racial segregation in the schools, and for marshaling support for research on the desegregation process. He represents a version of social psychology that set equally high value on both social and scientific responsibility. I mention these particular examples explicitly, since by the time Cook left for Colorado in 1963 and the group scattered, the kind of activity to which they devoted themselves no longer characterized the mainstream of American social psychology.

The interweaving currents of postwar social psychology were given more stable and legitimate definition by Lindzey's two-volume *Handbook* (1954) for which I was supposed to have done a chapter on attitudes that I was unable to write, to my great chagrin and annoyance. Soon after this excellent critical survey of the field had been promulgated, the mainstream took a turn, at once deepening and narrowing. The precipitating event was the publication of Festinger's *Theory of Cognitive Dissonance* (1957) shortly after his arrival at Stanford in 1955.

Festinger was already influential in social psychology from his studies of social pressures in informal groups and of social comparison processes. Among the students and associates of Kurt Lewin, he was clearly preeminent in theoretical inventiveness and experimental ingenuity, but the impact of his dissonance theory was greater by an order of magnitude. It shaped the dominant style of experimental social psychology for almost two decades.

The appeal of the theory and of the research that supported it was enormous. The theory was simplicity itself. Not only had it the virtue of being indigenous to social psychology, but its range of application seemed to extend even to animal behavior. Festinger especially emphasized its non-obvious predictions that, in the interesting cases, ran counter to prevailing expectations in terms of incentives or reinforcement principles. What students and colleagues seemed to find especially appealing was the Festinger style of experimentation, manipulating "social reality" through clever stage management to create conditions for which testable predictions could be derived—in spite of the total impossibility of counting the numbers of consonant and dissonant "cognitive elements" or of measuring the intensity of states of dissonance directly. There was no doubt about the ingenuity of the enterprise or the challenge that it posed to bright investigators.

Nevertheless, I had early doubts about the strong claims made for dissonance theory, and in a encyclopedia article (Smith, 1968), I ventured that the appeal of non-obvious predictions could be a snare; the theory as it was qualified and restricted by later research might in the long run turn out to account for some relatively minor perturbations of social behavior, but not for the main effects. Festinger told me at the time that he thought such criticism was inappropriate for an encyclopedia, but I have not come to regret the judgment or having expressed it in print.

It was the side effects of the torrent of dissonance research that especially dismayed me. A normative pattern of deceptive, manipulative laboratory experimentation was established that seemed to me bad for the field, both ethically and intellectually. The cleverness of the experiments seemed on the whole to exceed the human and scientific significance of the cumulative results. Social psychology became narrower, with less interest in socially and humanly important problems. Ambitious young social psychologists who sought to stake out new territory for themselves came to model their mini-theories on Festinger's, whether the issue be "reactance," "ingratiation," or whatever. Experimental social psychology was at risk of becoming an increasingly arcane enterprise for the principal edification of social psychologists, existing for academic career advancement more than for the advancement of knowledge—not quite the "fun and games" of which Ring (1967) complained in an opening salvo of the "crisis of social psychology" (tedious as the concept has become, I cannot avoid mentioning it), but not very satisfactory as natural or human science, either.

But I am arriving at the "crisis" prematurely. There are other important strands in the postwar picture to be brought into view. One is the exchange theory of Thibaut and Kelley (1959), who applied the pay-off matrices of game theory to a rationalistic analysis of interpersonal and group processes. Hal Kelley recently told me that his fruitful collaboration with John Thibaut was marriage-brokered by Gardner Lindzey in connection with arrangements for their chapter in the *Handbook* (Kelley & Thibaut, 1954). One may complain, as I have, that exchange theory ideologically reflects egoistic features of our contemporary competitive society and neglects the possibility of uncalculating commitments. All the same, the explicit articulation of a theory of social behavior in terms of what amounts to an up-dated and sophisticated utilitarianism was a substantial contribution that helped shape the contemporary mainstream of social psychology.

My reconnaissance of our well-springs would be misleadingly out of balance were I to fail to take note of what we owe to three exceptionally creative individuals: Muzafer Sherif, Fritz Heider, and Solomon Asch. They belong with Lewin and Newcomb on any list of great social psychologists. A crusty, difficult individualist, Sherif had an uncanny sense of significant problems and how to tackle them in ways that did not lose the problem in the method. Think of the span of his contributions, temporally and conceptually: *The Psychology of Social Norms* (1936), *The Psychology of Ego-Involvements* (Sherif & Cantril, 1947), *Social Judgment* (Sherif & Hovland, 1961), *Group Conflict and Cooperation* (Sherif, 1967), and later volumes with Carolyn Sherif almost until today. Social psychology would be much impoverished without his input.

Fritz Heider was an armchair theorist, not a researcher, but the richness of his phenomenological conceptualization of "commonsense psychology" (Heider, 1958) has been mined only very partially in the subsequent development of various versions of balance theory (Cartwright & Harary, 1956; Newcomb, 1968) and of attribution theory (Jones & Davis, 1965; Kelley, 1967), topics that have occupied an important place on the agenda of experimental social psychology in recent decades.

Reflecting the Gestalt perspective of his mentor, Max Wertheimer, Solomon Asch (1952) uncovered a number of significant social psychological problems, ranging from how prestige suggestion should be conceived (we would now speak of source effects and social influence) to the nature of conformity to the perceptual judgments of others and how people integrate information to form impressions of personality. His systematic textbook remains a model organization of the field from a coherent point of view and is still relevant as a critique of currents that persist in the mainstream. He and his colleagues acquired me as a devoted admirer in other respects when I visited Swarthmore for several years in the 1950s as external examiner to their honors program. In contrast to the frantic rat race of "publish or perish" that seemed so prevalent elsewhere—which I think has diminished the quality of our scientific literature, thus impeding the development of our science—the intellectual curiosity of Asch and his Swarthmore colleagues was intrinsically motivated. Asch's complete intellectual integrity was illustrated for me by his acceptance and further pursuit of what to him were most surprising and unwelcome findings about perceptual conformity, disconfirming his Gestalt expectations that with full information perceptually available, people ought to behave rationally.

A Peripheral Perspective on the Present

The cognitive social psychology that is presently predominant obviously emerges from the confluence of many of the sources that I have just reviewed. Surely it is also fostered by the current dominant position of cognitive, information-processing formulations in psychology at large. Good, important work is obviously being done, though I think that social psychological processes of interactive resonance—that is, fad and fashion and swings of the pendulum—have resulted in a shared view of human social behavior that is out of balance. My bet is that in a few years our currently prevalent assumptions will appear to have been both too individualistic (compare Sampson, 1977) and too neglectful of the affective side of social life. In the latter regard, I applaud the renewed theoretical attention to affect by Tomkins (1980) and Zajonc (1980). The people that I know are not all rational, and sometimes they care about each other in uncalculating ways.

My early background in wartime exposure, in the Social Relations Department at Harvard, and in the staff support of interdisciplinary research at SSRC has left me out of sympathy with the main directions that social psychology has taken since the mid-1950s. By now it should be clear that I yearn for a social psychology that is integrally linked with the psychology of personality. (I really believe in the conception of APA Division 8, Personality *and* Social Psychology!) I yearn for a social psychology that is genuinely interdisciplinary, that takes seriously the responsibility to provide the linkage between individual and sociocultural levels of analysis. I yearn for a social psychology that bears usefully on human problems—not so much in the technological spirit of human engineering as in the emancipatory spirit (Habermas, 1971) of empowering people to cope more competently. Of course, I would be more foolish than I think I am if I did not have some doubts that it is mainly I, and not the rest of the field, that is out of step! After all, I am not *that* far from retirement. Yet the more I take advantage of my senior status to try to gain a philosophic perspective on our activities as psychologists, the more I am convinced that the positivist tradition in which I was raised and to which the mainstream of the field still adheres is essentially misguided.

This is not the place to rehearse the complex issues that are involved. Here, I merely declare my conviction that a scientific psychology that aspires to deal adequately with human social behavior must be in key respects a historical science that studies its phenomena in their historical and cultural context. In line with Asch's (1952) research on conformity, I take comfort that I am not out of step with Gergen (1982) in these views.

In trying to be an ahistorical natural science, experimental social psychology has put most of its eggs in the basket of attempting to understand abstract social psychological processes, which it is hoped are independent of culture and history. Not all this effort has been wasted, I am confident, but the extreme emphasis has been unwise. If Gergen and I are right to any substantial degree, it would make sense to balance the investment in would-be ahistorical science with considerably more concern for attaining substantive social psychological understanding of concrete domains of actual social life. We need to get more *content* back into social psychology if we are to earn our keep.

As it is, we know a good deal about prejudice and intergroup relations. At the boundary of our field, we know something about electoral behavior. Thanks to the women's movement, we are learning fast about the social psychology of gender. A good deal is also known about behavior in concrete organizational contexts, but after the time of Kurt Lewin, social psychology left this area, by default, to specialists in management and industrial-organizational psychology. Because we have been so busy in the pursuit of abstractions, there are broad unexploited opportunities for social psychological attention.

Present urgencies call for many more of us than the stalwart few who are already involved to study the psychological impact of life under nuclear threat, and to contribute psychological insights to the pursuit of conflict resolution and peace. Other examples: Why not, with Frank (1973) and Brehm (1976), break through the artificial boundaries between social and clinical psychology in the study of psychotherapeutic processes (see also Weary & Mirels, 1982)? By the same token, why not, with Blank (1982) crash the equally arbitrary boundaries between social psychology and the psychology of adult development? Why leave family processes to the family therapists and sociologists?

Social psychology has more competences for research than ever. Our technical competence is cumulative, and recognition of the historically and culturally bounded nature of many of our phenomena and formulations need not imply laxity of method. Our substantive understanding is at least partially cumulative, too, as anyone can ascertain by reading the better textbooks from successive decades. Paradoxically, I believe it could become more cumulative than it has been were we to recognize explicitly the contextual boundedness of most of our findings. To be context-bound and not to know it is a sure ticket to social scientific oblivion. Admittedly, there *has* been some movement recently toward a more varied portfolio of research than exclusive investment in the laboratory study of social processes in the abstract, but more movement in that direction would make social psychology interesting and useful to more people than just social psychologists, who have sometimes seemed to be the main consumers. An awareness of our heritage may help us in taking firm steps in these new directions.

NOTE

1. I contributed an autobiography as of more than a decade ago to Krawiec's collection (Smith, 1972).

References

Adorno, TW., Frenkel-Brunswick, E., Levinson, D. J., & Sanford, R. N. *The authoritarian personality.* New York: Harper & Row, 1950.

Allport, F. H. *Institutional behavior.* Chapel Hill: University of North Carolina Press, 1933.

Allport, G. W. Attitudes. In C. Murchison (Ed.), *A handbook of social psychology.* Worcester, MA: Clark University Press, 1935.

Altemeyer, B. *Right-wing authoritarianism.* Edmonton, Alberta: University of Alberta Press, 1981.

Asch, S. E. *Social psychology.* Englewood Cliffs, NJ: Prentice-Hall, 1952.

Blank, T. *A social psychology of developing adults.* New York: Wiley, 1982.

Brehm, S. *The application of social psychology to clinical practice.* Washington, DC: Hemisphere, 1976.

Brown, J. F. *Psychology and the social order.* New York: McGraw-Hill, 1936.

Cartwright, D., & and Harary, F. Structural balance: A generalization of Heider's theory. *Psychological Review,* 1956, 63, 277–293.

Chein, I., Gerard, D. L., Lee, R. S., & Rosenfeld, E. *The road to H: Narcotics, delinquency, and social policy.* New York: Basic Books, 1964.

Deutsch, M., & Collins, M. E. *Interracial housing.* Minneapolis: University of Minnesota Press, 1951.

Festinger, L. *A theory of cognitive dissonance.* Evanston, IL:Row, Peterson, 1957.

Frank, J. D. *Persuasion and healing* (Rev. ed.). Baltimore, MD: Johns Hopkins University Press, 1973.

Fromm, E. *Escape from freedom*. New York: Farrar & Rinehart, 1941.

Gergen, K. *Toward transformation in social psychology*. New York: Springer-Verlag, 1982.

Habermas, J. *Knowledge and human interests*. Boston: Beacon Press, 1971.

Heider, F. *The psychology of interpersonal relations*. New York: Wiley, 1958.

Hovland, C. I., Janis, I. L., & Kelley, H. H. *Communication and persuasion*. New Haven, CT: Yale University Press, 1953.

Hovland, C. I., Lumsdaine, A. A., & Sheffield, F. D. *Experiments in mass communication: Studies in social psychology in World War II* (Vol. 3). Princeton, NJ: Princeton University Press, 1949.

Jones, E. E., & Davis, K. E. From acts to dispositions: The attribution process in person perception. In L. Berkowitz (Ed.), *Advances in experimental social psychology* (Vol. 2). New York: Academic Press, 1965.

Kardiner, A. *The individual and his society*. New York: Columbia University Press, 1939.

Kelley, H. H. Attribution theory in social psychology: In D. Levine (Ed.), *Nebraska symposium on motivation* (Vol. 15). Lincoln: University of Nebraska Press, 1967.

Kelley, H. H., & Thibaut, J. W. Experimental studies of group problem solving and process. In G. Lindzey (Ed.), *Handbook of social psychology* (Vol. 2). Reading, MA: Addison-Wesley, 1954.

Klineberg, O. *Social psychology*. New York: Holt, 1940.

Krech, D., & Crutchfield, R. S. *Theory and problems of social psychology*. New York: McGraw-Hill, 1948.

LaPiere, R. T., & Farnsworth, P. R. *Social psychology*. New York: McGraw-Hill, 1936.

Lasswell, H. D. *Propaganda techniques in the World War*. London: Routledge & Kegan Paul, 1927.

Lewin, K. The conceptual representation and the measurement of psychological forces. *Contributions to Psychological Theory*, 1938 1(4).

Lindzey, G. (Ed.) *Handbook of social psychology* (2 vols.) Reading, MA: Addison Wesley, 1954.

McGuire, W. J. The nature of attitudes and attitude change. In G. Lindzey & E. Aronson (Eds.), *The handbook of social psychology* (Vol. 3): Reading, MA: Addison-Wesley, 1969.

Murphy, G., Murphy, L. B., & Newcomb, T. M. *Experimental social psychology* (Rev. ed.). New York: Harper, 1937.

Murray, H. A. et al. *Explorations in personality*. New York: Oxford University Press, 1938.

Myrdal, G. with Stirner, R., & Rose, A. *An American dilemma: The Negro problem and modern democracy* (2 vols.). New York: Harper & Row, 1944.

Newcomb, T. M. *Social psychology*. New York: Dryden, 1950.

Newcomb, T. M. Interpersonal balance. In R. P. Abelson et al. (Eds.), *Theories of cognitive consistency: A source book*. Chicago: Rand McNally, 1968.

Parsons, T., & Shils, E. A. (Eds.). *Toward a general theory of action*. Cambridge, MA: Harvard University Press, 1951.

Ring, K. Experimental social psychology: Some sober questions about frivolous values. *Journal of Experimental Social Psychology*, 1967, 3, 113–123.

Sampson, E. E. Psychology and the American ideal. *Journal of Personality and Social Psychology*, 1977, 35, 767–782.

Sarbin, T. R., & Adler, N. Self-reconstitution processes: A preliminary report. *The Psychoanalytic Review*, 1970–71, 57, 599–616.

Schein, E. H., Schneier, I., & Barker, C. H. *Coercive persuasion: A socio-psychological analysis of "brainwashing" of American civilian prisoners by the Chinese communists*. New York: Norton, 1961.

Sherif, M. *The psychology of social norms*. New York: Harpers, 1936.

Sherif, M. *Group conflict and cooperation: Their social psychology*. London: Routledge & Kegan Paul, 1967.

Sherif, M., & Cantril, H. *The psychology of ego involvements*. New York: Wiley, 1947.

Sherif, M., & Hovland, C. I. *Social judgment*. New Haven, CT: Yale University Press, 1961.

Smith, M. B. Social psychology and group processes. *Annual Review of Psychology*, 1952, 3, 175–204.

Smith, M. B. Attitude change. In *International encyclopedia of the social sciences* (Vol. 1). New York: Macmillan, 1968.

Smith, M. B. Toward humanizing social psychology. In T. S. Krawiec (Ed.), *The psychologists* (Vol. 1). New York: Oxford University Press, 1972.

Smith, M. B., Bruner, J. S., & White, R. W. *Opinions and personality*. New York: Wiley, 1956.

Steiner, I. Whatever happened to the group in social psychology? *Journal of Experimental Social Psychology*, 1974, 10, 94–108.

Stouffer, S. A., Suchman, E. A., DeVinney, L. C., Star, S. A. and Williams, R. M., Jr. *The American soldier* (Vol. 1). Princeton, NJ: Princeton University Press, 1949a.

Stouffer, S. A., Cottrell, L. S., Jr., DeVinney, L. C., Janis, I. L., Lumsdaine, M. H., Smith, M. B., Star, S. A. Suchman, E. A., & Williams, R. M., Jr. *The American soldier* (Vol. 2). Princeton, NJ: Princeton University Press, 1949b.

Thibaut, J. W., & Kelley, H. H. *The social psychology of groups*. New York: Wiley, 1959.

Tomkins, S. S. Script theory : Differential magnification of affects. In H. E. Howe, Jr. & R. A. Dienstbier (Eds.), *Nebraska symposium on motivation* (Vol.26). Lincoln: University of Nebraska Press, 1980.

Weary, F., & Mirels, H. (Eds.). *Integrations of clinical and social psychology.* New York: Oxford University Press, 1982.

Wilner, D. M., Walkley, R. P., & Cook, S. W. *Human relations in interracial housing.* Minneapolis: University of Minnesota Press, 1955.

Woodworth, R. S. *Experimental psychology.* New York: Holt, 1938.

Zajonc, R. B. Feeling and thinking: Preferences need no inferences. *American Psychologist,* 1980, 35, 151 75.

Chapter Two

Quest for Power?

Participants in psychology, the behavioral sciences, and the mental health professions ought to take some satisfaction, I suppose, when a competent historian devotes her talents to analyzing the role of advice from psychological experts in the public affairs of the United States since World War II: it is, at least, testimony to the social importance of our field. But as an active participant in precisely the period of American cultural history that Ellen Herman covers in *The Romance of American Psychology: Political Culture in the Age of Experts*, I find her revisionist historical perspective troubling. It may be that my own vested interest in a less cynical view of our attempted contributions has made me a somewhat jaundiced commentator; on this point, readers will have to judge for themselves. In any case, my reservations about Herman's book, which are substantial, will form a large part of the content of this essay-review.

It should be said at the outset that Herman has done her homework thoroughly. Her accounts are mostly very well informed, based upon appropriate sources that are scrupulously referenced. The book is social history with a critical theme. It is well written and engages the reader in challenging appraisals. Thus, it is not at all surprising that the recent lengthy review in *Contemporary Psychology* by her fellow historian, Lawrence J. Friedman,[7] is so strongly favorable. This is the sort of book that good contemporary historians do.

In fairness to the book and its author, it should also be noted at the outset that its title is misleading. The book is not about American psychology, notwithstanding an even more misleading statement on the dust jacket (for which the academic publisher must bear responsibility):

> A quiet academic discipline two generations ago, psychology has become a voice of great cultural authority. . . . How, and more important why, has this fledgling science become the source of the most potent ideology in contemporary America?

Psychological expert advice is at issue, and the academic discipline of psychology is not a focus. Indeed, Herman writes:

> My use of the term "psychology" does not stop at the margins of an academic discipline or the boundaries of a professional job category. Rather, it indicates an emphasis on analyzing mental processes, interpersonal relationships, introspection, and behavior as a way of explaining both individual and social realities. *(p. 5)*

The behavioral sciences (first so-called with the blessing of the Ford Foundation in the years immediately after World War II) and the mental health professions are all involved, and mostly this merging of rather disparate enterprises seems warranted. Herman justifies it in terms of her critical concern to detect implicit ideology:

> Scientific discovery or clinical practice, technological innovation or philosophical inquiry, theoretical understanding or practical application—these represented different forms of the same enterprise, at least as far as the relationship between knowledge and power was concerned. *(p. 11)*

To the extent that the reader has reservations about what may seem to be the author's own ideological assumptions about freedom and control in the spirit of post-Foucault[6] historiography, the broad sweep of her critical brush may appear problematic. Again, direct quotation is the best way to communicate Herman's agenda for the book:

> Understanding the recent history of psychological experts is critical to understanding psychology's place in contemporary society. That history, the subject of this book, is based on an extraordinary quest for power. Enveloped in a climate of catastrophic global militarism and divisive national debate over the realization of racial and sexual equality, psychological experts shaped the direction and texture of public life deliberately, with results that were striking and unprecedented. *(p. 5)*

Deliberate quest for power? Striking and unprecedented results? These are strong claims indeed!

Herman's story begins with World War II, which

> . . . offered psychologists unprecedented opportunities to demonstrate the practical worth of their social theories, human sciences, and behavioral technologies in making and shaping public policy. *(p. 5)*

After brief attention to the experience of World War I, in which the role of psychologists in testing draftees put psychology on the map for practical relevance, she devotes three full chapters to psychological activities in World War II, among them: the work of Alexander Leighton and his colleagues on the management of a relocation center for Japanese Americans; psychological warfare; personality and culture studies as applied to Germans and to Japanese; the study of civilian morale, including that of minority groups, and the psychology of prejudice; publication in 1950 of Adorno and colleagues' *The Authoritarian Personality*;[1] the studies led by Samuel Stouffer[12] on soldier attitudes and morale, including the morale of Negro troops; the Strategic Bombing Survey, which cast doubt on the effectiveness of saturation bombing on enemy morale; the identification of psychoneurotic vulnerability; and the treatment of "normal neurosis" induced by combat stress. These are indeed, for the most part, activities that have often been pointed to with pride; as such, they are sitting ducks for revisionist analysis.

In the main, Herman cannot be faulted on the accuracy of her accounts. However, the reader who is entirely dependent on her for knowledge of these wartime activities may miss the essence of their contribution because of the author's focus on implicit assumptions and latent agendas. For example, she guides the reader to conclusions such as:

> [T]he war had shown that controlling personalities, shaping attitudes and feelings, and guiding democracy through an era of emotional turbulence were major responsibilities of government. They were also things that psychological experts did best. . . . *(p. 81)*

And:

> In spite of important tactical differences between clinical schools and tendencies, the postwar era they all envisioned was founded on the professionally unified project that emerged from World War II: to enlarge psychology's jurisdiction. *(p. 123)*

Readers will be particularly interested in Herman's insightful discussion of how psychiatric experience during the war led to a refocusing of attention on the "normal" psychopathology of citizen-soldiers, as discovered in induction screenings and, subsequently, in the stresses of combat. I think she is right in seeing this as a major factor in changing psychiatry from a marginal profession of alienists, a development paralleling the postwar role of the Veterans Administration in the creation of modern clinical psychology.

What fails to come through in Herman's account of the role of psychologists and their professional cousins in World War II is the task-oriented spirit that dominated their contributions. Unlike the first World War, the second one was not an occasion for flag-waving patriotism on the part of psychological professionals, any more than it was on the part of combat-weary GIs. Rather, it was a time of total mobilization for a consensually necessary cause. Yes, there were disciplinary and professional leaders who were looking out for the interests of their constituencies, but at the time they mainly saw themselves as seeking ways in which each constituency could make its own distinctive (and doubtless over-valued) contribution to the war effort. The real professionals whom I knew in John Flanagan's Aviation Psychology Program and in Samuel Stouffer's Research Branch were devoted to the jobs they were doing, with no sign of second thoughts about advancement for themselves or the professional disciplines they represented.

This may be the appropriate place to offer an illustrative anecdote, that, so far as I know, has not previously been reported. Fred Sheffield, an experimental social psychologist (later at Yale), was on temporary duty in the Mediterranean Theater as a civilian from Stouffer's organization when I joined the group in Algiers just after the Anzio landings in Italy. Fred had been up in Italy at the Fifth Army headquarters and, when it was discovered that he was a competent statistician, he found himself developing a system for analyzing battle and nonbattle casualty rates for the various army positions from the "morning reports" of each military unit—a system that was immediately put into effect and that provided the model for casualty statistics used in the European Theater after the Normandy invasion.

This is just one of many examples that might be cited of professionals using their training and imagination to do well what needed to be done. Fred Sheffield wasn't trying to advance psychology, though as a by-product of his achievement he surely helped the reputation of psychologists in that part of the army. Unacknowledged in *The Romance of American Psychology* is the devoted hard work and imaginative improvisation, rather than scheming for power and influence, that seem to me to have been major factors in laying the basis for the surge of psychology and the behavioral sciences immediately after the war. It is unfair and untrue to project our contemporary cynicism, developed for good reason since the Vietnam War, on our reconstructions of this earlier era.

The later 1940s and the 1950s were indeed a time of euphoria and hubris in the academic and professional community, as Herman accurately depicts. As she says, the leaders in the newly christened behavioral sciences saw few boundaries between public service, disciplinary advancement, and personal gain. The era of grantsmanship was just beginning. The new Department of Social Relations at Harvard, to which I returned from the war, together with the related programs of Rensis Likert and Donald Marquis at Ann Arbor and of Clark Hull and Carl Hovland at Yale (among leading programs that I knew well), shared an optimistic view of current progress in behavioral science and its applications that looks touchingly naïve in retrospect.

Still, I think Herman stretches things to subsume the intellectual outlook informing these programs as distortedly psychological, even in the broad sense in which I have quoted her above. Anthropologists like G. P. Murdock and sociologists like Talcott Parsons kept the relevance of culture and social structure firmly in view[2] even if their functionalism seems in retrospect to have fitted too comfortably with an ideology of adjstment and conformity. And the movement focused on the study of personality and culture and national character (an offspring of neo-Freudian psychoanalysis and cultural anthropology), to which Herman gives special emphasis, came to a crashing demise very early in the 1950s, though some of its assumptions reverberated a while longer.

Developments since the end of the Cold War convince me that the author is essentially correct about the link between wartime and postwar military agendas and the generous support received by psychology and the behavioral sciences, along with the hard sciences and advanced study in general. I remember at the time admiring the readiness of the Office of Naval Research (ONR) to support basic behavioral science, when ONR laid the basis for the National Science Foundation (NSF) by performing many of the functions that NSF later performed.

The broad support provided by ONR and NSF was certainly not constrained by narrow strategic considerations of the escalating Cold War. However, when the Cold War ended, the collapse of the alliance between academic science and government, as typified by Vannevar Bush's vision[3] of "the endless frontier," strongly suggests that underlying military and world-political considerations were primary motivations for the earlier generosity. Just now, the natural scientific community is having less success in promulgating a rationale for its support in terms of national economic competitiveness, while the behavioral sciences remain marginal to this arena. In this context, it seems ironic to read

Herman's assertions about psychology's actual power, not just its dreams of power. Despite some heady moments, the real thing was never as great as she imagines.

Herman's account of *The Romance of American Psychology* after the war is explicitly selective. At the outset she disavows the aim of producing

> . . . a comprehensive historical account of experts loyal to the psychological persuasion. During the postwar era, experts devoted considerable attention to other questions of social importance [than those on which she chose to focus], from crime and education to industrial relations. Their stories remain to be told. (*p. 7*)

Among issues that arose during the Cold War, Herman focuses on the Camelot affair, in which behavioral scientists were enmeshed in elaborate plans for covert research to back up counterinsurgency in developing countries, a fiasco that has already been well documented and analyzed. She examines the record of research, advocacy, and action in regard to race relations and prejudice, with attention to Gunnar Myrdal's *An American Dilemma*,[9] the work of Kenneth and Mamie Clark,[4] the Supreme Court case of Brown vs. Board of Education,[8] the Moynihan Report on the black family,[10] and the report of the Kerner Commission appointed in the aftermath of the Watts riots.[11]

She turns her attention as well to the "growth industry" of psychotherapy, especially for normal people, with particular reference to its postwar roots in governmental initiatives from the Veterans Administration and the National Institute of Mental Health (NIMH), to the community mental health movement, to the joint Commission on Mental Illness and Health (of which I was an officer) that laid the basis for deinstitutionalization, and to the popularity of Carl Rogers's humanistic psychology. And she explores the ambiguous psychological involvements with emerging feminism.

In her generally well-informed account, Herman recurrently stresses parallels between behavioral scientists' readiness to engage in covert manipulation during hot or cold wars and their propensity for social engineering in what her readers might regard as good causes. Although she reiterates and illustrates the assertion that psychological perspectives can be politically enriching and liberating, as well as manipulative and constraining, the net impact of Herman's panoramic treatment is that planned intervention based on supposed expertise is always suspect.

The skepticism favored by postmodern critical consciousness has its value, but I cannot help reading her book as a whole as congruent with the neoconservative stance that expansion of governmental activity is always bad; that aspiration to advise and influence government is always suspect; and that our faulty attempts to apply psychological perspectives in the interest of human betterment do more harm than good. Certainly, she drops gratuitous disparaging comments about a whole array of actors and events that I continue to hold in historical respect, whether it be major figures like Gordon Allport, Erik Erikson, and Gunnar Myrdal (Friedman's review' faults her treatment of Erikson and of Donald MacKinnon of the Institute of Personality Assessment and Research at Berkeley), or of events like psychologists' testimony in support of the Brown vs. Board of Education desegregation decision, of which I remain proud even if it didn't "solve" America's racial problems.

Inevitably, Herman makes some bloopers in regard to historical fact. One that could easily have been corrected is the statement that:

> In 1947 the American Psychological Association gave its institutional stamp of approval to the mushrooming practice of psychotherapy when it made clinical training a mandatory element of graduate education in psychology. *(p. 259)*

In fact, of course, in response to the recommendations of the Boulder Conference (an NIMH-sponsored gathering of key psychologists from throughout the nation), the American Psychological Association made practicum and predoctoral internship mandatory elements of the PhD in *clinical* psychology. Such occasional errors, to be expected on the part of an outsider to the subject discipline, ought to have been caught in the publisher's editorial process. But they are not the book's main defect.

As noted earlier, Herman deliberately focuses her inquiry narrowly and makes no aim to comprehensiveness. There are two major omissions, however, that seem entirely germane to her undertaking, and thus weaken her argument.

One is her avoidance of any consideration of trends in psychological, psychiatric, and behavioral science theory during the postwar period with which she deals. Any full treatment of these trends could, of course, merit a separate volume of its own, but it is surely relevant to a discussion of psychological claims to power and influence to recognize that the predominance of psychoanalysis in psychology and psychiatry peaked immediately after the war, and was followed by the steep decline that now leaves it most firmly entrenched in the English departments of our universities. At the same time, the claims of imperialistic "learning theory" in psychology—which found common cause with those of psychoanalysis in the work of Dollard and Miller[5]—disintegrated into the more modest and less coherent proposals of cognitive science, and the brain and the genome emerged as new foci of attention. So the ideas underlying psychological advice were continually changing, at least partly because of pressure from research evidence and professional experience.

The second omission has a different sort of relevance—that of the countercurrent in psychology and behavioral science that would give priority to matters of human welfare, social equity and justice, and the cause of peace. In psychology, this movement was typified by the Society for the Psychological Study of Social Issues (SPSSI), with which I have been identified for over half a century. SPSSI members and their counterparts in sister disciplines looked ahead, as they emerged from the war, to applying psychology and behavioral science toward these ends. They were mostly appalled by the Cold War.

Herman picks up the story of psychological opposition to government action with the Vietnam War, but there were many psychologists concerned with the "three Ps"—poverty, prejudice, and peace—who had been working long, hard, and for the most part futilely to be heard. During the brief interlude of the Johnson administration's War on Poverty, they were immensely gratified by the attention their voices received. For many, this was a high point. But the programs launched early in the Johnson years were soon undercut by the priorities of the Vietnam War, and it has recently become popular to disparage the results of even those initiatives that had both promise and, in fact, substantial positive effects. Psychologists of the SPSSI breed would have been gratified to have the power that Herman attributes to their profession in the years since World War II. The amount of real influence they were able to exert represents no more than a small blip in the historical record of the postwar period.

Herman concludes her book with a summary that begins thus:

Wherever they were located and whatever their immediate concerns, diverse psychological experts sought "a larger jurisdiction for psychology" during the years after 1940. I have tried to show that, to a remarkable degree, they achieved it. Delighted that psychology had finally attained some of the visibility and power they thought it deserved, they contemplated the happy prospect of "giving psychology away," consolidating their gains by making psychology an inextricable element of contemporary civilization rather than a factor dependent upon the fickle fortunes of one professional group or another. *(p. 313)*

This is too conspiratorial for my taste. Apart from its exaggeration of psychologists' hunger for power and the degree to which that hunger was consummated, this passage, like the book as a whole, conveys the author's tone of moral superiority over the mostly well-intentioned psychological "experts" of the recent past, and does so from a present perspective that is not necessarily more morally secure. Psychologists, behavioral scientists, and mental health professionals cannot avoid being creatures of their own time, then and now, though they do well to try to find ways to transcend its prejudices and limitations. Those of us concerned with social issues sometimes exhort our colleagues to change their priorities, and debates about competing policies and underlying values are important components of the political processes that, indeed, link both experts and the rank and file to history. But we should hesitate to engage in moral condemnation in the context of history. For reasons that would bear close examination, scholars who are unwilling to condemn even seemingly inhuman practices in alien cultures are quick to form negative judgments of their predecessors in their own. The case for and against historical relativism should be essentially equivalent to that in regard to cultural relativism. In today's critical mood, however, it doesn't work out that way, either for my students or for scholars at large.

If I have been at all generous to *The Romance of American Psychology*, despite my substantial disagreements with Herman's judgments and interpretations, it is because its accounts are mostly dependable and interesting, and the issues it raises are certainly worth debating. I calibrate my measured response against the overall approval accorded it by Friedman,[7] on the one hand, and by its outright condemnation as sloppy scholarship by a colleague of mine, a much younger psychologist, who found the book offensive. Readers in the mental health professions would be well advised to read the book and reach their own conclusions.

The Romance of American Psychology will, at the very least, offer some interesting history of their field and challenge them to consider historical and ethical issues that remain all too relevant today. It may also impart some dubious interpretations that could tend unnecessarily to undermine the morale of behavioral scientists and mental health professionals. *Caveat lector!*

References

1. Adorno, T. W., Frenkel-Brunswik, E., Levinson, D. J., & Sanford, R. N. (1950). *The authoritarian personality.* New York: Harper.
2. Becker, H., Gillin, J., Hallowell, A. I., Murdock, G. P., Newcomb, T. M., Parsons, T., & Smith, M. B. (1954). *For a science of social man: Convergences in anthropology, psychology, and sociology.* New York: Macmillan.
3. Bush, V. (1945). *Science: The endless frontier.* Washington, DC: Government Printing Office.
4. Clark, K. B., & Clark, M. P. (1950). Emotional factors in racial identification and preference in Negro children. *Journal of Negro Education, 19,* 341–350.
5. Dollard, J., & Miller, N. E. (1950). *Personality and psychotherapy: An analysis in terms of learning, thinking, and culture.* New York: McGraw-Hill.
6. Foucault, M. (1977). *Discipline and punish: The birth of the prison.* New York: Pantheon.
7. Friedman, L. J. (1996). Psychological advice and the public realm in America, 1940–1970: A study in mutability [Review of the book, *The romance of American psychology: Political culture in the age of experts*]. *Contemporary Psychology, 41,* 219–222.
8. Kluger, R. (1976). *Simple justice: The history of Brown vs. Board of Education and Black America's struggle for equality.* New York: Knopf.
9. Myrdal, G. (1944). *An American dilemma: The Negro problem and American democracy.* New York: Harper.
10. Rainwater, L., & Yancey, W. L. (1967). *The Moynihan Report and the politics of controversy* (includes the full text of *The Negro family: The case for national action,* by Daniel Patrick Moynihan). Cambridge, MA: MIT Press.
11. *Report of the National Advisory Commission on Civil Disorders.* (1968). New York: Dutton.
12. Stouffer, S. A. et al. (1949). *The American soldier* (2 vols.). Princeton, NJ: Princeton University Press.

Chapter Three

The American Soldier and Its Critics
What Survives the Attack on Positivism?

From the time of its publication, *The American Soldier* has evoked strong reactions from its readers—and, one would guess from the contemporary reviews, from some nonreaders as well. Reactions to it provide a kind of diagnostic test to display the array of convictions then prevalent about modern empirical, large scale, quantitative social research.

I volunteered to develop my topic for this symposium since I am aware that my own thinking about the proper aims and methods of social psychological research has shifted substantially since I was first an *American Soldier* contributor, then an enthusiastic participant in the postwar "behavior science" movement (see Smith, 1983). In the years since, I have been increasingly persuaded by criticisms of the positivism that this movement, and *The American Soldier*, variously represented. With many of my colleagues in psychology, I now regard the neo-behaviorism of Hull and Spence that dominated the psychology of the day as seriously mistaken—mainly because of its naive commitment to positivist philosophy. I agree with the evolutionary biologist Ernst Mayr (1982) that physics turned out to offer a most inappropriate case on which to base a *general* philosophy of science. With Gergen (1982), I now think that much of our subject matter in human psychology and the social sciences is essentially historical, and I am impressed by arguments that human symbolization, that is, language and culture, requires methods of interpretation very different even from the methods of the biological sciences (see Geertz, 1973; Bernstein, 1976). I have no residual hesitation about rejecting as firmly as I can the dogmatic side of positivism that would narrowly restrict the bounds of proper science in principle. But, as I took on this self-assignment, I was not as clear as I would like to be about the role of rigorous empiricism in the advancement of knowledge about human affairs. It seemed to me, therefore, that to reconsider the critical reaction evoked by the *American Soldier* in the light of my changed perspective might not only help me work through some unfinished personal business of a cognitive-emotional sort, given my earlier indiscriminate need to defend *The American Soldier* from its critics, but it might also help to sharpen our shared thinking about the empirical component of social science at a time when the assumptions of positivism can no longer be taken for granted.

So I reread the major contemporary reviews of the volumes, also the almost contemporary chapter by Daniel Lerner (1950) categorizing and summarizing the critical reaction. I found it a fascinating experience, a mixture of double-take and déjà vu. In sum, I was struck as much by continuities in critical perspective as I was by changes in my own standpoint and in what I take to be the prevailing intellectual climate. First, I need to summarize the initial critical reception.

The essentially friendly reviews need not delay us for long. John W. Riley's *ASR* (1949) review of Volume I is representative. Asserting that "These volumes . . . constitute as impressive a piece of scientific reporting as we are likely to see in a long time" (Riley, 1949:517), he singled out for special notice the essentially monographic studies of status mobility in the Army and of the Negro soldier, conceptual development in respect to "relative deprivation," and analytic development in terms of Stouffer's emphasis on consistency of replication rather than on strong statistical tests applied to single sets of observations. These features still seem to merit particular emphasis.

Nor does the mixed review of both volumes by Ethel Shanas (1949–50) in *AJS* pose a serious challenge. She wrote:

> In one sense the publication of these volumes is unfortunate. Young scholars, impressed by the number and stature of its contributors, its distinguished sponsors, and its size, may think that *The American Soldier* represents "scientific sociology" at its best. To use the method of study in this work as the *standard* for social psychological research would be regrettable. In the main, the method of study demonstrated is the devising and use of questionnaires to treat separate and scattered matters, without the guidance of coherent theory or careful formulation of theoretical premises. The result . . . is the accumulation of a vast body of discrete and unordered "data" and a treatment reflecting little use of any guiding or meaningful theory. (p. 594)

Although the negative tone of this statement cannot have pleased the authors, much the same reservations were expressed by Stouffer in Chapter 1, Volume I (Stouffer, Suchman et al., 1949), and in his (Stouffer, 1950) "Afterthoughts of a Contributor," as limitations that followed from the fact that the volumes were the by-product of research undertaken for practical, not scientific objectives.

Three major themes pervade the reviews that were flatly unfavorable. According to one theme, the scientific pretensions of the volumes were ridiculous, since only obvious and/or trivial results emerged, certainly not interesting or useful ones. A second asserted that the human value of the research was vitiated by its role in the service of the military establishment. It therefore represented manipulative technology, not research toward the increase of human freedom. The third, of most concern for my present purposes, attacked the enterprise as representing the inappropriate and ineffective extension of conceptual strategies of the natural sciences where they don't belong—a sin asserted to characterize the modern social and behavioral sciences generally.

Snide reviews of the first type came, for example, from a disgruntled retired Colonel Dupuy (1949) ("Actually, nothing in this work has not been set forth in one fashion or another by Col. Ardant du Picq, French Army, prior to the Franco-Prussian War. . . ."), and from what can only be regarded as a hungry and envious humanist-historian, Arthur M. Schlesinger, Jr. (1949) ("*The American Soldier* is an entirely harmless book . . . 'Social Science' as a whole is perhaps doing no present harm, except as it engrosses money and energy which might be put more wisely to other uses.") Balancing the old soldier's condescension was a laudatory review by General Gavin (1949) in the *New York Times*. I was surprised also to unearth a favorable comment by our present Secretary of Defense, Caspar Weinberger (1949), written when he was a young staff reviewer for the *San Francisco Chronicle*: "The methods, the conclusions, and the fact that such studies were once undertaken, should prevent many of the command mistakes which harmed morale in the last war and which might have led to disaster."

The definitive answer to the charge of obviousness, however, was given by Lazarsfeld (1949) in a classic expository review in *Public Opinion Quarterly*. One passage from this review is worth quoting in part for the benefit of newcomers:

Thus, . . . the argument is advanced that surveys only put into complicated form observations which are already obvious to everyone. . . . The reader may be helped in recognizing this attitude if he looks over a few statements which are typical of many survey findings and carefully observes his own reaction. A short list of these, with brief interpretive comments:

1. Better educated men showed more psycho-neurotic symptoms than those with less education. (The mental instability of the intellectual . . . has often been commented on.)

2. Men from rural backgrounds were usually in better spirits during their Army life than soldiers from city backgrounds. (After all, they are more accustomed to hardships.)

. . .

4. White privates were more eager to become non-coms than Negroes. (The lack of ambition among Negroes is almost proverbial.)

. . .

6. As long as the fighting continued, men were more eager to be returned to the States than they were after the German surrender. (You cannot blame people for not wanting to be killed.)

We have in these examples a sample of the simplest type of interrelationships which provide the "bricks" from which our empirical social science is being built. But why, since they are so obvious, is so much money and energy given to establish such findings? Would it not be wiser to take them for granted and proceed directly to a more sophisticated type of analysis? This might be so except for one interesting point about the list. *Every one of these statements is the direct opposite of what actually was found.* (pp. 379–80)

The second major critical theme has a broadly Marxist flavor. It was given its definitive statement in a review essay by Robert S. Lynd (1949: 22) for *The New Republic.*

These volumes carry magnificent promise and serious threat. On the one hand, social science is seen at work on the urgent affairs of contemporary man. . . . But, on the other hand, these volumes depict science being used with great skill to sort out and to control men for purposes not of their own willing. . . .

Scientists may rationalize the fact that they work on Caesar's problems by saying that at this stage in the development of the science of human relations the perfecting of research techniques is all-important. But one wonders again and again throughout these 1,600 pages: What kind of society would that society be which developed its skills not on war but on the problems of peace . . . ?

A bit later on, C. Wright Mills (1959) quoted the Lynd review in support of his choice of *The American Soldier* as a prime example of "abstracted empiricism." Of course, "abstracted empiricism," along with "grand theory," stood for the kinds of sterile social science that he deplored, in contrast to historically grounded theory that is critical, emancipatory, (cf. Habermas, 1959), and generative (cf. Gergen, 1982)—to apply terms from our own time anachronistically to Mills's ideals. The fact that the recent terms fit Mills's and Lynd's concerns so well suggests that in this respect, social scientists remain divided about their proper mission along much the same lines on which they were split when *The American Soldier* appeared.

On his part, Stouffer would have had little sympathy for the conception of "emancipatory" social science, and little understanding of it. His conception of applied social research embraced the human engineering model that Lynd and Mills deplored. There would, indeed, seem to be a basic incompatibility between the science-oriented ideal of highly technical and quantitative research and the emancipatory aim of empowering ordinary people to make wiser social decisions on their own behalf.

The third critical theme, using *The American Soldier* as a vehicle for attacking the positivistic conception of social science on the model of the physical sciences, is best exemplified by Nathan Glazer's (1949) very negative review essay in *Commentary*, which our Chairman told me he remembered finding especially infuriating. On that score, his memory is better than mine, but as I reread the essay, I could see immediately why both he and I would have regarded it as grossly unfair. All the same, if I take Glazer at his literal word, and if I let time loosen my ties of identification with the book, I now think that he made more of a case than I was then ready to grant. Let me explain.

The title of Glazer's essay is important in defining the perspective from which he reviewed the book: "*The American Soldier* as Science: Can Sociology Fulfill its Ambitions?" As Glazer saw it, *The American Soldier* exemplifies social science aping the physical sciences and the book has to be so judged. "The overpowering obsession with the physical sciences and their great achievement makes its mark on every page, and defines the general aim" (Glazer, 1949:488). At the very end of the long review, which up to that point can only be read as a hatchet job, Glazer (1949: 496) grudgingly admitted:

In the course of the efforts to create science, a great deal of interesting and valuable information about the American Army and the American soldier in World War II has been turned up (I have not reported on it here, since it was not my aim; . . . it is primarily as science that I consider *The American Soldier*).

We could not help reading this as saying, "It was not my aim to say anything good about this otherwise fine book!" Unfair!

What, though, of Glazer's case against *The American Soldier* as sociological science? He surely exaggerated "the overpowering obsession with the physical sciences," but some such obsession there surely was. Most of us in empirical, quantitative social research shared it, and it underlay the spirit of the behavioral revolution, the aspiration for an interdisciplinary, unified behavioral science in contrast with traditional speculative "grand theories." Actually, the strongest influence on Stouffer's own intellectual development was not any imaginary conception of physics but R. A. Fisher—who nevertheless represented the experimental rather than the natural history-evolutionary branch of biological science. In his methodological writings, Stouffer (1962) came close to viewing the experimental method (the method *par excellence* of the physical sciences) as a royal road to truth. It is ironic that though he sponsored experimentation, he never practiced it. I would now agree with Glazer (1949:489) that

If the writers of *The American Soldier*, and the branch of social science they represent, had taken . . . biology as a model, their presumption would have been less and their success in approximating it possibly greater.

As for Glazer's more specific criticisms—ways in which the book seemed to him bad science—they fall into three sets. First, he did not like the emphasis on attitude scales, for reasons that seem to have little to do with his main argument. To me, his most cogent criticism in this area concerned the substitution of (individualistic) measures of personal adjustment for indices of group morale that would have been more appropriate. This defect, if it is one, certainly does not derive from any fixation on the conceptual approaches of physical science. Second, he noted that actual hypothesis testing, the stuff of the physical sciences, is absent from *The American Soldier*, and the nearest equivalent to an hypothesis, the concept of relative deprivation, is actually used in a rather slippery ad hoc way. The criticism here is not unlike that made in the Shanas (1949–1950) review. Indeed, *The American Soldier* is not a stellar example of mature scientific sociology. Insofar as aspirations got confounded with accomplishments in some of the claims made for it, Glazer had a point.

Glazer's third complaint concerns the treatment of prediction, and I think his criticism is on target. Surely, it was because prediction is a prime criterion of understanding in astronomy and the experimental sciences that Stouffer and his colleagues made such a fuss about the significant relationship between average infantry company scores on individual morale scales (collected in England before the invasion of Normandy) and nonbattle casualty statistics for the same companies after D-Day. I think Glazer was quite right that in the absence of a theoretically articulated account of the connections between these two sets of indices, this satisfying achievement falls far short of the role of prediction in the physical sciences. Stouffer tended to value prediction in its own right as a symbol of science and a matter of practical achievement, rather than as a criterion of the correctness or utility of theoretical formulations.

What in *The American Soldier*, I asked, survives the attack on positivism? Before addressing that question directly, let us bring the foregoing discussion into focus by trying first to answer the question, What survives the attack from its immediate critics?

For one thing, many nontrivial facts about relationships of varying degrees of complexity survive as raw materials for history, for social criticism, and even for systematic social science. So *The American Soldier* stands up quite well against the criticism of obviousness and triviality from which Lazarsfeld defended it. But to view these facts as "the 'bricks' from which our empirical social science is being built," as Lazarsfeld (1949) put it in the passage that I quoted, is to take a much more Baconian view of the scientific enterprise than now seems tenable. Science isn't built of bricks in that way.

As I see it, Lynd's (1949) critical attack also leaves *The American Soldier* essentially unscathed. In effect, Lynd wished that the book had presented a kind of research that it did not present, but he showed considerable respect—respect mixed with disapproval—for what it was. One may agree with Lynd that a different kind of research, under different auspices, is needed if democratic and libertarian values are to be advanced by research that empowers people better to recognize and act upon their options—some sort of "science for the people." One may deplore the social engineering conception of applied research. But Lynd's criticism hardly invalidates the book as it stands, a by-product of such applied research.

The kind of attack mounted by Glazer (1949), part of his campaign against positivist sociology, brings us back to our primary question. But Glazer's assault on positivistic sociology has much less drastic consequences for how we regard *The American Soldier*, I think, than he supposed. If the authors had followed Glazer in mistrusting any philosophy of social science based on the physical sciences, they might have set about the secondary analysis and write-up of the Research Branch archive under somewhat different self-instructions. They would probably have been less owlish in featuring prediction. But I do not see why the basic strategies of index construction and data analysis that they developed under Stouffer's leadership would have had to be altered.

The more radical subsequent attacks on positivism (e.g., see Gergen, 1982) bring even these strategies into question. To the extent that theoretical presuppositions enter into the very constitution of facts and "data," the evidential status of facts and data comes into doubt, as, for that matter, does the probative status of scientific hypotheses and theories. For some, the undermining of previous dogmatic assurance in the security of "scientific method" seems to have given license for untrammelled speculation in disregard of evidence. If we cannot aspire to a firm and timeless science of social behavior that is as secure from doubt as Newton's Cosmos once seemed to be, why anything goes. It is a humpty-dumpty world of wishful conceptualization.

That is not the way I read the demise of positivism. I welcome the release from arbitrary, dogmatic restrictions on kinds of data, concepts, and methods. We give up the misleading model of the physical sciences as a guide to our formulations about people in society and culture. We give up the expectation that many of our abstract formulations about social life have context-free validity outside history and culture—but not our extreme interest in ones that seem to approach such validity! We recognize that scientific truths are always provisional, not absolute. But we do not give up for the sphere of human life, personal and social, the powerful invention of science as a social enterprise under the discipline of evidence and mutual criticism, an enterprise which seeks to be as cumulative as it can in the pursuit of understanding. We retain much of the strategy of what Bernstein (1976) called empirical theory in the broadly positivist tradition. Our aspirations are more modest than they were in the days of postwar behavioralism, but they are also less vulnerable.

From this more down-to-earth standpoint, we can respect the achievements of *The American Soldier* in the development of survey analysis as one fallible, useful set of research strategies and tactics, and we can acknowledge indebtedness to Stouffer as leader of the enterprise. Throughout his career, Stouffer was a master of empirical analysis in a style of inquiry that may have been rather closer to the data than is optimal for the development of theoretical conceptions with powerful generality. (It remained for Merton and Kitt [1950] to explicate and generalize in an account of reference-group theory the theoretical notions involved in relative deprivation and other seemingly unrelated findings close to the data.) He had the knack of making social data answer to his questioning as they can never "speak for themselves" (see Smith, 1968). If *The American Soldier* was no model for theoretically guided, hypothesis-testing research (which it never pretended to be), it has surely turned out to have been a fine model indeed for the secondary analysis of a rich archive of data collected for other purposes. If it has been influential, I think the influence has been to the good.

One aspect of Stouffer's analytic strategy in *The American Soldier* deserves special comment because of its contemporary relevance: his systematic use of replicated analyses to substantiate his generalizations, in preference to single statistical tests of pooled data. For example, Table 9 in Chapter 5, Volume I (Stouffer, Suchman, et al., 1949:228), "Summary of Attitude Profiles Showing Differences Between Matched Groups of Soldiers in Favorableness on Various Attitudes Reflecting Adjustment to the Army," "rests on the analysis of comparisons of 8,554 pairs of percentages, each percentage in turn being based on the responses of anywhere from forty to several hundred soldiers." This kind of strategy, characteristic of Stouffer's approach though the particular example is a unique *tour de force*, can fairly be described as anticipating the currently fashionable method of meta-analysis (Glass, 1976; Glass et al., 1981). Incidentally, Stouffer's procedure as he applied it to Research Branch data escapes the problem of bias in the reporting of nonsignificant findings, to which contemporary meta-analysis is vulnerable.

All told, *The American Soldier* seems to me to hold up very well, both against its immediate critics as read in the light of today's somewhat different context of assumptions, and against my attempt to bring to bear my own skepticism about the positivist philosophy of science. Some of the faith in big behavioral science may sound innocent and dated; this has little to do with the substance. Methods of survey analysis have been substantially strengthened in the years since, but those employed in *The American Soldier*, which helped launch the tradition, remain impressive. Substantively, *The American Soldier* is not timeless hypothetico-deductive science of the sort that Stouffer most admired, but as a descriptive analytic account of its topic, it is evidential, disciplined, and assuredly valuable. Its concern with developing systematic evidence of high quality does not date. The attack on positivism, in rejecting its dogmatic and stultifying aspects, need not and should not be read as an attack on the need for imagination and discipline in the creation of usable evidence, in the style of *The American Soldier*.

References

Bernstein, R. 1976 The Restructuring of Social and Political Theory. New York: Harcourt Brace Jovanovich.

Dupuy. R. E. 1949 "Review of S. A. Stouffer et al., *The American Soldier*, Vols. 1 and 2." Christian Science Monitor, June 2:18.

Gavin, J. M. 1949 "Review of S. A. Stouffer et al., *The American Soldier*, Vols. 1 and 2." New York Times, May 29:3.

Geertz, C. 1973 The Interpretation of Cultures. New York: Basic Books.

Gergen, K. J. 1982 Toward Transformation in Social Knowledge. New York: Springer-Verlag.

Glass, G. V. 1976 "Primary, secondary, and meta-analysis of research." Educational Researcher 5:3–8.

Glass, G. V., B. McGaw, and M. L. Smith 1981 Meta-analysis in Social Research. Beverly Hills: Sage.

Glazer, N. 1949 "*The American Soldier* as science: Can sociology fulfill its ambitions?" Commentary 8:487–96.

Habermas, J. 1959 Knowledge and Human Interests. Boston: Beacon.

Lazarsfeld, P. F. 1949 "*The American Soldier*: An expository review." Public Opinion Quarterly 13:377–404.

Lerner, D. 1950 "*The American Soldier* and the public." Pp. 212–51 in R. K. Merton and P. F. Lazarsfeld (eds.), Continuities in Social Research: Studies in the Scope and Method of *The American Soldier*. Glencoe, IL: Free Press.

Lynd, R. S. 1949 "The science of inhuman relations." New Republic 121 (No. 9):22–25.

Mayr. E. 1982 The Growth of Biological Thought. Cambridge, MA: Belnap Press.

Merton, R. K., and A. S. Kitt 1950 "Contributions to the theory of reference group behavior." Pp. 40–105 in R. K. Merton and P. F. Lazarsfeld (eds.),

Continuities in Social Research: Studies in the Scope and Method of *The American Soldier*. Glencoe, IL: Free Press.

Mills, C. W. 1959 The Sociological Imagination. New York: Oxford University Press.

Riley, J. W., Jr. 1949 "Review of S. A. Stouffer et al., *The American Soldier*, Vol. 1." American Sociological Review 14:557–59.

Schlesinger, A. M., Jr. 1949 "The statistical soldier." Partisan Review 16: 852–56.

Shanas, E. 1949–1950 "Review of S. A. Stouffer et al., *The American Soldier*, Vols. 1 and 2." American Journal of Sociology 55:590–94.

Smith, M. B. 1968 "Stouffer, Samuel A." In International Encyclopedia of the Social Sciences. New York: Macmillan and Free Press.

Smith, M. B. 1983 "The shaping of American social psychology: A personal perspective from the periphery." Personality and Social Psychology Bulletin 9:165–80.

Stouffer, S. A. 1950 "Afterthoughts of a contributor." Pp. 195–211 in R. K. Merton and P. F. Lazarsfeld (eds.), Continuities in Social Research: Studies in the Scope and Method of *The American Soldier*. Glencoe, IL: Free Press.

Stouffer, S. A. 1962 "Some observations on study design." Pp. 290–99 in S. A. Stouffer, Social Research to Test Ideas. New York: Free Press.

Stouffer, S. A., E. A. Suchman, L. C. DeVinney, S. A. Star, and R. M. Williams, Jr. 1949 The American Soldier, Vol. 1: Adjustment During Army Life. Princeton, NJ: Princeton University Press.

Stouffer, S. A., A. A. Lumsdaine, M. Harper Lumsdaine, R. M. Williams, Jr., M. B. Smith, I. L. Janis, S. A. Star, and L. S. Cottrell, Jr. 1949 The American Soldier, Vol. 2: Combat and Its Aftermath. Princeton, NJ: Princeton University Press.

Weinberger, C. W. 1949 "Review of S. A. Stouffer et al., *The American Soldier*, Vols. 1 and 2." San Francisco Chronicle, June 5:20.

Chapter Four

A Forgotten Classic
Murphy's Integrative View of Personality

Six major works published in the two decades encompassing World War II institutionalized personality as a subfield of psychology for research and teaching. Of these, the books by Allport (1937), Murray (1938), Murphy, and Kelly (1955) were primary. The collection edited by Hunt (1944) reflected the juncture of interests in personality and psychopathology, just before the postwar burgeoning of professional clinical psychology; and the several editions of the text by Hall and Lindzey (1947), with their identification and presentation of classical personality theories, provided a staple for teaching. Psychologists no longer have reason to be interested in the excellent Hunt volumes, because the books were superseded by other collections and handbooks long ago. Hall and Lindzey (1978) is still in print, though integrative texts are becoming more popular. Of the primary books, only Gardner Murphy's *Personality: A Biosocial Approach to Origins and Structure* (New York and London: Harper, 1947)—the book retrospectively reviewed here—is essentially forgotten, as is Murphy himself, who at midcentury was among the prominent American psychologists.

This lapse of disciplinary memory is understandable though, as I hope to show, unfortunate. The volume is long (about 1,000 pages) and fully packed, much too big for use as a textbook. Murphy's style is graceful but symphonic; the 41 chapters follow one another without the props of internal subdivisions and summaries. When I bought the book on publication, I remember dipping into it rather than reading it consecutively and thinking that it flowed along pleasantly but unmemorably, rather like a Bruckner symphony (I am not a Bruckner fan). This reaction is quite unfair to the content, which attempted to integrate an enormous range of literature from psychology and adjacent fields toward general formulations about human personality.

The literature that he considered is dated, of course, though Murphy brought to it perspectives that he developed in interchange with a brilliant interdisciplinary cluster including Margaret Mead, Gregory Bateson, Karen Horney, David Levy, Ruth Munroe, Robert and Helen Lynd, and Kurt Goldstein. Murphy seems to me to have been quite successful in his aim to produce

> not so much a safe-deposit vault for jealously guarded facts as a companion for the investigator who likes to see problems defined in terms of the directions in which they might lead; an explorer's kit, containing, to be sure, some standard tools, and also some maps. Some of the maps are sober, some eccentric, no doubt; but all are drawn in the belief that any map of a far country encourages more travel than an architect's finished representation of the doorway as it is here and now. (p. x)

It is Murphy's continually thoughtful, responsibly speculative framing of psychological issues that has enduring value.

The title of the book accurately identifies its approach, which is biosocial and developmental and concerned with personality structure. Murphy is explicit that the biological and the sociocultural are not empirically separable categories: It is the active biological human organism that participates in society, enacts culture, and is modified in turn by its sociocultural involvements. The book moves from the biological to the cultural and social. The first part, Organic Foundations, deals with heredity, individual constitution, the biology of motivation, and organic traits. A section titled Learning also includes chapters on symbols, values, and conflict. The Personal Outlook deals with the perceiver (anticipating the New Look wave to which Murphy and his students contributed), imagination, dreams, and creativeness. There follows extended treatment of the self in The Self, including consideration of psychoanalytic mechanisms. A section titled Wholeness focuses on personality structure and issues of continuity, discontinuity, and typology, with chapters on projective methods. The final section, Individual and Group, draws with intelligent discrimination on the contributions of the culture-and-personality movement just culminating and considers the perspective of situationism sympathetically but opts for a version of field theory (to which I return next).

This review essay is concerned with the present relevance of Murphy's book. I will therefore first consider selectively respects in which Murphy was ahead of his time; maybe we can still learn from his way of putting things. Then I will point to aspects of the book that are clearly out of date. So doing is a useful exercise, as it bolsters our morale to see evidence of real progress, at a time when the very concept of progress in human science is being challenged.

Murphy's conception of field theory permeates the book and represents very articulately a perspective that personality theory has only recently reattained after the long detour occasioned by Mischel's (1968) situationism.

> *We cannot define the situation operationally except in reference to the specific organism which is involved; we cannot define the organism operationally, in such a way as to obtain predictive power for behavior, except in reference to the situation. Each serves to define the other; they are definable operationally while in the organism-situation field.* For the writer it was the errors made when personality tests were used without the benefit of field theory that first forced a formulation in this direction; for others it will be the clinical sterility of a therapy based on the isolated individual. (p. 891)

Murphy's field theory—an orientation parallel to but independent of Lewin's—is not burdened with Lewin's topological baggage and amounts to what we would now call transactionalism, following Dewey (Dewey & Bentley, 1949). From this standpoint, Allport and Kelly look old-fashioned in their focus on the encapsulated personality, and even Murray's interactionism of needs and press falls short.

A second respect in which Murphy anticipated present-day concerns is his treatment of the self, which, along with his cognitive-affective examination of the person as perceiver-conceiver, forms the conceptual center of the book. Again, direct quotation is necessary to convey the flavor of his discussion, which proposes usage that would have avoided much confusion had it been generally adopted:

> [T]here is an organism, which among its functions includes the function of observing and knowing. Among the things which it observes and knows are its visible surfaces, its vocal cadences, its muscular strains. Being a more or less integrated system of responses, the organism appropriately orders these diverse impressions into an integrated whole and agrees to call it by the name which others have given it, just as it accepts the names that are current for other distinguishable wholes. In the same way it begins to cogitate on the nature of this totality, paying more and more heed to those aspects of it which others fail to note; the inner world becomes important. From the diverse knowing and thinking processes a conceptual

unity is deduced. The self is a thing perceived, and it is also a thing conceived; in both senses it is constantly responded to. A large part of the behavior that constitutes personality is self-oriented behavior. The system of *responses to* the self [will be considered under the term the ego]. (p. 479)

None of the other personality theorists contemporary with Murphy link so directly with our present conceptions of selfhood.

Another undated feature of Murphy's *Personality: A Biosocial Approach to Origins and Structure* is his stress on the culture-specific basis of Western individualism.

[T]he term "ego" as used in western culture is regarded as axiomatically a competitive term. Egoism is set in opposition to altruism. . . . It is difficult to conceive of selfhood except in terms of a commodity obeying economic laws—the more and better selfhood a person has, the less is available for others. . . . But . . . the economic order is itself in some degree an expression of the self-attitude rooted very deeply in the fundamental outlook of the culture. (pp. 524–525)

Such critical awareness of the cultural perspective has yet to penetrate the mainstream of personality and social psychology.

Murphy's cultural orientation came from his intellectual participation in the culture-and-personality movement, which mainly involved the collaboration of cultural anthropology with neo-Freudian psychoanalysis and psychoanalytic ego psychology. His use of the culture-and-personality literature is sophisticated and, I think, not to be faulted in hindsight. The movement came to an abrupt crash after World War II, largely because of reaction against the folly of wartime and postwar studies of "national character," and the cross-cultural study of personality has only recently begun to recover in a different intellectual climate. I think current workers in this field should find much stimulation in reading Murphy's critical and tentative distillation of the culture-and-personality literature written just before the movement was aborted.

When we come to Murphy's treatment of heredity, we are reminded of the large advances in molecular and behavioral genetics since his time. Yet Murphy was able to state clearly the way to talk sensibly about heredity and environment, a matter of pernicious confusion up to the present:

[No] quantitative generalization regarding the relative importance of nature and nurture [is ever possible], . . . [E]very trait is completely and absolutely a hereditary tendency brought to its fulfillment by a specific environmental pressure. But the *variability from person to person* in respect to each trait within any sample of people under any sample of conditions can always be treated with respect to the question: How is the variability of individuals related to the variability of stock and of environment? (p. 56)

Present-day readers will also note the essential absence of treatment of psychometric approaches to the measurement of personality (no anticipation of the Big Five factor traits) and the confident attention paid to projective tests: It was the heyday of the Rorschach and the TAT. They will note that Murphy shares the metaphor of tension reduction, then universal, in discussions of motivation, though my sense is that current personality theory has still to get its treatment of motivation in order. What will probably strike present readers as strangest is Murphy's idiosyncratic treatment of learning in terms of his own version of conditioning (essentially stimulus substitution) and *canalization*, a term he adopted from Janet to refer to the differentiation of modes and objects involved in the satisfaction of needs. Instrumental learning à la Thorndike and Skinner is ignored except as it is included in canalization, and his interest in contributions from Gestalt psychology has little impact here. What Murphy wrote about canalization makes considerable sense to me, but his usage never caught on either in research on motivational learning or in personality psychology.

In her excellent scholarly biography of her husband and collaborator, Lois Murphy (1990) identified some other ways in which the book would be written differently today. One is the matter of Gardner's tendency to emphasize the positive:

> In this book on personality there is a dearth of tycoons, pirates, Mafia godfathers, corrupting politicians, as well as serial murderers: even for the sake of extending science, Gardner did not consort with rascals. In the half-century that we were together, he mentioned two "evil men," Hitler in World War II and Richard Nixon subsequently. (p. 210)

And, in an area in which she herself was to be a major contributor, she notes further lacks:

> [T]he book reflects the limitations of psychology in the first half of the twentieth century. The index includes anxiety, but not courage . . . ; insecurity but not competence, trust, or confidence; sensitivity but not coping or mastery; trauma but not resilience; narcissism but not generativity. The

fact that Gardner does include both empathy and sympathy as well as tact, cooperation, curiosity, integration, and love, points to his values and his concern with positive and socially valuable aspects of personality. (pp. 214–215)

In his own critical look at his topic near the end of the book, Murphy suggests the promise of regarding

personality not as a state or form of organization but as a direction of development. . . . Personality would thus become not a recognizable cross section but a multidimensional trend phase of a complex developmental process. The data for such a psychology of personality are not available and programmatic discussion of their future role would be presumptuous. It is, however, likely that the concepts in the present volume . . . will be regarded, two or three generations hence, as minor fragmentary contributions to an essentially dynamic, temporally oriented view of personality. (p. 918)

Elsewhere, he notes the yet-to-be-realized promise of the longitudinal studies then in progress.

In a final chapter titled "The Skeptical Psychologist," Murphy makes an eloquent case for the open, tentative approach he has taken toward an integrative view of personality. He also suggests—hints rather than puts directly—the value of openness to more cosmic boundaries of personality. Murphy's standing in mainstream psychology was always partly clouded by his career-long interest in psychical research, about which the skepticism of other psychologists approached the dogmatic. Only readers aware of this side of Murphy's commitments will interpret his final chapter as I read it here.

In sum, Murphy's *Personality* is a book well worth remembering. To return to a question I raised at the outset, why is it so much less remembered than Allport (1937), Murray (1938), or Kelly (1955)? I suggested that its length and style pose one kind of barrier. More important, I think, is the fact that it is essentially a very broad, intellectually speculative attempt at integration, not the presentation of a highlighted personal theory. There are no easy hooks to hang disciplinary memory on, like Allport's (1937) functional autonomy of motives, Murray's (1938) needs and press and TAT, or Kelly's (1955) personal constructs and REP test. Murphy's transactional approach infuses the entire book, and his pioneering conceptualization of self does not stand out figurally. Contributions toward integration may be important to the development of a science, but it is their misfortune to be absorbed rather than remembered.

References

Allport, G. W. (1937). *Personality: A psychological interpretation.* New York: Holt.

Dewey, J., & Bentley, A. F. (1949). *Knowing and the known.* Boston: Beacon.

Hall, C., & Lindzey, G. (1947). *Theories of personality.* New York: Wiley.

Hall, C. S., & Lindzey, G. (1957). *Theories of personality.* New York: Wiley.

Hall, C. S., & Lindzey, G. (1978). *Theories of personality* (3rd ed.). New York: Wiley.

Hunt, J. Mc V. (Ed.). (1944). *Personality and the behavior disorders* (2 vols.) New York: Ronald.

Kelly, G. A. (1955). *The psychology of personal constructs* (2 vols.) New York: W. W. Norton.

Mischel, W. (1968). *Personality and assessment.* New York: Wiley.

Murphy, L. B. (1990). *Gardner Murphy: Integrating, expanding, and humanizing psychology.* Jefferson, NC: McFarland.

Murray, H. A., et al. (1938). *Explorations in personality.* New York: Oxford University Press.

Chapter Five

Personology Launched

This retrospective review of *Explorations in Personality* (Murray, 1938) was published two years late. It should have come out in 1988, the 50th anniversary of the book's publication, when Murray was still alive and would have been fully able to appreciate it. (He died on June 23, 1988, at the age of 95 [Smith & Anderson, 1989].) But *Explorations* is still very much alive. New generations of psychologists ought to get acquainted with it.

I have vivid memories of my first encounter with the book. It was just after I had taken an upper-division course in personality with Lewis Terman, in his last year of teaching at Stanford, in which we had used the new texts by Stagner (1937) and Gordon Allport (1937). Stagner's was a good, solid textbook that had priority but was not memorable. Allport's, as we all know, was a classic—scholarly, philosophical, magisterial, and focused on the mature Ego. Then, Murray's *Explorations* burst forth upon us. The device on its dust jacket (presumably designed by Christiana Morgan) showed a mandala with the sun above, a sperm whale central, and an octopus below, with the inscription, "Let not him who seeks cease until he finds, and when he finds, he shall be astonished." It was numinous, Jungianly archetypical, magically enticing. And the contents were engrossing, unlike any psychology we had read: voluminous prolegomena and schemata for the study of personality by Murray and reports of a stunning array of investigative procedures, featuring especially the interpretation of imaginative productions, by Murray and the talented group of collaborators that he had assembled and inspired, including such later luminaries as Erik Erikson, Jerome Frank, Donald MacKinnon, Saul Rosenzweig, Nevitt Sanford, and Robert White. And one—sadly, only one—illustrative case study by White. We students hastened to read the book without anybody's assigning it. Its rich array of conceptual and empirical strategies for studying the depths and heights of personality drew us to psychology with a magnetism that was missing in Stagner and Allport.

Later, when I was a graduate student at Harvard just before and after World War II (and I went to Harvard mainly because Murray and Allport were on the faculty), Murray was present only from time to time. When he was there, the sun shone, the whale heaved, the octopus became dimly visible in the depths. All of us in the old Harvard Psychological Clinic on Plympton Street ("wisteria on the outside, hysteria on the inside") felt that we were living at the peak when Harry was with us. He catalyzed intellectual enthusiasm and creativity not only by his own brilliance and "sanguine surplus," but also by his continual public cherishing of the inchoate ideas that we were encouraged to present to each other and to him. Those were great times, paralleled, I imagine, by times shared nearby at MIT with Kurt Lewin by another segment of the same generation of American psychologists (Patnoe, 1988). So this review is primed by preconceptions and feelings that are not at all objective. For me and for many others, *Explorations* embodied Murray's charisma and enticed us to commitment to the field that it substantially redefined.

From today's perspective, Murray's innovations in *Explorations* in the 1930s are remarkable. As a trained and accredited Freudian analyst who had no respect for psychoanalytic orthodoxy or fear of deviation, he proclaimed what was, in effect, an open, catholic ego psychology before ego psychology was popular in analytic circles and at a time when psychoanalysis had pariah status in academia. An admirer of Jung, who had opened up new perspectives for Murray at the midlife beginning of his career in psychology, but no religious Jungian, he produced an eclectic system for the description of personality (with hosts of variables somewhat in the spirit of his earlier immersal in biochemistry) that was at least as much indebted to the unpopular William McDougall as to either Freud or Jung. (Murray's *needs* have the psychological characteristics of McDougall's *instincts*, or *propensities*, including their integration of cognitive, affective, and conative aspects and their investment in psychological objects to form *sentiments* as structural components of the affective life [McDougall, 1921, 1937].) Drawing on the perspectives of his mentors and friends, the great philosopher Alfred North Whitehead and the great physiologist L. J. Henderson, he developed a holistic conception of personality much in tune with modern systems theory as later expounded by James G. Miller (1978), who subsequently became a student, colleague, and friend. In principle, the subject matter of Murray's *personology* (his preferred term for the psychology of personality) had the person's full intact life as its macro-unit, with the goal-directed behavioral episode as the micro-unit, still at a "molar" level. In fact, he never engaged in longitudinal research, but as Block (1981) and White (1981) make clear, Murray's conceptualization called for the difficult longitudinal research that was to come later.

Murray's conception of personality as presented in *Explorations* should not have been at all vulnerable to later criticisms of "trait theory"; indeed, his conception of personality as process had a strongly Heraclitian flavor, with temporary *regnancies* commanding the person's resources. He also gave emphasis to his concept of *press*—affordance and induction from the psychological environment—to complement *need*, producing a genuinely interactional, if not transactional, psychology, a framework for thinking about personality and behavior that stands up very well today (although it is only psychologists in his explicit tradition who still use the term *press* for sentimental reasons).

For many of his contemporaries, it was Murray's catalogue of needs and his creative sponsorship of projective techniques, especially the Thematic Apperception Test (TAT) that he developed with Christiana Morgan, that constituted the primary contribution of *Explorations*. The elaborately instantiated taxonomy of human motivation in terms of 20 manifest needs (from *n* Abasement to *n* Understanding, alphabetically), 7 more introduced too late for full, systematic use in the studies reported, and 8 latent or repressed needs (together with a host of other internal factors, traits, and attributes) was certainly not Murray's main theoretical contribution, but it has turned out to provide a very useful checklist of relevant personality descriptors. Later investigators, particularly David McClelland (1985) and his students, have pursued the study of particular needs from Murray's list with a more closely codified treatment of evoked fantasy—thus *n* Achievement (McClelland, Atkinson, Clark, & Lowell, 1953), *n* Affiliation (Shipley & Veroff, 1952), and *n* Power (Veroff, 1957; Winter, 1973).

The subsequent history of projective techniques, which *Explorations* did so much to launch, is still controversial. Murray (1967) later preferred to call them *eductors*. During the 1940s and 1950s, the TAT and the Rorschach were at the top of the kit bag of the emerging profession of clinical psychology, which was then still more involved in testing than in psychotherapy. Research to validate projective techniques was mainly nonsupportive (Lindzey, 1961), but it was probably the shifting focus of professional concern from testing to therapy, more than discouraging evidence, that ended psychologists' love affair with projective techniques. Murray's treatment of the TAT and other imaginative productions actually stands up quite well in the present more skeptical climate. He did not offer a cookbook scoring system. Rather, he saw evoked fantasy as a more accessible semiequivalent to the dream, open to systematic analysis along lines that currently fashionable jargon would call *hermeneutic.* The TAT still seems better than the Rorschach as an eductor of interpretable responses.

By the end of the 1960s, when Mischel's (1968) *Personality and Assessment* appeared, it seemed for a while as though the holistic, dynamic approach to personality that Murray stood for was being interred, along with Allport's and, indeed, with any structural/dispositional account of the person. The pressures of the grant system of research support and of the publish-or-perish context of academic career advancement were very hard on people who wanted to do research in the style of *Explorations,* which Robert White (1981) described as "exploring personality the long way" in his classic appreciative account of how *Explorations* was produced. It just didn't make career sense for young psychologists to invest in research that lacked the prospect of quickly quantized payoffs. Laboratory studies of situational effects, studies of variables rather than of persons, held the day. Carlson (1971) gave the definitive characterization of the disastrous consequences for personology.

During those lean years, the Institute for Personality Assessment and Research (IPAR) at the University of California, Berkeley, explicitly continued the Murray tradition under MacKinnon's (1975) leadership. It was also kept alive in industrial/organizational psychology. The multifaceted observational approach to personality assessment first displayed in *Explorations* and further developed under wartime pressures by another stellar team of psychologists led by Murray (Office of Strategic Services Assessment Staff, 1948) continued to be applied in the American Telephone and Telegraph assessment center studies (Bray, 1982; Howard & Bray, 1988). While academia doubted, the business world profited by Murray's approach. By the late 1970s, the climate was beginning to change, and psychology was once more recognizing the existence of personhood in an interactionist framework much like Murray's (also Gardner Murphy's and Kurt Lewin's) of four decades earlier (Magnusson & Endler, 1977). Since then, personology has enjoyed a small renaissance, heralded particularly by the publication of major longitudinal studies of personality development (e.g., Block, with Haan, 1971). We can therefore now look back on *Explorations* in a spirit that is more appreciative, less polemical than would have been possible only a little while ago. We can see it as launching an enterprise of personology that once more is vigorously alive in psychology.

As a launching platform, *Explorations* presented a very incomplete Gestalt. The research that the book reported used a number of interviews and experimental procedures on a single set of 51 paid subjects of student age. Murray's inspired idea was to have all the investigators with their different hypotheses and methods feed their results and their understandings of individual differences into a diagnostic council of senior staff, who would then arrive at a consensual formulation of each personality. Their construction of the life would then feed back into fuller understanding of people's responses to the various procedures. At the insistence of the publisher, however, *Explorations* presented only a single case thus described. Thus, the substantive payoff of the elaborate conceptualization and procedures is very incompletely presented. In a subsequent study at the Harvard Clinic that was substantially modeled on *Explorations*, I participated in a similar venture that used diagnostic council discussion to agree on qualitative formulations (Smith, Bruner, & White, 1956), so I share in the subjective conviction that the strategy serves to approach the "truth" about people in some sense. At IPAR, individual quantitative ratings were pooled instead, to avoid possible distortions from social influence processes in diagnostic council discussion (MacKinnon, 1975). I am aware of no research venture after *Explorations* that followed its promising example of using information from a variety of other procedures to throw light on the meaning of subjects' responses to particular experimental situations. Experimental personality research has simply not been done from such a person-focused perspective.

Over the years after World War II, Murray offered partial revisions of his concepts and hoped to complete a major, fully revised system. It was one of his Icarian ambitions that he was unable to bring off. (Murray identified with his formulation of the "Icarus complex," which included unrealistic ambition [Murray, 1955].) Although we can regret the occasion for his disappointment, personologists of the present generation probably doubt that such an objective was feasible—or, to put it another way, we probably suppose that, even if Murray *had* managed to produce a new full version of his system, the science of personology might still not be greatly advanced from where it stands today. That may seem to be a grim judgment. All the same, I think it reflects our more modest conception of what a systematic personology can achieve.

In psychology at large, the age of grand systems, essentially contemporaneous with *Explorations*, is long gone. All the more reason to be skeptical of the merit of grand systems in an area that we are coming to see participates as much in the characteristics of the humanities as in those of the natural sciences. With his background in medicine and biochemistry, Murray could not help thinking of personology as a natural science, even while his own participation in the life of the creative imagination made him a humanist. The tension between the scientific and the humanistic world outlooks surely played a part in Murray's own creativity, but it did not receive explicit recognition in his systematic formulations. I suspect that Murray the ex-biochemist would have loved to have left as his legacy a system of needs and press, actones and themas, which would do for personality what Mendeleyev's periodic table did for 19th-century chemistry. That no longer makes sense. He also wanted to write the definitive psychobiography and critical analysis of Herman Melville—his Icarian ambition on the humanistic side.

In the chapter that he prepared for Sigmund Koch's massive *Psychology: A Study of a Science*, which drew the curtain on the age of systems, Murray adds the following comment on his career shift from physiology to psychology, almost as an aside:

> Also influential to some degree were the impressions that (1) human personality, because of its present sorry state, had become *the* problem of our time—a hive of conflicts, lonely, half-hollow, half-faithless, half-lost, half-neurotic, half-delinquent, not equal to the problems that confronted it, not very far from proving itself an evolutionary failure; (2) that psychoanalysis had already made appreciable progress in exposing and interpreting the deeper processions of the mind; and (3) that my temperament was more suited to the making of coarse maps of newly explored areas than to the refinement of relatively precise maps of familiar ground. (Murray, 1959/1981, p. 11)

Murray's concern with the crisis of our times comes through in his later work but is tacit in *Explorations*. In that seminal volume, he did much more than provide a coarse map. By precept, example, and the charisma that he somehow managed to transmit by means of the printed page, he essentially launched the modern psychology of personality. Recent longitudinal research in the study of lives is beginning to realize the promise held forth by Murray's classic.

References

Allport, G. W. (1937). *Personality: A psychological interpretation*. New York: Holt.

Block, J. (1981). Some enduring and consequential structures of personality. In A. I. Rabin, J. Aronoff, A. M. Barclay, & R. A. Zucker, *Further explorations in personality*. New York: Wiley.

Block, J., with Haan, N. (1971). *Lives through time*. Berkeley, CA: Bancroft.

Bray, D. W. (1982). The assessment center and the study of lives. *American Psychologist, 37*, 180–189.

Carlson, R. (1971). Where is the person in personality research? *Psychological Bulletin, 75*, 203–219.

Howard, A., & Bray, D. W. (1988). *Managerial lives in transition: Advancing age and changing times*. New York: Guilford Press.

Lindzey, G. (1961). *Projective techniques and cross-cultural research*. New York: Appleton-Century-Crofts.

MacKinnon, D. W. (1975). IPAR's contribution to the conceptualization and study of creativity. In I. A. Taylor & J. W. Getzells (Eds.), *Perspectives in creativity*. Chicago: Aldine.

Magnusson, D., & Endler, N. S. (Eds.). (1977). *Personality at the crossroads: Current issues in interactional psychology*. Hillsdale, NJ: Erlbaum.

McClelland, D. C. (1985). *Human motivation*. Glenview, IL: Scott, Foresman.

McClelland, D. C., Atkinson, J. W., Clark, R. A., & Lowell, E. L. (1953). *The achievement motive*. New York: Appleton-Century-Crofts.

McDougall, W. (1921). *An introduction to social psychology* (14th ed.). Boston, MA: John W. Luce. (Original work published 1908)

McDougall, W. (1937). Organization of the affective life: A critical survey. *Acta Psychologica, 2*(3), 233–346.

Miller, J. G. (1978). *Living systems*. New York: McGraw-Hill.

Mischel, W. (1968). *Personality and assessment*. New York: Wiley.

Murray, H. A., et al. (1938). *Explorations in personality*. New York: Oxford University Press.

Murray, H. A. (1955). American Icarus. In A. Burton & R. E. Harris (Eds.), *Clinical studies of personality* (Vol. 2, pp. 615–641). New York: Harper.

Murray, H. A. (1967). Henry A. Murray. In G. Lindzey (Ed.), *A history of psychology in autobiography* (Vol. 5, pp. 283–310). New York: Appleton-Century-Crofts.

Murray, H. A. (1981). Preparations for the scaffold of a comprehensive system. In E. S. Shneidman (Ed.), *Endeavors in psychology: Selections from the personology of Henry A. Murray*. New York: Harper & Row. [Reprinted from S. Koch (Ed.). (1959). *Psychology: A study of science*]

Office of Strategic Services Assessment Staff. (1948). *Assessment of men: Selection of personnel for the Office of Strategic Services*. New York: Rinehart.

Patnoe, S. (1988). *A narrative history of experimental social psychology: The Lewin tradition*. New York: Springer-Verlag.

Shipley, T. E., Jr., & Veroff, J. (1952). A projective measure of need for affiliation. *Journal of Experimental Psychology, 43*, 349–356.

Smith, M. B., & Anderson, J. W. (1989). Obituary, Henry A. Murray (1893–1988). *American Psychologist, 44*, 1153–1154.

Smith, M. B., Bruner, J. S., & White, R. W. (1956). *Opinions and personality*. New York: Wiley.

Stagner, R. (1937). *Personality*. New York: McGraw-Hill.

Veroff, J. (1957). Development and validation of a projective measure of power motivation. *Journal of Abnormal and Social Psychology, 54*, 1–8.

White, R. W. (1981). Exploring personality the long way: The study of lives. In A. I. Rabin, J. Aronoff, A. M. Barclay, & R. A. Zucker (Eds.), *Further explorations in personality*. New York: Wiley.

Winter, D. G. (1973). *The power motive*. New York: Free Press.

Chapter Six

Beyond Aristotle and Galileo
Toward a Contextualized Psychology of Persons

Psychologists of my generation will recognize the implicit reference in my title immediately: to Kurt Lewin's (1931) classic paper that introduced most of us to the excitement of his ideas when we read it as the initial chapter of *A Dynamic Theory of Personality* (Lewin, 1935). When Lewin wrote about "The Conflict Between Aristotelian and Galilean Modes of Thought in Contemporary Psychology" over a half a century ago, it was indeed a breath of fresh air. Along with a very few other books and papers, it stands out saliently in my memory as having had a large part in forming my enduring perspective in psychology. It surely played a similar role for many others, by no means just Lewinians. We cannot readily recall its content since we've absorbed it, and built it into the fabric of our thought.

I turn back to Lewin's essay because it represents the physicalist tradition in psychological theory at its best, free of many faults that tainted the behavioristic expressions of positivism. All the same, the hermeneutic and contextualist critique of positivism should leave us dissatisfied with Lewin's version of a Galilean strategy for psychology. In one respect, thus, I am using this occasion for my own "me-too" endorsement of post-positivist theorizing, joining with Harré and Secord (1972). Harré (1984), Gergen (1973, 1982), and Shotter (1984) among others.

My second concern here is to focus attention on the need for a culturally and historically contextualized approach in personality theory. For accidental reasons (if it is fair to call Gergen's [1973] intervention accidental), the case for a historically contextual approach in the human-oriented personality/social sector of psychology was made first in the especially hostile territory of experimental social psychology. Personality psychology was then in the doldrums symbolized and promoted by

Mischel's (1971) anti-personality text, and personality theory was most aptly represented by the competing chapter-versions of timeless human nature presented in the successive editions of Hall and Lindzey (1957). The task of re-formulating personality theory in the post-positivist mode remains largely to be done, though we are seeing some encouraging new developments in the current renaissance of personology.

Finally, this occasion[1] lets me talk some sense about post-positivist perspectives in psychology. As usual, the conceptual innovators have not been very reasonable. *If* a contextualized psychology of persons is to be advanced, we need a more plausible version of contextualism than is being argued by the leading polemicists. This is also an effort, therefore, to domesticate a contextualized approach, to accommodate it to its prospective role of defining a new mainstream of theorizing at the softer, more human end of the psychological spectrum.

Lewin's Formulation Revisited

To begin with, then, let us turn back to Lewin's attack on what he saw as Aristotelian features of the psychology of fifty years ago. Lewin made it clear, by the way, that the target of his objections was not the writings of the historical Aristotle but rather the styles of conceptualization generally favored in medieval natural science, in contrast with those of modern physical science as heralded by Galileo. He was also explicit in disavowing any stand on physicalist reductionism, while arguing that conceptual approaches effective in physics could also be appropriate for psychology.

Many features of his argument are still pertinent and persuasive today. Thus his objection to *essentialist* modes of explanation—to instinct or trait or factor theories, for example, in which causes are sought in the properties of the individual taken in isolation—as contrasted with his Galilean strategy: "*The dynamics of the processes is always to be derived from the relation of the concrete individual to the concrete situation,* and, so far as internal forces are concerned, from the mutual relations of the various systems that make up the individual" (p. 41, italics are Lewin's). In social and personality psychology, we are still struggling to regain and substantiate in research the interactionist approach that Lewin formulated so clearly, which for long was misinterpreted in social psychology as a mere situationism.

Lewin's sophisticated treatment of the role of the situation is well illustrated in his incisive disposal of the heredity-environment issue, in a passage that follows from his criticism of the concept of an "optimal" situation as developed in the psychology of mental test performance:

> . . . [The] question at the center of discussion of the situation is, quite in the Aristotelian sense, how far can the situation hinder (or facilitate). The situation is even considered as a constant object and the question is discussed: which is more important, heredity or environment? Thus again, on the basis of a concept of situation gotten by abstraction, a dynamic problem is treated in a form which has none but a statistical historical meaning (p. 39).

That is, the question usually put about the relative influence of heredity and environment admits no general answer, only a particular historical one limited to a particular population under particular environmental conditions. Much of the heat dissipated in disputes about heredity vs. environment in the intervening years could have been conserved had Lewin's analysis been grasped more widely.

Another central point, still valuable, was Lewin's insistence on the lawfulness of the individual case and the potential misleadingness of statistical generalization, especially when tied to essentialist conceptualization. Merely actuarial prediction in psychology falls short of understanding as it ducks the challenge to analyze the underlying processes.

In his own day, Lewin had to face considerable debate about his insistence on contemporaneous as vs. historical causation. The issues in that debate are not those that concern us now. Looking back, I think it is fair to say that in an imaginary state of ideally complete knowledge, the historical lines of explanation favored then by followers of Freud, Hull, and Skinner converge with Lewin's preferred version of contemporaneous causation. If you know everything, you could use the past to construct the present situation. The trouble is, we don't have and won't have complete historical knowledge about the life-long sequence of anybody's person-situation interactions, nor do we or will we ever have valid X-ray vision to detect the momentary array of personal and situational determinants of behavior, to fill in the data required in principle by Lewin's analysis. In regard to *this* argument, it is only fair to say that historical and contemporaneous strategies are both required, neither is self-sufficient, and using them together, we still have a hard enough time!

Having paid our respects to the continuing relevance of Lewin's critique of conceptualization in psychology, we must now note some fundamental ways in which his vision seems dated. Lewin saw his efforts as contributing to the emergence of a theoretically systematized psychology modeled on the physics of Newton and Einstein. His version of "field theory" was less simply mechanical than the associationist behaviorism of Hull and Spence, but his conception of the goal of scientific endeavor in psychology was essentially the same as theirs: a fully articulated and mathematicized, deterministic, timeless system of axioms and postulates, theorems, and coordinating definitions. Many of us cannot believe in that goal any more, not just because we have been chastened by the failure to make discernable progress toward achieving it, but more fundamentally because our conception of the scientific enterprise, in general and especially as it bears upon the science of people, has changed. The hegemony of logical positivism is over, though the news of this state of affairs has not yet spread to all quarters.

As I see it, at least two distinct lines of challenge have been successful in ending its unquestioned hegemony in psychology. On the one hand, the timeless validity of psychological explanation has been called into question, especially by Gergen (1973) in his claim that social psychology is an essentially historical discipline. (He has since [1982] come forward with still more radical challenges to the positivistic interpretation of the human sciences.) On the other hand, the very nature of explanation in the human sciences has been challenged, questioning not only the models of linear causation traditional in psychology (and built into the usual design of experiments) but also the interactive "field" determination characteristic of Lewin and the Gestalt theorists, and the recursive feedback loops of more recent cybernetics and general systems theory, from a point of view that stresses meanings, intentions, and rules instead. (Harré and Secord [1972]. Harré [1984], and Shotter [1984] are recent exponents of this line of attack, under the banner of rule-role or ethogenic theory, or interpretative or "hermeneutic" approaches.) The two lines of attack readily merge, since meanings, intentions, and rules are formulated and constituted in terms of symbol systems that are culturally and historically provided. If we are to take these two lines of criticism as seriously as they demand, we perforce must go beyond Lewin's vision of a Galilean psychology, though we can retain most of his insights into the limitations of Aristotelian strategies that still persist in psychology a half century later.

Even in the latter respect, some of Lewin's strictures against Aristotelian features of psychological analysis need reconsideration, in the light of post-Galilean developments in the formulation of human action. Lewin objected to the intrusion of anthropomorphic concepts, of value concepts, and of dichotomous formulations into psychological theory. But if our meanings are constructed within culturally provided symbol systems, and if our conduct is governed by how we construe ourselves and our world, then to the extent that our conceptions of one another and of the social world are riddled with anthropomorphic concepts and value concepts and (if George Kelly [1955] was right) also with dichotomous ones, there is a *prima facie* case that we ought not to exclude concepts of these kinds arbitrarily from our more formal psychological theories. At least, our theories must make a place for accounts of how such concepts participate in constituting our human nature as it has emerged in culture and history. Developments in cybernetics and information science since Lewin's time also legitimize new interpretations of the Aristotelian principle of teleology, another item on Lewin's hit list.

Cultural and Historical Context in Personality Theory

As I have already noted, it seems surprising that the challenge to ahistorical systematic science on the softer end of psychology has been debated primarily in the ultrapositivist context of experimental social psychology rather than in personality psychology, where, on the face of it, the case would seem to have been more obvious and potential receptivity greater. Traditional theories of personality, the sort presented in Hall and Lindzey (1957), have characteristically been put forward in universalistic, ahistorical terms. Even such an influential theorist as Allport (1937), who was explicitly critical of the dominant positivist tradition and open to European phenomenological and existential trends, remained blithely history- and culture-bound (and in Lewin's terms, also Aristotelian in his emphasis on the psychophysical systems of the abstracted individual).

Perhaps one reason that personality psychology was slow to respond to the vulnerability of mainstream positivism was the ill fate of the culture-and-personality movement of the 1930s and 1940s. In the work of Mead (1939), Benedict (1934), Kardiner (1939), Hallowell (1955), Du Bois (1944), and others, interesting and important problems were addressed concerning the linkage of economy, child rearing, modal personality, and the coherence of cultural beliefs and institutions. As a collaboration between anthropology, psychoanalysis, and to a small extent psychology, the movement was a major step toward focusing awareness on the cultural context of personality. But writers in this tradition mostly assumed the universal validity of some version of neo-Freudian psychoanalysis or of neobehaviorism rather than remaining open to more radical ways in which the organization and dynamics of personality might vary across cultures. And the soon-recognized excesses of wartime interpretations of national character sped a decline of interest in the field, more rapid and complete than the similar decline in the status of psychoanalysis. Only a few contemporary writers in psychological anthropology continue the older culture-and-personality tradition (e.g., Le Vine, 1973; Spiro, 1967). I am encouraged, now, by the resurgence of interest in essentially the same area, under the more cognitively framed aegis of "culture and self" (see Heelas & Lock, 1981; Marsella, De Vos, & Hsu, 1984).

In principle, cross-cultural variation and historical change should have essentially the same conceptual implications for a science of personality. Each brings in contextual considerations that our traditional theories have ignored. In fact, the historical perspective on personality is even more underdeveloped than the cross-cultural. Most of the salvos charging "history-boundedness" that get fired in the theoretical disputes of psychology are themselves likely to be history-bound. That is, the critic challenges the universalist claims of the theory being criticized, on grounds of its unwitting determination by its historical context—while assuming the universal validity of his or her *own* preferred theoretical position. Much of the feminist criticism of Freud seems vulnerable in this respect. Freudian theory is charged with reflecting the prejudices and pathologies of patriarchal bourgeois society in turn-of-the-century Vienna. Indeed, it does reflect them, but one's judgmental tone is different if one sees the Freudian accounts, say, of penis envy, castration anxiety, and the super-ego merely as false projections of male prejudice, or whether one rather sees them as not-so-bad metaphors for the fate of the sexes in *that* society at that time. Along these lines, I am continually impressed by the difficulty my students seem to have in attaining any degree of *historical* relativism of perspective, students who are enthusiastically imbued with the spirit of *cultural* relativism. It takes confrontation with cultures that sanction infanticide or clitoridectomy to shake their nonjudgmental stance. Unlike us Americans, the Buga-Buga can do no wrong, but our parents and grandparents can never be forgiven their benightedness.

If we look for a treatment of personality that is truly contextual historically, the tradition of Marxist scholarship, particularly in the Frankfurt school, comes especially to the fore. Horkheimer (1936), Marcuse (1955), and Fromm (1941) drew jointly on Marxism and psychoanalysis to give substance to a line of theorizing linking personality to social structure in historical perspective, a research tradition that paralleled the culture-and-personality collaboration of psychoanalysis and anthropology but had little contact with it. Fromm in particular laid out in *Escape from Freedom* (1941) a sophisticated neo-Freudian, revisionist Marxian account of the interplay of social history and "social character" in accounting for modern vulnerability, especially in Germany, to fascism and nazism. As he further developed his ideas about a historically grounded characterology (1947), they provided the basis for Riesman's (1950) popular and still provocative analysis of tradition-directed, inner-directed, and other-directed character types in recent history and the contemporary United States.

And Riesman's analysis gave me, in turn, a convenient framework to put competing theories of selfhood in historical context. It seemed to me that the Freudian super-ego and the integral Allportian ego or "proprium" both represent conceptions of personality congruent with the historical predominance of Riesman's inner-directed type (metaphorically "gyroscopic"), whereas the unintegrated—or disintegrated— ideas of selfhood linked to Laing (1959) (*The Divided Self*), Lifton (1976) (the protean self), Gergen (1971), and the dramaturgical approaches (Goffman, 1959; Sarbin, 1977) could occur only to authors who take for granted the personality orientations that Riesman labeled as other-directed (metaphorically, governed by radar). If these theories are seen as addressed to salient features of the character structure of their time, they need not be forced into confrontation as mutually exclusive versions of universal human nature. We have recently been reminded by Shweder and Bourne (1982) that tradition-directed conceptions of the person are still much alive in the contemporary world. By their analysis, such conceptions of concretely situated behavior may correspond more closely to Lewin's process-oriented Galilean ideals than do our Aristotelian folk habits of trait attribution.

The most articulate call for an explicit historically contextual approach to personality has come not from the central territory of the field but from its borders, in the interdisciplinary area of life-span or life-course human development, a still-recent movement that got its start as an orientation to gerontology but has become a mainstream orientation of human development and developmental psychology. If we consider the metatheoretical hemming and hawing about history and science in social psychology, and my own hemming and hawing here about historical aspects of the psychology of personality, it is remarkable how little metatheoretical fuss has been made about the role of history in formulations of human development: the concern there has been primarily *methodological*, and it seems to be taken for granted by developmentalists that history can contribute to good science. It would never occur to them to pose the issue as it came to be framed in social psychology: social psychology as history *versus* science.

A central methodological feature of the life-span approach was drawn from the highly technical but essentially atheoretical discipline of demography: the concept of birth *cohorts* (cf. Ryder, 1965), sets of people who enter the course of history at about the same time. The life-span approach stresses the importance of distinguishing between the effects of aging as such from cohort effects—consequences of a particular intersection with history that were commonly confounded with age effects in the earlier literature on aging, which depended on cross-sectional rather than longitudinal research. Making this clear distinction led initially to a radical revision of our understanding of the fate of intellectual abilities (since the older people in any U.S. cross-section were also less well educated, more likely to be immigrants). More recently, attention to cohort differences is turning out to be just as fruitful in throwing light on the impact of historically structured life events on personality development (Elder, 1974). Current empirical research on personality development not only is open to historically contextual contributions but is actively seeking them out.

In considering the need to bring cultural and historical context into the study of personality, and the efforts that have been made to do so, I have passed over an issue of conceptual strategy that needs to be looked at explicitly. How radical should we be in our contextualism? Do we envisage the cultural and historical context primarily as providing *content*—values of variables and parameters, so to speak—within structures and relationships that are humanly universal? Lewin would have had no difficulty with this sort of contextual formulation, so it becomes understandable why Sarbin (1977) could classify him as a contextualist. The culture-and-personality theorists with their commitment to neo-Freudian or neobehavioristic principles fall at the same universalistic pole of contextualism, which is implied by the old anthropological postulate of the "psychic unity of mankind." At the other pole is a radical contextualism that amounts to a thoroughgoing relativism. Should we be open to the possibility that the rules of the game change with contextual effects: that a few? some? most? structures of personality and principles of personality development and interpersonal relations differ with the historical and cultural context?

Elsewhere, I have noted in passing Edelstein's (1983) criticism of the extreme relativism that radical contextualism implies, which undercuts any justification for basing recommendations for applied social practice on scientific results. Edelstein finds such a demoralizing, even nihilistic view exemplified in Kessen's (1979) essay, "The American Child and Other Cultural Inventions"; social psychologists will recognize it in Gergen's (1982) recent writings, and in aspects of the current treatments of selfhood by Harré (1984) and by Shotter (1984). The intellectual challenge is drastic, and it has to be taken seriously.

Edelstein's way of taking it seriously seems to me so well formulated that I will quote him at greater length:

> Neo-universalist programs [that challenge extreme relativism], obviously, run into difficulties. Their proof-systems rest on plausibilities that differ from the validational conventions of the accepted probabilistic methodologies. They have to reach beyond relativistic and particularistic knowledge and to construct, both from synchronic and diachronic dimensions of child development, an over-arching yet dynamic structure of the whole, which encompasses both the contexts of child development and the dynamics of transformation affecting childhood and its organization. . . . [The] immediate impression from child studies is that contextual embeddedness and societal change deeply affect child development. Two consequences emerge from this observation: *First*, the study of child development, if it is to be adequate to its object, both represents and, to some extent presupposes the study of the developmentally relevant structures and parameters of the society itself. *Second:* The culturally relative data that such studies yield need to be ordered in view of a criterion or theory that transcends them.

Edelstein's own life experience in Iceland with the extraordinary sudden transition after World War II from the age-old traditional world of subsistence farming and fishing to a modern stratified society gives especial authority to his sociologically framed attempt to escape from the nihilistic implications of extreme relativism. On the social-historical side, he draws on the traditions of Marx and Weber for an analysis of the major world-wide dimensions of "modernization"—a process that also provides for the newly universal institution of formal schooling and a novel social definition of childhood and youth in relation to this impacting institution. In the modern world, affluent or poor, bureaucratic schooling replaces the transparently valid ways in which the child used to become a participating member of the family enterprise *through* participation, with an abstract and rational age-graded system for inducting new members to the roles that society requires of them—one that tends to be opaque in its justification for participants. In his view.

> . . . the contradictions affecting the interaction between development and the social structures which both generate and constrain development appear to limit its course towards cognitive and moral autonomy and functionally adequate self-identity and to channel socializing forces towards the production of the orally dependent, alienated, angry or depressive type that Lasch (1979) has described.

At the same time, the requirements imposed by modernity result in the emergence of Piagetian sequences of cognitive development, not as biological givens but as non-arbitrary historical emergents. Such a contextualized view indeed presupposes frames of interpretation that transcend the culturally and historically relative: there is no royal road to their attainment, validation, or correction. I will return to the broad issue contrasting radical and limited contextualism later.

Contextualism Reconsidered

So far, I have been discussing historically and culturally contextualized approaches in psychology from what seems to me a fairly down-to-earth perspective, in terms of their motivation, their variants, and some of the conceptual problems to which they give rise. I have not given any explicit attention to "contextualism" as a distinctive metatheoretical or philosophical model. But such a model is exactly what Sarbin (1977), Reese, and Overton (Reese and Overton, 1970: Overton and Reese, 1973) have been promoting, in espousing the classic formulation by the Berkeley philosopher Pepper (1942) as the basis for metatheoretical criticism and prescription in social, developmental, and personality psychology. We need to look more closely at Pepper's conception of contextualism.

Contextualism for Pepper is one of four relatively successful "root metaphors" underlying the various metaphysical systems that thoughtful people have developed. He explains the idea of root metaphor as follows:

> A man [he wrote before we were self-conscious about sexist style] desiring to understand the world looks about for a clue to its comprehension. He pitches upon some area of common sense fact and tries to understand other areas in terms of this one. This original area becomes his basic analogy or root metaphor. He describes as best he can the characteristics of this area, or, if you will, discriminates its structure. A list of its structural characteristics [categories] becomes his basic concepts of explanations and description. . . . In terms of these categories he proceeds to study all other areas of fact. . . . As a result of the impact of these other facts upon his categories, he may qualify and readjust . . . so that a set of categories commonly changes and develops. (p. 91)

Pepper's four major root-metaphors include formism, mechanism, contextualism, and organicism. The root metaphor of formism hinges on similarity and leads to classificatory systems like those of Plato, Aristotle, and the Scholastics. That of mechanism hinges on the machine, be it a clock, a dynamo, or a computer, and, as our presently dominant world view, it deals in terms of cause and effect. Contextualism is harder to grasp.

> When we come to contextualism, we pass from an analytical to a synthetic type of theory. It is characteristic of the synthetic theories that their root metaphors cannot satisfactorily be denoted even to a first approximation by well-known common-sense concepts such as similarity, the artifact, or the machine. . . . [Could it be that his metaphor of root-metaphor is breaking down? MBS] The best term out of common sense to suggest the point of origin of contextualism is probably the historic event. And this we shall accordingly call the root metaphor of this theory. (p. 232)

Pepper has in mind the "dynamic dramatic active event," the act-in-context, and it turns out that the family of philosophical systems that he is thinking of is the American pragmatism of Peirce, James, Dewey, and Mead in which he himself was raised.

There are similar problems with organicism:

As with contextualism, so with organicism, no ordinary common-sense term offers a safe reference to the root metaphor of the theory. The common term "organism" is too much loaded with biological connotations . . . and "integration" is only a little better. Yet there are no preferable terms. . . .

Actually, the historical event which is the root metaphor of contextualism is a nearer approximation to the refined root metaphor of organicism than any common-sense term. This is so true that it is tempting to regard these two theories as species of the same theory, one being dispersive and the other integrative. It has occasionally been said that pragmatism is simply idealism with the absolute left out, which in our terms would be to say that contextualism is simply dispersive organicism. (p. 280)

It is clear that Pepper's concern here is with the underlying category system of absolute idealism in the style of Hegel, Bradley, and Royce. He is definitely not considering the holistic biological conceptions of organism so prominent in the history of psychological theorizing.

This is of course not an appropriate occasion for detailed criticism of Pepper's classic analysis, nor do I have the philosophical capability for it. The little I have already said, however, may suffice to make the point to those who take their Pepper at second hand via his contextualist advocates in psychology: that his typology constructed for the analysis of philosophic systems need not necessarily suit our different purposes as psychologists. The lines of cleavage that he finds between the major philosophical outlooks are inherently arbitrary to a degree. Why should we expect them to draw the distinctions that are most relevant to psychological theorizing? Formism and mechanism, yes: we can readily apply these root metaphors to the clarification of our theoretical assumptions. Recent psychologists have had little truck with absolute idealism, so Pepper's version of organicism doesn't meet our needs. When we move from old fashioned machines and dynamos as models to general systems theory, to computers, cybernetics, and information science, the meaning and boundaries of mechanism get obscured in ways that Pepper gives us no help with. Why should we expect such help from what he published in 1942? His detailed treatment of the categories of contextualism in terms of change and novelty in the quality and texture of events does not seem to me to make fruitful contact with our real problems of conceptual strategy in dealing with context in psychological theorizing. In no way does he tackle the phenomenological, hermeneutic, and dialectical traditions, which now seem very relevant to psychology.

Have we perhaps been drawing on Pepper's terminology for polemical purposes, without finding his actual analysis of much real use?

I am challenging the authority of Pepper in our domain not only because he does not highlight the distinctions that may be most important for us, but also because I am not ready to accept for psychological theorizing his strong argument against eclecticism: that one cannot legitimately criticize one "world hypothesis" or philosophical system in terms of another; that we should not compromise or combine them; that our root metaphors shouldn't be mixed. In specific regard to the tasks of psychology, I remain convinced that the phenomena of selfhood can only be grasped by some kind of deliberate mixing or alternation of causal-explanatory (mechanistic) and interpretative (contextual and hermeneutic) points of view, root metaphors if you like.

As I have argued elsewhere (Smith, 1978a), our reflexive self-awareness and all that goes with it in our existence as embodied persons indeed thrusts us into two worlds—the world of the natural sciences in which we look for causal explanation following strategies that are no longer readily sorted into Lewin's Aristotelian vs. Galilean dichotomy, and a human symbolic and cultural world of meaning and value that requires of us an interpretative approach. These worlds empirically intersect in us as persons, as human actors. We psychologists who wish to give an account of personhood—or as applied practitioners want to use our psychology to advance human ends—cannot avoid dealing with our topic in both the causal and the interpretative mode. Indeed, some of the most fruitful foci of our research in recent years involve concepts like locus of control or self-efficacy or learned helplessness in which self-attributed meanings—aspects of the interpretative world—have been subjected to causal analysis of their conditions and consequences (see Smith, 1983). From a perspective influenced by existentialism, we seem indeed to be creatures intrinsically linked to mixed metaphors. To constrain our psychological accounts to one "root metaphor" is humanly wrong!

Toward a Contextualized Psychology of Persons

Though I think it is wrong, it may nevertheless be fascinating, provocative, and useful to push a self-consistent point of view as far as it will go. That is how I interpret the recent ventures of Gergen (1982). Harré (1984), Shotter (1984) and Sarbin (1977), all in one way or another "contextualist," all creatively unreasonable, all making major forays into the territory of personality study.

In his radical reaction against positivism, Gergen seems to me to have cast off anchor from the evidential, empirical base that is essential to any enterprise that has a call upon the label "science." Our theories indeed have an ideological aspect, and he is right that we partly negotiate our generative conceptions of social theory among disputants, just as, according to Goffman (1959), we negotiate a socially validated conception of ourselves. But this is a partial truth, part of the truth, not the whole truth. Even though what we take as evidence, as *data*, is subject to debate, the never-finished business of the scientific enterprise requires a critical if never fully conclusive concern with evidence. I am not ready to dismiss the concept of human science, as it seems to me Gergen virtually proposes.

Harré (1984) and Shotter (1984) have published ambitious works in the British tradition of Wittgenstein (1953) and Ryle (1949), a tradition that takes its philosophic stance in the clarification of everyday language. They set an agenda for psychology unconnected with natural science. Harré, whose treatment is the more systematic, spells out many implications of a view that takes the radical option between the contextualist alternatives as I posed them earlier. Both authors make major claims toward the radical reconstruction of personality theory. Psychologists of personality have not hitherto been part of their audience. They should be. Yet I think Harré and Shotter have proposed a valuable elaboration of only one side, a partial view, of what is needed for an adequate psychology of persons.

In the course of a long and productive career, Sarbin, on his part, has advanced the dramaturgical metaphor of personhood as a major spokesman for "role theory." He has also been one of Pepper's prominent advocates. In various passages I read him as adopting a radical option of contextualism that places the historic event in a broader context of virtually Heraclitian flux. Yet at the same time he is able to call both Lewin and Piaget contextualists in psychology. The concept of contextualism does get slippery! I have to classify Sarbin, too, among the creatively unreasonable, since he persists in pushing the valuable dramaturgical metaphor or model well beyond the territory that it can handle comfortably—thus, on the empirical side, in his recent treatment of schizophrenia (Sarbin and Mancuso, 1980).

For my part, I want to put Pepper aside, and simply insist on the importance of much more attention to historical and cultural *context* in personality psychology than has been characteristic of the field. I welcome the contribution of the contextualist radicals, as opening important new perspectives on being a person, perspectives that also provide useful linkage to the symbolic interactionist tradition in sociology. But I want also to keep open the issue highlighted by Edelstein. In placing personality theory in its cultural and historical context, must we give up aspirations for transcendent, universalistic formulations? Not without trying as hard as we can to attain them, I would urge. But as a matter of strategy. I agree with the symbolic anthropologist Clifford Geertz (1973):

> In this area [of human studies], the road to the general, to the revelatory simplicities of science, lies through a concern with the particular, the circumstantial, the concrete . . . (p. 53),

a concern organized, he urges, by analyses at multiple levels from the biological to the cultural, with especial concern for the interplay between levels. A strongly contextual approach, in the weaker sense, but with no commitment at all to a single root-metaphor!

In my view a contextualized version of personality theory need not deny universals or be embarrassed by them. Surely some follow from our common biological make-up, the results of our evolutionary history genetically encoded. Others must be entailed by common social and cultural consequences of the life cycle of individuals and families, everywhere. Still others would be expected from the universal human existential predicament of self-aware mortality. A different type of universalist consideration might come from uniformities of social history, of the sort emphasized by Edelstein. Our formulations in context should capture such transhistorical, transcultural features, and we should be delighted when we find them.

Our attempts at general theories of personality have been severely history-and-culture bound, so we need to do better. In psychoanalysis, which has been so central in the course of personality study, the move toward a more hermeneutic formulation is a step in the right direction. (See, for example, Ricoeur [1970]: Schafer [1976].) But the challenges in personology, at least as I see them, can be more fully specified in terms of a set of orienting questions. In offering them as my shopping list. I partly summarize points that I have been trying to make: partly I introduce an even larger agenda schematically.

1. How can we formulate a psychology of personality that recognizes adequately the culturally and historically contextual nature of personality, and deals adequately with the sources of individuality in particular settings, in terms that aspire to *transcend* cultures and history and particular settings? This has emerged as the central question in this essay.

2. How can we give an account of personality that allows for degrees of unity or disunity or conflict, and degrees of self-determination or external control—without *postulating* absolutes of unity or Protean dispersion, or of free will or external programming? Such openness seems to be required by the range of cultural and historical variation. The challenge, thus, is to create a "morphogenic" theory in Allport's (1961) sense, a theory that does not assume or prescribe any single potential to be actualized, any predetermined goal.

3. How can we regain a *biosocial* conception of personality? Murphy (1947) was working along the essential lines, but his influence faded because he was so reasonable!

4. How can we reconstruct a *dynamic* theory of personality, without the metaphor of libido energy or its equivalent, which has been made obsolete by the revolution of information science?

5. How can we integrate an intentional, phenomenological psychology of meaning with a causal, explanatory psychology? As I have been urging, an adequate psychology of personality has to deal with both facets.

Perhaps a relatively abstract formulation like Silvan Tomkins' (1979) script theory, one in close touch with the general psychology of affect and cognition, may provide the framework within which these issues can be dealt with productively; perhaps the growing edge may turn out to lie in life-span developmental psychology.

These issues indeed involve considerations of metatheoretical strategy that carry us beyond the Aristotelian and Galilean alternatives that Kurt Lewin (1935) had in mind when he proposed his *Dynamic Theory of Personality*. The reigning positivism of his day has fallen in a scientific revolution. For the area of personality study, I have urged that we scrutinize our present theories critically to question aspects in which they are history-and-culture bound; that we accept more limited objectives with explicitly restricted historical and cultural reference as entirely legitimate; but that we remain responsive to the big challenge to find theoretical footholds that transcend history and culture. In this endeavor, moreover, I would carefully distinguish rejection of dogmatic positivism or scientism (Chein, 1972)—I am all for that—from complete skepticism about the role of evidence in psychological inquiry. I want to retain, though critically, the indispensible element of empiricism that lets us hold onto the ideal of a human science, a science of persons that is corrigible and partly cumulative, the more so because it is attentive to the historical and cultural context of personhood.

NOTE

1. The occasion was the author's delivery of the presidential address before the Division of Theoretical and Philosophical Psychology of the American Psychological Association in Toronto in August 1984.

References

Allport, G. W. *Personality: A psychological interpretation*. New York: Holt, 1937.

Allport, G. W. *Pattern and growth in personality*. New York: Holt, Rinehart, and Winston, 1961.

Benedict, R. *Patterns of culture*. Boston: Houghton-Mifflin. 1934.

Campbell, D. T. *Descriptive epistemology: Psychological, sociological and evolutionary*. William James Lectures (Preliminary draft), Harvard University, 1977. (Unpublished.)

Chein, I. *The science of behavior and the image of man*. New York: Basic Books, 1972.

Du Bois, C. *The people of Alor: A social-psychological study of an East Indian island*. Minneapolis: University of Minnesota Press. 1944.

Edelstein, W. Cultural constraints on development and the vicissitudes of progress. In F. S. Kessel and A. W. Siegel (Eds.), *Psychology and society: The child and other cultural inventions*. New York: Praeger, 1983.

Elder, G. H., Jr. *Children of the great depression: Social change in life experience*. Chicago: University of Chicago Press, 1974.

Fromm, E. *Escape from freedom*. New York: Farrar and Rinehart. 1941.

Fromm, E. *Man for himself. An inquiry into the psychology of ethics*. New York: Rinehart, 1947.

Geertz, C. *The interpretation of cultures: Selected essays*. New York: Basic Books, 1973.

Gergen, K. J. *The concept of self*. New York: Holt, Rinehart, and Winston, 1971.

Gergen, K. J. Social psychology as history. *Journal of Personality and Social Psychology*, 1973, 26, 309–320.

Gergen, K. J. *Toward transformation in social knowledge*. New York: Springer-Verlag, 1982.

Goffman, E. *The presentation of self in everyday life*. Garden City, N.Y.: Doubleday, 1959.

Hall, C. C., and Lindzey, G. *Theories of personality*. New York: Wiley, 1957.

Hallowell, A. I. *Culture and experience*. Philadelphia: University of Pennsylvania Press, 1955.

Harré, R. *Personal being: A theory for individual psychology*. Cambridge, Mass.: Harvard University Press, 1984.

Harré, R., and Secord, P. F. *The explanation of social behavior*. Oxford: Blackwell, 1972.

Heelas, P.L.F., and Lock, A. J. (Eds.) *Indigenous psychologies: The anthropology of the self*. New York and London: Academic Press, 1981.

Horkheimer, M. *Studien über Authorität und Familie*. In M. Horkheimer (Ed.) *Schriften des Instituts für Sozialforschung*, Vol. 5. Paris: Alcan, 1936.

Kardiner. A. *The individual and his society*. New York: Columbia University Press, 1939.

Kelly, G. A. *The psychology of personal constructs*. New York: Norton, 1955.

Kessen, W. (1979). The American child and other cultural inventions. *American Psychologist*, 34, 815–820.

Laing, R. D. *The divided self*. London: Tavistock, 1959.

Lasch, C. *The culture of narcissism: American life in an age of diminishing expectations*. New York: Norton, 1979.

LeVine, R. *Culture, behavior, and personality*. Chicago: Aldine, 1973.

Lewin, K. The conflict between Aristotelian and Galilean modes of thought in contemporary psychology. *Journal of Genetic Psychology*, 1931, 5, 141–177.

Lewin, K. *A Dynamic theory of personality: Selected papers*. New York: McGraw Hill, 1935.

Lifton, R. J. *The life of the self: Toward a new psychology*. New York: Simon and Schuster, 1976.

Marcuse. H. *Eros and civilization*. Boston: Beacon, 1955.

Marsella, A. J., De Vos, G. and Hsu, F. K. (Eds.) *Culture and self*. New York: Methuen Press (Tavistock Publications), 1984.

Mead, M. *From the south seas: Studies of adolescence and sex in primitive societies*. New York: Morrow, 1939.

Mischel, W. *Introduction to personality*. New York: Holt, Rinehart, and Winston, 1971.

Murphy, G. *Personality: A biosocial approach to origins and structure*. New York: Harper, 1947.

Overton, W. F., and Reese, H. W. Models of development: Methodological implications. In J. R. Nesselroade and H. W. Reese (Eds.). *Life-span developmental psychology: Methodological issues.* New York: Academic Press, 1973.

Pepper, S. C. *World hypotheses: A study in evidence.* Berkeley and Los Angeles: University of California Press, 1942.

Reese, H. W., and Overton. W. F. Models of development and theories of development. In L. R. Goulet and P. B. Baltes (Eds.). *Life-span developmental psychology: Research and theory.* New York: Academic Press. 1970.

Ricoeur, P. *Freud and philosophy: An essay on interpretation.* New Haven: Yale University Press, 1970.

Riesman, D. *The lonely crowd. A study of the changing American character.* New Haven: Yale University Press, 1950.

Ryder, N. B. The cohort as a concept in the study of social change. *American Sociological Review,* 1965, *30,* 843–861.

Ryle, G. *The concept of the mind.* London: Hutchinson, 1949.

Sarbin, T. R. Contextualism: A world view for modern psychology. In A. W. Landfield (Ed.). *Nebraska Symposium on Motivation,* 1976. (Vol. 24). Lincoln: University of Nebraska Press, 1977.

Sarbin, R. R., and Mancuso, J. C. *Schizophrenia: Medical diagnosis or moral verdict?* New York: Pergamon Press, 1980.

Schafer, R. *A new language for psychoanalysis.* New Haven: Yale University Press. 1976.

Shotter, J. *Social accountability and selfhood.* Oxford: Blackwell, 1984.

Shweder, R. A., and Bourne, E. J. Does the concept of the person vary cross-culturally? In A. J. Marsella and G. M. White (Eds.), *Cultural conceptions of mental health and therapy.* Dordrecht, Netherlands, and Boston: D. Reidel, 1982.

Smith, M. B. Humanism and behaviorism in psychology: Theory and practice. *Journal of Humanistic Psychology,* 1978a, 18 (1), 27–36.

Smith, M. B. Perspectives on selfhood. *American Psychologist, 1978b, 33,* 1053–1063.

Smith, M. B. Hope and despair: Keys to the socio-psychodynamics of youth. *American Journal of Orthopsychiatry,* 1983, *53,* 388–399.

Smith, M. B. The metaphorical basis of selfhood. In A. J. Marsella, G. De Vos, and F. K. Hsu (Eds.). *Culture and self.* New York: Methuen Press (Tavistock Publications), 1984.

Spiro, M. *Burmese supernaturalism: A study in the explanation and reduction of suffering.* Englewood Cliffs, N.J.: Prentice Hall, 1967.

Tomkins, S. S. Script theory: Differential amplification of affects. In H. W. Howe, Jr. and R. A. Dienstbier (Eds.), *Nebraska Symposium on Motivation 1973* (Vol. 36). Lincoln: University of Nebraska Press, 1979.

Wittgenstein, L. *Philosophical Investigations.* Oxford: Blackwell, 1953.

Part II

Toward an Understanding of Selfhood

Commentary

My involvement with personality and selfhood has consistently favored the holistic study of individual lives, as promoted by both Allport (1937) and Murray (Murray & others, 1938). My baptism of fire in such a personological approach came in my early collaboration with Jerome Bruner and Robert White in a study of how the opinions that ten adult men held about the Soviet Union at the beginning of the Cold War reflected features of their personalities and contributed to their functioning (Smith, Bruner, & White, 1956). In that research, Bob White was our leader in the tradition of Harry Murray's (1938) *Explorations* at the Harvard Psychological Clinic, which was the model for our study at the clinic. Bob was an amazingly competent and creative psychologist of personality who combined the different virtues of Allport and Murray with ones distinctively his own without the major limitations of each. Since he was so dependably helpful and modestly self-effacing, his substantial contributions to motivational and personality theory and personological research have been insufficiently appreciated (cf. Smith, 2002).

Each of us was responsible for integrating and presenting one of the three cases treated at full length in the book. "Hilary Sullivan," presented here in chapter 7, was my primary responsibility. I still remember with pride and pleasure that Murray's collaborator and paramour Christiana Morgan sat in at the meeting of the Diagnostic Council (of the senior investigators in our study) when I presented my initial formulation about Sullivan, and that she wrote me a laudatory note thereafter.

I reprint the case here for several reasons. For one, it represents work at the juncture of personality and social psychology, illustrating as it does the functional approach to the psychology of social attitudes. For another, I think it exemplifies rather well a kind of qualitative research that contributes appropriately to human psychology that aspires to be scientific. Qualitative research as careful natural history is a phase of empirical science that psychologists have tended to neglect in their fascination with experimentation and statistics. Still another reason is that it qualifies me as a personologist, a contributor to the holistic and dynamic study of individual personality in the trajectory initiated by Murray and White. Over the years, I have cherished participation in the small Society for Personology launched by Silvan Tomkins and Rae Carlson for the intellectual sustenance provided by the informal discussion in its annual meetings.

Starting from the broadly psychodynamic orientation of chapter 7, I have come like my fellow personologists to give more emphasis to the self-referential, reflexive aspects of personality, to selfhood. I particularly like Dan McAdams's (2001) treatment of people's sense of personal identity in terms of their life stories. Such a narrative approach has come to be quite widely shared by psychologists who see it as alternative to the natural scientific treatment of personality (here I would put Sarbin, 1986), and by others like McAdams who see it as improving the scientific status of psychology. McAdams (1995) provides an attractive framework for incorporating this relatively new focus in a general theory of personality, in terms of three standpoints or levels for the formulation of individuality. There is the level of *dispositional traits*, such as the currently popular Big Five, relatively decontextualized features of thought, feeling, and behavior. At a second level there are *characteristic adaptations*, including goals and motives, defense mechanisms, values and beliefs, and so on, "personal characteristics that are contextualized in time, place, or social role" (McAdams, 2001, p. 111.) The third level, that of integrative *life stories*, involves the person's ongoing project to provide her or his life with "some modicum of unity and purpose" (p. 111), with meaning. "Personality is a complex patterning of traits, adaptations, and stories" (p. 112). The functionalist approach represented by my treatment of Hilary Sullivan (chapter 7) was limited to Levels 1 and 2.

Chapter 8, "What It Means to Be Human," is my attempt to put selfhood in evolutionary and historical context. As my version of a scientifically oriented Origin Myth, its speculation holds up rather well after a quarter century. Probably the Neanderthals did not bury their dead in flower-lined graves, as I assumed following the anthropological wisdom of the day, but not much else is clearly wrong. My use of Ernest Becker's *Denial of Death* (1973) in highlighting the problematic consequences of the attainment of human self-awareness is given some empirical support by recent research on "terror management theory" (Solomon et al., 1991; Greenberg et al., 1986), also stimulated by Becker's speculations. The account I give of contemporary threats to meaning in the loss of various bases of death-defying hope lays a basis for discussions in chapters 9 and 19 of postmodernism as a response to these threats.

Chapter 9, "Selfhood at Risk," written in response to Kenneth Gergen's *The Saturated Self* (1991), was my first attempt to criticize the relativistic, demoralized postmodernism that Gergen came to epitomize for me. In its examination of our current cultural predicament, it goes beyond chapter 8, especially in drawing on Giddens's (1991) powerful sociological analysis of the grounds for alienation and moral confusion in what he calls the "late modern age." In its call for psychology to focus on strengthening people's shaken grounds for hope rather than contributing to postmodern fecklessness, it links with my earlier writings that put hopelessness at the core of much that is distressing about our present era (cf. Smith, 1983).

The last chapter in this part—chapter 10, "Self and Identity in Historical/Sociocultural Context"—was my contribution to an Australian conference on social psychological approaches to self and identity organized by Yoshihisa Kashima. It provides a brief historical perspective on psychological writing about selfhood since William James, and in particular looks back upon my own treatment of the topic a quarter century earlier in my presidential address to the American Psychological Association, "Perspectives on Selfhood" (Smith, 1978), to assess change and perhaps progress since then. I hope the reader will forgive some brief repetition from chapter 8. Prominent in regard to change is important recent work from the approach of cultural psychology (Cole, 1996; Markus & Kitayama, 1991), which emphasizes fidelity to indigenous conceptualization—and cross-cultural psychology (e.g., Triandis, 1989), which works with concepts intended to transcend particular cultures. I have not been a contributor to cultural or cross-cultural psychology, but I have been an avid consumer as a result of vivid exposure to developing societies in Mayan Chiapas and in Ghana.

References

Allport, G. W. (1937). *Personality: A psychological interpretation.* New York: Holt.

Becker, E. (1973). *The denial of death.* New York: The Free Press.

Cole, M. (1996). *Cultural psychology.* Cambridge, MA: Harvard University Press, Belknap Press.

Gergen, K. J. (1991). *The saturated self: Dilemmas of identity in contemporary life.* New York: Basic Books.

Giddens, A. (1991). *Modernity and identity: Self and society in the late modern age.* Stanford, CA: Stanford University Press.

Greenberg, J., Pyszcznski, T., & Solomon, S. (1986). The causes and consequences of a need for self-esteem: A terror management theory. In N. F. Baumeister (Ed.), *Public self and private self* (pp. 189–212). New York: Springer Verlag.

Markus, H., & Kitayama, S. (1991). Culture and self. *Psychological Review, 98,* 224–253.

McAdams, D. P. (1995). What do we know when we know a person? *Journal of Personality, 63,* 365–396.

McAdams, D. P. (2001). The psychology of life stories. *Review of General Psychology, 5,* 100–122.

Murray, H. A. & others. (1938). *Explorations in personality.* New York: Oxford University Press.

Sarbin, T. R. (1986). The narrative as root metaphor for psychology. In T. R. Sarbin (Ed.), *Narrative psychology: The storied nature of human conduct.* New York: Praeger.

Smith, M. B. (1978). Perspectives on selfhood. *American Psychologist, 33,* 1053–1063. Reprinted in M. B. Smith (1991), *Values, self, and society,* pp. 19–35. New Brunswick, NJ: Transaction.

Smith, M. B. (1983). Hope and despair: Keys to the sociopsychological dynamics of youth. *American Journal of Orthopsychiatry, 53,* 388–399. Reprinted in M. B. Smith (1991), *Values, self, and society,* pp. 233–245. New Brunswick, NJ: Transaction.

Smith, M. B. (2002). Robert W. White (1904–2001): Humanistic psychologist. *Journal of Humanistic Psychology, 42,* 9–12.

Smith, M. B., Bruner, J. S., & White, R. W. (1956). *Opinions and personality.* New York: Wiley.

Solomon, S., Greenberg, J., & Pyszczynski, T. (1991). A terror management theory of social behavior: The psychological functions of self-esteem and cultural world views. In M. P. Zanna (Ed.), *Advances in Experimental Social Psychology, 24,* 93–159. New York: Academic Press.

Triandis, H. C. (1989). The self and social behavior in differing cultural contexts. *Psychological Review, 96,* 506–520.

Chapter Seven

Hilary Sullivan

A Communist in belief though not a party member, Hilary Sullivan, one of the ten adult men studied by Smith, Bruner, and White (1956) at the Harvard Psychological Clinic, held opinions about Russia that were fraught with much more personal significance than those of the ordinary citizen. His attitudes illustrate vividly how a person's creative interpretation of the external world can play a strategic part in making difficult personal problems supportable.

Just as the personal significance of the world view of Chatwell, another subject of the clinic research, casts no light on the present validity of nineteenth century Liberalism, so our scrutiny of Sullivan's Communism can tell us nothing about the tenability of the Communist position in 1947. As we have repeatedly taken pains to observe, psychological interpretation must be carefully disentangled from *ad hominem* argument. We must also agree with Sullivan that he is "typical" only of himself. The psychological sources of Communist ideology in general are outside of our present concern.[1]

Our functional approach does, nevertheless, lead to some expectations in regard to people like the Communists who hold intense attitudes, and defines a limited sense in which we assume Sullivan to be "typical" of them. Whenever a person feels strongly about a topic, we run little risk in inferring that it has important personal meaning to him. The attitudes of a Communist should therefore provide unusual opportunity to trace out the adjustive functions that they serve. Deviant and unpopular, the views of such a person inevitably encounter attack from the public media of communication and perhaps from some of his circle of acquaintances. Unless he responds to such attack by consolidating his position and building it firmly into the structure of his going concerns, his dangerous opinions must succumb to social pressure and he ceases to be a Communist.

Introductory Sketch

Hilary Sullivan was a 48-year-old, self-educated man, the son of poor Catholic parents, who at the time of the study was making a precarious living working on weekly newspapers and occasional publicity jobs. Newspaper work had predominated in his spotty and variegated occupational career. His Communist beliefs were his most salient characteristic, both to himself and to the interviewers. Born a Catholic, he was no longer a believer. His physical health was good, except for a shoulder injury that prevented his attempting heavy work. Psychologically, he presented a history of claustrophobia and heavy drinking with delirium tremens, and described himself as "kind of nervous and high-strung." Nine years previously, his first wife had divorced him because of his drinking. An abstainer since shortly thereafter, he had remarried successfully five years before the study.

We got in touch with Sullivan through a person active in left Liberal circles whom we asked to suggest a pro-Russian subject. Sullivan was not told, however, that the study would concern Russia. When we explained over the telephone that we were studying "normal men," he insisted, to our perplexity, that he was not "normal," repeating the same point in the *Enrollment Interview*. From the very beginning, Sullivan was wary of our attempts to put him in a pigeonhole, especially any conventional one.

As he first appeared at the Clinic and we subsequently came to know him, Sullivan was a rather large man, with heavy, well-rounded physique, light hair graying at the temples, pink complexion, a large mouth, and indistinct eyebrows that made his blue eyes seem small, and his whole appearance rather that of a jolly piggy-bank. He dressed neatly, usually in a gray business suit. His face was expressive, ranging between joviality, deadpan pseudo-naïveté, and emphatic (sometimes mock-serious) contortion. In gait, he was awkward and a little confused, as though he might stumble over himself, while his gestures were abrupt, large, and not graceful. In general bearing, he gave the impression of being well-mannered, uncoordinated, and somewhat disoriented.

In talk, which Sullivan clearly enjoyed, he was prolific in disjunctive outbursts. He often failed to complete sentences, and there were frequent asides, self-contradictions, and immediately retracted paradoxical statements. While his grammar was good and his vocabulary rich, the effect was occasionally spoiled by his unsureness about words that he had more often than not employed correctly.

In his relationship with the members of the staff, Sullivan was warm, informal, and witty. He actively tried to establish relations on a level of informal equality. Often he seemed to be playing for an impression, waiting for the interviewer to give the appropriate reaction, to which he would respond gratefully. Characteristically he insisted on his own often paradoxical phrasing of his opinions; to the discomfiture of interviewers, he would often reject their reformulations of his meaning.

Sullivan's Values

Sullivan's attitudes toward Russia were part and parcel of his version of the Communist world view. We approach his opinions about the Soviet state as he himself would wish by first examining in outline the main features of his ideology and value system. The details will emerge later on.

(1) Sullivan was a Marxist and a non-party Communist. His understanding of the Marxist position was worked out adequately on the main points, but did not always embrace the details of doctrine.

(2) Through his Communist ideology, he consciously sought meaning and purpose in life.

> You're always seeking a stronger purpose for living. . . . I think we should justify ourselves.

Purpose was to be sought; it could not be taken for granted.

(3) The world was in flux. "We do not live in a static world," he liked to state; "my philosophy, so far as I understand it . . . I don't think . . . is a static thing." Education was therefore a "continuing process" for him, and he made much of Lincoln Steffens' dictum that schools should "teach the unknown," not the known. Experiment was good. Life was a constant, rather grim struggle for survival. The processes of historical change were inevitable and could not be evaded.

(4) The capitalist patterns were outworn, and fated to be replaced after an inevitable interval of Fascism by developments along the lines of the Russian experiment.

(5) Although historical processes were inevitable, the individual had the obligation to see the right and do his part, whatever its effectiveness.

The highest virtues, valued by Sullivan in their own right, were intellectual integrity, "savvy," and the courage of one's convictions. These were best embodied in his ideal, the independent radical Scott Nearing.

> I would like to have . . . the . . . the savvy of men like Scott Nearing, I'd like to have their courage, their stick-to-it-ivenes . . . their great faith in what they believe is right.

(6) However, people in general and himself in particular were to be excused when they fail to show these virtues. It was too much to expect a person to escape "the pattern." Not everyone could be Scott Nearing. People were basically trustworthy and good, and

> When they let you down, there's an economic reason. . . . I don't blame them. I blame the pattern.

Even ideological opponents in the Republican camp could be accepted in these terms. "They *are* good men, you know, according to their lights."

> Now this *J*, he's a splendid fellow. Marvelous fellow. He sees Communists under the bed . . . but he's a likeable fellow . . . he's got integrity. . . . Well, gee whiz, just because they don't agree with you . . . your social and economic beliefs. . . . There're other likeable things about them.

Communism was the second of two ideologies which Sullivan's life had encompassed. By his late twenties, some years before he was to embrace the Communist philosophy, he had gradually fallen away from the Catholicism in which he grew up, though most of his friends were Catholic. When we encountered him, he was neither religious nor anti-Catholic. He said:

> I appreciate those people who have the faith. They've certainly got something that we haven't. But I haven't got it and there's no use trying to kid myself that I have. There's nothing there for me to lean on. . . . I recognize the fact that everybody reaches for some spiritual thing and for some reason or other they think that there's something beyond . . . they reach instinctively for something higher. I know they do it . . . but I don't, and it's instinctive and there must be some reason for it. I don't know what the reason is. If there is a reason, it has not been explained to me in a sensible manner.

His account of the satisfactions that he found in religion emphasized forgiveness, dependence, and hope:

It was a solace. You'd go to church. Go to confession. You'd come out . . . forgiven. Now. . . . And this atmosphere in which they brought you up . . . when things were bad, you'd go and see the priest . . . have a calm talk and feel better for it. You'd pray, and hope. It's hope that they preach. And of course, life everlasting.

From the perspective of his second ideology, he looked back on his earlier faith as a "crutch."

We were quickly alert to possible equivalences in his two faiths, an interpretation on our part that Sullivan soon came to suspect and to reject vehemently. Contrasts in the personal meanings that Catholicism and Communism had for him proved most illuminating in regard to the functional grounding of his political views. To pursue this analysis, however, we need closer acquaintance with his strivings and predicaments. These topics will occupy us later after we have examined his views on Russia.

Sullivan on Russia

In the third session at the Clinic, Sullivan was explaining to the interviewer on *Personal Values and Religious Sentiments* how he became a Socialist. We break into the transcript at this point.

E: You'd call yourself a Marxian Socialist, would you?

S: Yes.

E: There're Socialists and Socialists and Socialists.

S: I'd call myself a Communist. That's what I'd call myself.

E: That must bring trouble on your shoulders, I should think.

S: I don't go out of my way telling everybody I'm a Communist, though. That's the closest. Like Scott Nearing. If somebody says, "Well, are you a Communist?", well, Scott says, "Not at the moment." You know.

E: Because he didn't have his card?

S: Well, no, because the Communist Party of America he'd disagree with, because he thought that they were the tail to the foreign policy of Russia.

E: And how would you feel about that?

S: I would feel exactly the way he did . . . that I was interested in the theory of the thing . . . as a revolutionary theory.

E: You don't care particularly about Russian Communism? You are interested in Communism as a general thing . . . to apply to. . . .

S: No. . . . I'm. . . . There has been an experiment in Russia . . . a social experiment. Well, they made mistakes . . . the same as we in our social experiment made mistakes. In our Constitution we had chattel slavery. [Umhum] Well, we abolished it, but we killed an awful lot of guys off before we did. But the thing is, we did. Well, so they have made a lot of mistakes. So we, I think, are in an admirable position to profit by their mistakes. Well. Because Russia was a pre-capitalist state . . . ah . . . there are certain things in . . . in . . . that happened in the Union of Soviet Socialist Republics that wouldn't apply in our. . . . So I'm in favor of adapting these things. And I'm in favor of letting these people work out this alternative.

E: Umhum. How do you see the future in those terms? Do you think that some sort of Socialism or Communism will be a likely possibility in America?

S: Well . . . yes. Because I think we're the only [laugh] capitalist nation left.

E: What sort of a time-schedule do you see that taking place in?

S: Well, we will simply go on trying to make a system . . . an outmoded system . . . work and then the forces from the left will disorganize the forces from the right. And the forces from the right will rush in and you'll have Fascism as the last dying gasp of capitalism. [Said very forcefully and slowly with pauses between words.]

E: You think Fascism will be a stage that we'll have to go through before we have Communism?

S: Right. Yes.

E: And you're reconciled to that pretty much, then?

S: Yeah. I'm pretty sure . . . that's going to happen.

E: It's inevitable, so you think. . . .

S: I think it is happening.

E: What do you see as the thing to be done under that view of things, then? You don't think there's any hope to avert the stage of Fascism?

S: No. None.

E: So what is the thing which you find most important to do?

S: Well, the thing most important to do is to . . . preach a doctrine of one world, united nations, and that's sort of self-preservation, because if we don't have it, we're likely to be vaporized [laugh].

The *Open-Ended Interview on Russia* conducted the following week by the same interviewer formally broached the topic of Russia as follows:

E: You remember when we were starting out on this thing, I told you we were going to be interested in some of your opinions on current affairs as well as in who you are. And, at this point, I'd like to start in on that part of our project. We've decided to concentrate mainly on attitudes toward Russia, because we think that's a good hot subject that most people have opinions on as it's pretty much in the news nowadays. And we think it's important in itself to find out about. So that from now on you'll probably be hearing quite a bit about Russia—or we'll be hearing from you. To start out, this evening what I'd like is for you to tell us as much as possible in your own words just how you feel about it, and why. So, to start with, you can just start anywhere and tell me some of the things you feel about Russia.

S: Well, of course I feel very very kindly toward Russia as a country . . . and towards the Russians. I have a book on Russia [laugh] which I think I've told you about. And . . . it just occurred to me the other day I should probably go through it again. Well, I think the Russians have an alternative to capitalism . . . at least they are seeking an alternative. They're engaged in a great experiment and I think we should be sympathetic towards any people engaged in an experiment the aim of which is to benefit most of them. That applies to what you people are doing here tonight.

E: You see the Russian development as an experiment.

S: As an experiment. Now I know . . . or, I feel, I don't know . . . I feel this way . . . ah . . . They are enjoying a very great measure—I'd say GREAT, all caps . . . of success, because the press of this country is blowing its top about it and resorting to every means to discredit it. Well, I only can see from that the thing is working out very well, because if it wasn't working out, why get excited about it! On the other hand, they have told us prior to the war that these Russians were very very stupid people, peasants, left their tractors out in the fields, couldn't repair them—all that sort of thing—it didn't get anywhere. The kind of myth they gave me when I was a kid. And I believed them for a while.

E: You think that the existence of all these rumors about Russia proves that there must be something there?

S: Yes. Definitely. Yeah. Well, then came the war. And the Russians did know something about manufacturing, production. The rocket gun . . . I think they were very successful with that. And they captured more equipment from the Germans than we sent to them in lend-lease. So I think that destroys that myth.

E: You think that their war achievement is something that convinces you that they . . .

S: Well, of course, I didn't need convincing, because I liked them. I like Slavs. I like Lithuanians. I lived with them. I know. In other words, how could you tell me that a Lithuanian of Pole or a Russian was stupid when I lived with them and knew that they were pretty good mechanics.

E: You knew them as people.

S: Yes, as people. Because I lived in a polyglot—that's the word, isn't it? I lived in a polyglot community.

Here begins an historical account that need not be quoted. As these selections indicate, Sullivan's attitudes toward Russia formed an integral part of his central ideology.

While Sullivan knew and had thought much about Russia, the differentiation in his attitudes did not show itself in a pattern of praises and reproofs. Except for minor Russian mistakes in planning, which he admitted defensively but could not specify even under the pressure of the *Stress Interview*, he was favorable toward Russia in every respect. His attitudes were nevertheless highly differentiated in a cognitive sense; he reacted with discrimination to many facets of Russia, of which some were important to him while others he had to explain away. The basic formula was apparent in his initial statements. Elsewhere he stated it succinctly as follows:

> That it is a social and political experiment and that it is the alternative to a system that has had its historical purpose.

The principal guises in which Russia entered his ken can be summarized as (1) Russia as an experiment in social welfare, (2) Russian Communism as the only alternative to a moribund capitalism, (3) Russia as in basic ideological conflict with the United States, and (4) Russia as a temporary "police state."

Time and again Sullivan underlined Russia's significance as an experiment. "I see Russia showing us a way," he told us. "It's the only country where youth has any hope. They try to say that youth has hope in this country. I don't believe so." This social experiment he saw as enjoying a large measure of success, evidenced by Russia's war performance and by the violence of opposition to her in the rest of the world. The experiment extended to treatment of minorities, industrial progress, cultural progress, etc., etc. Even greater was the success he foresaw in the future:

> I also think that they are a strong people, and they have ideals and that they will see it through. And I think . . . of course to me it's the only hope.

Russia for him was the sole source of hope. The United States, once a strong and fortunate country, was already entering an inevitable stage of Fascism. There was no hope nor security nor real Democracy here.

Everybody you talk to is worried about what is going to happen to them.

Sullivan saw the two countries in basic ideological conflict.

E: What do you think some of the main sources of disagreement are between us and Russia?
S: There is one main source. Ideology.

But Russia had been playing realistic power politics like the other great powers:

I think that the Russians are having in mind what took place after World War I and their experiences in the League of Nations, which weren't very happy—but they learned a lot about world politics and diplomacy. And so they said, "This time we are at least equal to these boys and we'll not be tossed around." So they expanded their borders. For what reason? Just to bargain, because that's the way diplomacy and treaties are made. They're bargaining counters yet. I don't see why they should, but that's the way they have to be made. . . . Of course it's all right for us to do that. . . . [Gives example of U.S. obtaining Japanese mandate islands.]

The United States had its inevitable role cut out for it:

I can't see where American policy can be anything else than what it is, being a capitalist nation . . . and the last one left [laughing]. I can't see.

The future was dubious, threatening, but somehow vague:

Well, there's two great powers . . . there's Russia and the United States and their ideologies are at variance . . . they cannot accept . . . they cannot . . . their premises are simply. . . . So they will collide. The only thing that can prevent their colliding is that England will come in with Russia and therefore the balance . . . is . . . will be so great that it will probably stop a collision. At any rate, if that happens, we probably will not be vaporized.

At another point Sullivan made a different prognosis:

The question is, if Russia is a strong power and surrounded by nations supporting her, will Uncle Sam attack her? I think not. However, there is one group in this country that wants war and they may go on anyhow.

Elsewhere in his immediate reactions to the Truman Doctrine he asserted that "this is the first phase of World War III."

I happened to pick up the *Monitor* that night and there it was commenting on Truman's speech. And I thought, "There he goes [laugh]. He's moving faster than I thought. Gee, this is two years ahead of time." He didn't give me a chance to catch up with it. But I wasn't shocked or anything by it.

The relatively high degree of inconsistency or confusion in his thinking about the possibility of war, while scarcely peculiar to Sullivan, raises the question of personal determinants since it contrasts so sharply with the orderly progression of events that he envisioned at an historical level.

It was when he considered Russia as a temporary "police state" that Sullivan came closest to qualifying his altogether favorable judgment, yet even here he could not see the cloud for the silver lining.

> E: Some people have compared German Nazism with Russian Communism. I wonder how you react to that comparison.
>
> S: Well, German Nazism was totalitarianism for the benefit of the few, not for the people. The present form of Russian government is a totalitarian government for the benefit of all.
>
> E: You don't have any reaction against totalitarianism in itself?
>
> S: Yes. Ah . . . I've been brought up to believe . . . and I think rightfully so . . . that we should have a measure of freedom . . . movement, speech . . . and all that sort of thing. But, as I've said before, there's a state of martial law. Now when there's a state of martial law, you have totalitarianism. And when that emergency is over and the thing is secure, then you go back to your Russian Constitution. I don't know whether you ever read it or not . . . but you'll see that it's quite an instrument. And you can see how it works. But, the thing that we forget is that they are in a state of emergency—a state of war.
>
> E: That is something that would justify practically any emergency measures?
>
> S: Yes. And that they were a feudal state, and they had such a gap to bridge, and at the same time had to contend with enemies from without. And also enemies from within, because they had the counter-revolution.
>
> E: You think they really had a counter-revolution there?
>
> S: Oh, yeah. Any revolution has a counter-revolution. Suppose you didn't believe . . . you know, in Russia . . . then what would you do? You'd work in the underground. In fact it's in every country. Do you mean to say that there couldn't be an underground in Russia? Of course there can be an underground in Russia. There can be an underground anywhere. There is an underground. Let's be realistic about this [laugh]. If

there isn't an underground, why do you have the NKVD—the secret
police?

E: You think that was a necessary thing, with the counter-revolution
there?

S: Yeah. Well, yeah. The police state doesn't appeal to me very well. A
police state. But it evidently is necessary. I don't know whether it is or
not. But it evidently is necessary, because of the counterrevolution—
the movement to overthrow the thing. And they had a plot and plans
to throw the thing over, and they were taking every measure to protect
it.

As soon as the pressure let up, he believed, Russia would become more
liberal.

They know that they have to relax and give people civil liberties. Otherwise you have your underground.

Hilary Sullivan knew much about Russia and was favorable in every
respect. A few of the miscellaneous aspects that his opinions took cog-
nizance of may be noted briefly. None was of central importance to him.

Russia's role in World War II rated his strong approval. Russia had
stayed out of the first phase of the war only to prepare herself better,
Sullivan held, and when the invasion came, the Russians had done a
"marvelous job." Self-preservation and the love of country had come
before ideology in accounting for their splendid performance, but that
was only natural.

Sullivan also approved of Russian religious policies.

Well, of course, I think the Russians take a very very sane view on the
religious issue. They, according to the Constitution and the Workshop
book, say that you can practice atheism or you can practice Christianity
. . . but it seems that what we object to over here is the atheism. In other
words, organized religion over here can sabotage any group of people that
might be atheists . . . and the same thing holds true for people who have
some religious faiths.

Morality was no problem. Russian family customs are like ours, he said,
except that nursery schools are provided that make families possible for
working mothers.

Russian industrial progress came in for equal praise. "In ten years I
think they'll leave us so far behind that we can't even hear the band."

Similarly with the arts and sciences and virtually anything else an interviewer could bring up.

> S: Now . . . I think that in Russia the work that you people are engaged in would find a . . . a . . . readier sympathy and cooperation than in this country.
>
> E: You think they are interested in fostering research?
>
> S: Yes, and the arts, and all the humanities. And I think that by pooling all these things they're going to make them great. I think their leaders are sincere . . . and . . . I recognize the fact that they are revolutionaries . . . that they are. . . . I like their idea of agreeing on programs . . . and whenever they set out to accomplish a program, those people that get in the way or try to sabotage it, they get out of the way. I think that's very logical, to my mind.

Alienated as he was from the premises of conceivable American policy toward Russia, he saw little that he could do about it. Events would pursue their inevitable course. He had little hope that other Americans could be brought to share his goals:

> E: So it's pretty much a course of events out of control of the American people, whether we get along with Russia or whether we don't?
>
> S: Yeah. Well, the American people, of course, if they *knew*, but they don't know . . . and the American people don't know how to think. They say, "Oh, this is the best country in the world." That's what they say, 365 days in the year. "This is the greatest country in the world. Why should we give them anything?" . . . all that sort of thing . . . over and over again. They'll go to the polls . . . and they'll vote wrong. Well, we have a record, according to one man. *They Also Ran*, by Irving Stone, which is a biography of the presidents who ran. It's pretty poor. Pretty poor.
>
> E: Do you think there's any hope so far as educating the people to see things the way they really are?
>
> S: No.
>
> E: Just got to wait for the clock to run down.
>
> S: Yes. I can't see any hope at all. Gee, I thought that after this war the boys would at least . . . going over across there . . . seeing those different things . . . having bull sessions . . . and it never affected them at all.
>
> E: The veterans don't think any differently than they did before?
>
> S: No, no. They join the American Legion and become a bunch of strikebreakers just like their fathers.
>
> E: I should think you'd find this pretty discouraging, since you're trying

to do something about all this, to find that you're just butting against a wall.

S: Yeah, but it's better to be doing something you believe in. . . . Well, if you have an ideal to work for, it's kind of nice. You'd miss it.

Here was a man who had garnered considerable information about Russia in the service of his ideology. In fact, only Chatwell and another subject in the clinical research, Kleinfeld, both men with more formal education than he, equaled his score on the *Information Test*, 50 correct out of 53 items. Two of his errors on this test deserve special comment. One revised recent history in Russia's favor: he checked an item to indicate his belief that "Russia declared war on Japan shortly before [not after] the first atom bomb was dropped." The other revealed some ignorance of fundamental facts: he thought that "The present Communist government in Russia seized power from the Czar [not the Kerensky government]." But he could not have attained his high score without considerable knowledge of many facets of Russian affairs. Where had he gleaned his information?

Not primarily from books; he had read rather few books about Russia. On these, to be sure, he leaned heavily, but he depended primarily on newspapers, lectures, and pamphlets, and on much enjoyed conversations with friends who shared his sympathies. Unlike Lanlin, still another subject, Sullivan did not habitually draw on "line" sources for hypotheses to test out against a wider array of "filler" sources. His line was internalized, and did not require direct reinforcement from without. He himself was the Marxist authority who told him the "correct" position to take. For keeping up to date, he much preferred the *New York Times* to the *Daily Worker*, which he did not particularly respect. The staff member who conducted the *Conformity Interview* summarized it thus:

> He does not even bother with the leftist press or magazine sources except for an occasional casual interest. His point is that from reading the *Christian Science Monitor* or the *New York Times*, with particular reference to the financial section . . . it is possible for him to arrive at his own conclusions which will be a solid Marxist analysis corresponding closely with what the *Worker* or the *New Masses* think. Naturally the liberal magazines and newspapers are too wishy-washy to please him. He is from personal experience well aware of the way in which news distortion takes place.

Much of his time was spent in systematic reading of his favorite papers.

We may now summarize Hilary Sullivan's opinions about Russia in terms of our descriptive scheme.

Differentiated Object of Attitude

Russia for Sullivan was above all a promised land, living testimony to the possibility of a better world. The crux of his attitude concerned the contrast between Russia as a hopeful experiment in social welfare and the moribund capitalism of the United States. Other features of the object were highly elaborated, but for the most part secondary. Conflict between Russia and the United States was of more concern to him than to many of our subjects, but took second place to the ideological matters that Russia symbolized for him. The police state features of Soviet society, a source of some embarrassment to him, were relegated to the background.

Saliency

Sullivan stands by himself among our subjects in the central place accorded Russia and Communism in his scheme of things. With him, Russia was extremely salient, a continual focus of preoccupation.

Time Perspective

Sullivan's hopes rested entirely on the long run. This well-elaborated historical perspective provided the justification he needed for Russia's momentary shortcomings; it also included grimmer expectations about the period of Fascism that, according to Marxist dogma, the United States must pass through before being able to follow Russia's lead. American relations with Russia in the shorter run, with the attendant possibility of atomic war, appeared more cloudy to him; he had settled on no single conclusion among the several contradictory guesses that he ventured from time to time with less than usual coherence.

Informational Support

Diligent combing of the quality press and other sources equipped Sullivan with a rich background of factual detail in elaboration and support of a position that did not depend for guidance on his sources of information.

Object Value

To an extreme degree, Russia appeared to Sullivan in positive guise. Differentiated as were the cognitive details of his picture, each facet shared in the positive affect that adhered to everything that the Soviet Union was and stood for. Whatever aspect might be brought up, he was certain to approve of it. The threatening outlook in Russian-American relations was an inevitable historical development detached from his feelings about the Soviet Union. If blame were to be assigned, it would go to the United States—but he hardly could blame even this country for fulfilling its historic role.

Orientation

Sullivan's orientation can only be called one of approach, but it was approach to an ideological ideal rather than to a source of events in the real world. For all the fervor of his views, Sullivan was not a Party member. Reading, talk, and revery were the primary avenues by which he "approached" Russia and Communism, though he had, to be sure, engaged in activities in support of Communist causes.

Policy Stand

His stand on American policy could only be negative. Favoring support for the U.N. was the closest that he came to a positive stand, but this appears to have been more a random thought than a considered position. We did not believe that policy stand had much relevance to his attitudes as they functioned for him.

What manner of man had arrived at these singular views?

Sullivan's Life and Enterprises

Personal History

Hilary Sullivan was born in 1898 as the oldest son (and second child) of poor Catholic parents in Whitney, a Connecticut textile town where his father worked as a knitter. His mother was born in Ireland, where she had some education; his father, native born, had only grammar school education but showed unusually broad interests for his background. There followed six younger children in the next twelve years, three of whom lived to maturity. Home life was not pleasant. Mrs. Sullivan sought to control the family by playing off the children against each other and against their father, showing traits that had recently contributed to her institutionalization as paranoid. Larry worshipped his father, and with the death of the latter from tuberculosis when Larry was fifteen, the beatification was complete. This bereavement was followed in a couple of years by the death of his younger brother, probably also of tuberculosis.

With his father's death, Larry's formal education was interrupted, after parochial school and not quite two years of high school. Although he had not found school rewarding, he had already begun to read omnivorously. Toward the end of the First World War he left his first full-time job as baggage-master at the Whitney station to join the Navy. He never saw sea duty, returning after a short but dreary experience to his railroad job. In 1920 he was back in the Navy for a brief period. From this first contact with the wide world, he was left with pleasant memories of European architecture and museums, but with a vast disrespect for the Navy and strong repugnance toward the shipboard homosexuality that he had witnessed.

After a brief and dissatisfied period of local jobs on his second return to civilian status, he took off with a reckless friend for four years of "bumming" around the country. This period of irresponsibility terminated in 1924 with the tragic accidental death of his friend. Back once more in Whitney, Sullivan worked periodically in the mills, escaping to New York for sprees when he would buy himself a hotel job and sell "booze" on the side. In 1925 he obtained a minor newspaper job, and was engaged, somewhat irregularly, in newspaper work until about 1933.

During his late twenties, Sullivan was troubled by claustrophobia in theaters and subways, and it was then and in his early thirties that he drank most heavily on his periodic sprees. His thirty-first or thirty-second year found him suffering from delirium tremens after such a bout.

When he was thirty he married a woman of similar social background who had been a factory worker since she was twelve. After eight years, his drinking led to divorce, and his wife obtained custody of their one child, a son. Meanwhile, his newspaper work had become a depression casualty and he was trying first in one way and then in another to make a living, by pursuits ranging from selling beer or Christmas cards to employment on the W.P.A. The divorce and the separation from his son left him at a nadir which had the virtue at least, as he put it, of allowing him once more to start from scratch. "I was trapped. . . . When the world topples down over your ears, it's better because you can start building again."

Following the divorce, his new life was marked by satisfying work on a W.P.A. Writers Project. At the same time he gave up drinking permanently and moved into respectable quarters in Providence that symbolized his changed life. With the onset of World War II, he took up, conscientiously, manual work in the textile mills, only to give it up shortly because of his shoulder. There followed a succession of war-connected jobs as guard, clerk, and investigator. At 44 he married a semi-professional woman, an "intellectual companion," who was one of the last of his social group left after the reshufflings of the war. Moving shortly thereafter to Boston, he returned in 1945 to newspaper work of an irregular sort that left him much freedom but brought in a fairly satisfactory income.

Sullivan's social ties in earlier years seem mostly to have been to a succession of cronies who were his companions in drink and work and play. More recently, he had cultivated a small circle who discussed politics and world affairs. His radical beliefs, which crystallized in the late 1930's, increasingly became the center of his life.

During his earlier years, he at first took little note of the soapbox talks that were his first contact with Communism. Gradually, we are led to gather, he began to take them more seriously. As late as 1930, however, he had written in favor of Mussolini, who perhaps appealed to his inner longing for a strength to bring order out of chaos. But this peccadillo was hardly the expression of a coherent ideology. His radical beliefs seem to have taken form about the time of the W.P.A. Writers Project. Among his co-workers were several avowed Communists, who would air their heretical views on the job. Sullivan himself had been warned, when he was taken on the project as a political favor, not to get involved in political arguments but to "keep his yap shut." This advice he followed, even to the extent of avoiding the Communists after hours. Nevertheless, his own convictions were taking form, and the prestige that the project held in his eyes doubtless served to invest with particular significance the opinions he heard expressed there. In desperate need for a guiding philosophy of life, Sullivan borrowed the appropriate ideas so auspiciously brought to his attention. But his Communism was not adopted *in toto* by conversion: it was, rather, a structure that he built for himself.

Present Enterprises

The main areas of interest and endeavor that stood out in Sullivan's current pattern of life can be listed, with some overlap, under four headings: making a living, Communism, self-improvement and self-fulfillment, and friendship.

"My whole life has been concerned with getting a living," Sullivan told us. Security could not be taken for granted. "The whole of life is a problem: how to survive." And again, "I never use the gold standard; I always use the hamburg standard." Starting with severe poverty, he had never been economically secure, however much his insecurity may have been of his own contriving. Although, like Chatwell, he liked to day-dream of the self-sufficient security of a farm, and more seriously considered seeking a municipal job, he had come to accept in practice a minimal level of security. The prospect of being on relief did not represent an unknown horror. For the most part, a job was simply a way of feeding himself, and when that was done he had little further interest in it. Speaking of the possible municipal job, he said:

> Well, if you have felt economic pressure all your life, then you simply have to take safeguards. That's a safeguard. Whether I'll take it or not I don't know. Now I'm enjoying myself with not too much work.

His first newspaper job and his position with the W.P.A. Writers Project, in both of which he took real pride, led him to depart from this point of view. At the time of the study, he still appeared to take considerable satisfaction in being a semi-professional man on the one hand, and a free-lance, for the most part his own boss, on the other.

Communism, we have seen, formed the pivot of Sullivan's coherent philosophy of life. In his daily life it provided the raison d'être for his favorite activity, reading and talk about political and economic affairs.

Ever since his boyhood discovery of books Sullivan had pursued self-improvement through the constant reading of books and newspapers and through seeking out intellectual discussions. In the last five years he had branched out into a new line, that of oil painting. Thus through his own endeavors Sullivan had achieved a culture that removed him from his working-class background. Far from mere rungs in a ladder of social success, however, his intellectual and cultural pursuits had become essential to his picture of himself. These attainments together with his sharp Communist perspective on affairs enabled him to value himself as an intelligent and cultured person who was "in the know" and, seeing the true nature of society, lived by no shams himself.

It was in the context of friendship that most of Sullivan's political and economic ideas were worked out. He valued highly the friends who dropped in for discussion and coffee. His present marriage appeared to be only another instance of this friendship pattern. Sullivan liked people, and said, according to his ideology,

> I feel that most people are trustworthy and when they let you down there's an economic reason. . . . I've always believed that and I always will!

Although intellectual friendship was his ideal, he fostered informal friendliness in whatever his environment might be. "If I'm going to work on a job," he told us in the *Interview on Personal Values*, "I'll make it as pleasant as possible for myself and everybody around me." With those who disagreed with him, he was likely to play the clown, a role about which he felt ambivalent.

> *S:* I find it pretty hard to be cross with people, to maintain a grudge.
> *E:* That can't be too much of a handicap, is it?
> *S:* Well, no. If I insist on it, I have to laugh at myself. I feel ridiculous to myself.
> *E:* You tend to view yourself with somewhat of a humorous eye?
> *S:* Yeah. I see myself as a . . . character.
> *E:* You like to see yourself in that role?
> *S:* Well, no. I don't like to see myself in that role too often. Because that's wearing the cap and bells. And, you know . . . they say . . . "The fellow's a clown." Well, I don't want to be going around as a clown. But, if you're a character, they're liable to put the cap and bells on you. . . . If I talk to somebody whose mind I know is pretty closed, I just kid with him. And he kids back with me. I say, "Hello, Tovarich." When I go into a fancy restaurant, I say, "Anything for the workers?" [laughter] It's pretty hard for anyone to take offense.

On this surface level of his present activities some obvious sources of both satisfaction and difficulty may be discerned. Satisfactions came from the intellectual and cultural life he had fashioned for himself—from his perennial discussions over coffee with his wife and his friends, from his reading, from his painting, but also from the baseball games that he and his wife both enjoyed. Being a newspaperman still had its fascination and meant something to him for the semi-professional status it conferred, as well as for the inside view it afforded behind public personages and events. And, looking inwards, he could take satisfaction in the sophistication and integrity with which he saw behind appearances and forsook bourgeois "hypocrisies" for the hard but predestined realities as portrayed in the Communist ideology.

Yet there were also major problems facing Sullivan in his pattern of living. Some of them are already apparent. As it had always been, his source of income was still insecure. His commitment to Communism also entailed various difficulties. In a time of decreasing tolerance, his very opinions endangered his livelihood and his relations with others. His concession to economic pressures in not joining the Communist Party involved, in his eyes, a compromise in integrity that was only compounded by the "venality" of his job activities according to his Communist standards. Finally, the "cap-and-bells" technique he had worked out for getting on with people who differed with him sat poorly with his self-esteem.

Significant Emotional Relationships

We return for a closer look at Sullivan's early family relationships, which turn out to have been deeply influential on his outlook on life and on the Communist opinions that became so salient to him. Larry's father, whom he fondly remembered after thirty years, "didn't have any faults, except being ill, of course, always having a little touch of T.B." He was the

> finest looking man I ever saw . . . just handsome. A gentle person. . . . One of the earliest memories is entertaining us with all kinds of sounds of birds and animals, and songs. . . . Going up to meet him when he came home from work, and he'd take the youngest on his shoulders and two or three piling onto him.

In a family of much confusion and disturbance, he was the center of peace and serenity.

I'd say his strongest point seemed to me to be that he had a kind of kindly, calm philosophy. For example, when my mother was blowing off her top and sprinkling holy water on everybody from top to bottom in the house, raising Hell, my father would sit calmly and look out of the window. And he'd sort of try to calm things.

Although Mr. Sullivan occasionally punished with a strap, Mrs. Sullivan was the main disciplinarian. For the most part Larry got from his father a kind of warmth and comfort that children more usually find in their mothers.

Mr. Sullivan emerged from Larry's adult eulogies as a vivid, talented person of broad and contagious interests. "The minstrel type of Irishman," sensitive and humorous, he figured in his son's recollections as a great entertainer who could do imitations, recite Shakespeare, play semi-pro baseball, and take part in amateur plays in spite of having had only a grammar school education. Larry remembered being roused by his father in the middle of the night to see Halley's comet; the children were brought up to share in his lively interest in the larger world. In general, "he was just a marvelous man . . . and we could never get enough of him."

While the father was busy and tired and little available for his boys to confide in, Larry early became aware of his strong views on Trade Unionism, according to which "the lowest word in our house was the word *scab*." In fact, as Larry took pains to point out, Father was something of a radical for his day, who would quote from the early writing of Hearst and Brisbane "in great gobs," and once tried unsuccessfully to organize his plant.

The impact of his father on Sullivan's personality seems to have been large. The reasons for his particularly strong attachment must be sought in the total family scene. But in this attachment we may find the origin of most of his enduring interests and values, as well as some of his characteristic techniques of adjustment, including things as diverse as his interest in baseball, his "cap-and-bells" role, his intellectual curiosity and cultural interests, and an incipient radicalism. He believed that his father would agree with his contemporary views.

While Father was all hero in Sullivan's family drama, Mother was all villain. He may have overdrawn the picture from his present perspective, but there is no doubt that she created an exceedingly bad family situation. As matriarch and disciplinarian she commanded no respect. She was given to constant harangue and "mental punishment," rubbing it in how poor they were and how the children were bringing disgrace on the family. Her especially vicious technique, from Larry's point of view, "was to play one of us off against the other."

> She didn't force you to do anything. She was a person who got you to do things by guile . . . never gave me or anyone else any affection that I know of. I've asked and they say no. . . . Impressing on me how important . . . not "how important" but how *imperative* it was to bring home what I made . . . and that they'd starve and all that sort of thing. And she always impressed on us how hard she worked . . . always telling us that our father was no good . . . which was all a lie.

"The chief ideal in the home," Sullivan tells us in another connection, "was to be smart so as not to bring shame on the family." From his mother Larry felt a pressure to conform, to maintain appearances, for which she offered little recompense. Even at an early age, conformity had acquired unpleasant meanings for him.

To give Larry even more grounds for feeling exploited, she rankled his boyish pride by making him wear hand-me-downs, including girls' clothes. Later, after Larry's first return from the Navy to work in Whitney, she took all his savings to buy a new house, complaining afterwards to others that he didn't give her any money. In sum, Sullivan came to hate his mother vigorously and explicitly. On talking it over with his brother recently, they agreed that "when the O'Brians put her on a boat in Ireland they were glad to get rid of her." On probing, we gathered that he did not come to a full realization of this hatred until later years, but it must have underlain his childhood reactions.

Some fairly direct consequences of this miserable relationship to his mother may be surmised. One is the apparent lack of emotional depth in his marriages, and some tendency to reserve his stronger emotional ties for men. A second is his frustrated need for dependent well-being, perhaps at the root of his alcoholism. Thirdly, the guilt and conflict that must have been aroused by his childish hatred may have been a prime source of the burden of anxiety which he has carried throughout his life. Her carping criticism of his father continuing even after his death ("He could have lived," he quoted her as saying, "if he'd stayed up at the hospital but he wanted to come home and give all of you the T.B.") contributed to Father's complete beatification. His mother had raised all the possible criticisms, and he rejected them. The pattern has echoes in his later unwillingness to admit Russia's slightest defect.

Through her part in a family situation that left Larry with serious problems of adjustment, his mother had important indirect effects on his attitudes. More directly, she also impressed him with poverty, contributing to an underdog identification compatible with his later Communism. One may surmise that it was from her, too, that Sullivan first learned the meaning of exploitation.

In general, Larry's siblings were unimportant in his life. An older sister, who subsequently died, maintained the balance in the family, but he and the younger siblings did not confide in her.

> None of us confided in anybody. We just sort of talked things over among ourselves. We had pretty much the same things to bear—discussed things, not very thoroughly. I suppose if you could say it, we tried to forget Mother. We accepted things as a part of existence. We were all a clan . . . and all of us survived. That's about all.

There was no important sibling rivalry that he can remember.

Perhaps his experience of sibling solidarity acquired special significance when, at a later time, his Communist ideology was taking form. In his early family experience he had made acquaintance in prototype with the leading characters in the Marxist *dramatis personae*: the exploiter in his mother, the working-class martyr in his father, and the union of the oppressed among his siblings. It seems to us both idle and improbable to advance the sort of speculation that would see in Sullivan's later Communism simply the repetitive elaboration of his familial struggles. Much more plausible, we think, is the conjecture that in his family he acquired certain pervasive attitudes toward himself and others that found congenial resonances in Marxism, more congenial ones than in his earlier Catholic solution to his problems.

The significant figures in Sullivan's adult life seem to have had little direct influence on his sentiments or personality. In the past, his important personal ties had all been with men his own age with whom he worked, drank, or bummed around the country. The most conspicuous of these was the companion of his wanderings from 1921–24, whom he described as a reckless character who would try anything. The violent death of this friend was another devastating personal bereavement; he was not, however, a source of Sullivan's present ideas or sentiments. His present friends, who mostly shared his left-wing views, entered his circle only after he had arrived at the radical position. So far as we can tell from his account, personal ties followed and confirmed his radicalism rather than created it.

It is no longer possible to reconstruct clearly the meaning to Sullivan of his first marriage. As he described her, his first wife showed the traits of a compulsion neurotic. During the first few years of their marriage they got along "pretty well" though with little emotional intensity. The greatest blow from their divorce was the loss of his son, with whom he was maintaining intermittent and deliberately casual contact.

This was his account of how his second marriage came about:

> This girl has always lived away from home, never had a home and she's a marvelous companion. And the group we knew went away to war . . . broke up, so we were the only ones left. She was working in one place and she said . . . I said, "You've got a problem and I've got a problem; let's get married." And she said, "We will, some day." And we'd meet and meet and talk about it, and then we got an apartment . . . and so [laughs] we got married.

The bond between them, it appears, was their common problem of parental rejection. We may further surmise, as other information confirms, that their relation rested mainly on intellectual companionship. She agreed with many of his political ideas, though she would sometimes protest his exclusive preoccupation with them. Retaining her job and her own circle of friends, she was not dependent on Sullivan financially or otherwise.

The Personal Setting of Sullivan's Opinions

Capacities and Traits

Taken together, our battery of tests showed Sullivan to possess a superior intelligence the functioning of which was considerably impaired. The *Wechsler-Bellevue Adult Intelligence Test* showed him to best advantage, with a full I.Q. of 128, a Verbal I.Q. of 134, and a Performance I.Q. of 118. His score on this test places him just within the "very superior" group, or the top three per cent of the general population, and leaves him tied for third place among our ten subjects. His *Wells-Alpha* score of 119, while not outstanding and in eighth place among our subjects, nevertheless supported the *Wechsler* in regard to his good intellectual level, particularly since he had had so little formal education. The *Rorschach*, however, revealed a "relatively low level of mental functioning . . . either consistent with an average endowment, or else due to an impairment by a disorganizing emotional factor," the latter interpretation being required by the other test results.

Though he was well endowed, his capacity for organized and abstract thought was limited. For example, his none-too-successful attempts at classifying the blocks of the *Vigotsky Test* were interpreted by the examiner (working in ignorance of other personality and opinion data) as follows:

> Although this performance gives no evidence of a high level of conceptual thinking, disorganization and blocking seem to be more outstanding features than the actual lack of abstract thinking. It is notable that S has some ideas about the required logical procedure; thus he realizes that categories once tried have to be "out," knows that he should be able to find the required categories by comparing the samples, and generally tries to find a "formula." His performance, however, does not conform to these fragmentary verbal expressions. . . . Yet the perceptual factor is not given free play either—S obviously does not feel right about just following the perceptual tendencies, and constantly strains for a more logical approach, which results merely in blocking. This pronounced discordance is probably typical of S's thinking in general. . . .

The *Rorschach* analyst, also working independently, described his approach to problems as "careless and superficial, lacking in organization and precision, as well as in effort," while the *Wechsler* report remarked,

> His generally poorer performance scores seem due to his tendency to overgeneralize and ramble, a characteristic more suitable to high Verbal scores but inadequate for Performance tests. Consistently in these latter tests he overlooked detail.

These intellectual qualities were manifest in Sullivan's attitudes toward Russia. His opinions, we have seen, showed a subtlety and elaboration that could only be possible for a person of his high verbal ability. Yet the discordant, over-generalizing, disorganized quality of his thought processes also left its unmistakable mark. Apart from the loose, disjunctive way in which he presented his opinions, his sweeping judgment that Russia was *entirely* good would come easily only to a person so constituted.

Sullivan's other abilities may be passed over quickly. He rated himself "poor" in mechanical and in business ability. In artistic ability he thought himself excellent; artistic sensitivity was an important part of his self-image. What he told us of his aesthetic bent was in keeping with scores in the 7th and 8th deciles for artistic, literary, and musical interests on the *Kuder Preference Blank*. While he enjoyed music and art without a highly cultivated taste, he painted quite well for a self-taught amateur. The other abilities on which he gave himself an "excellent" rating—social, entertaining, memory, and intuitive abilities—were all based, as he explained them, on his interest in people, liking for them, and real gifts at getting along with them.

Turning to Sullivan's temperamental qualities, we note that his emotional life was drawn in strong if somewhat blurred colors. In his behavior as we observed it, as well as in the interview and projective test material, substantial evidence pointed toward strong and impulsive emotionality that was rather inadequately controlled. His many bereavements typically left him distraught, and he mentioned instances of emotional outbursts and fits of temper. The intense affect of his attitudes toward Russia was therefore characteristic of him.

Perhaps the crucial underlying fact of Sullivan's affective life was the high level of his anxiety, indications of which pervaded his history and his behavior and test records at the Clinic. At times, it had been not only manifest but nearly overwhelming. Early in his childhood he had been troubled by dreams of being buried alive; later he was beset with claustrophobia and fears of falling from high places. The theme of being "trapped" ran through several episodes in which his enterprises were at a nadir, and recurred in his *Free Association Hour*. When his life pattern collapsed with his divorce, he felt completely disoriented and wondered if he were going insane. At the time of the study, he told us in an interview after the end of the regular series, he had occasional spells of extreme depression and disorientation, when he would get the feeling that he was the only person in the world, feel utterly lost, and shake all over as he began to come out of it. These brief attacks occurred irregularly, perhaps once a month. He felt that he had become able to cope with them, mainly by sitting down to write or sketch. Besides this catalogue of gross disturbance, to which should be added his former alcoholism, there is the indication of emotional disturbance on the *Rorschach*, and his general disorganization and lack of coordination. The resultant picture is that of a person with strong predispositions toward anxiety which for the most part were brought under control. The control, however, was neither entirely dependable nor very efficient; his disorganization and impaired test performance bore witness to the struggle. The closest Sullivan came to a frank realization of his plight was his paradoxical remark:

> My whole life is worry, so now I do not worry. I say, "What the Hell can I do about it!" I do the best I can.

Aside from his occasional sieges of depression, his prevailing mood of superficial, somewhat "slap-happy" joviality appeared to be a defense against his underlying distress. Alcohol was a means by which he once reinforced the euphoric component of this mood:

> It mellows and expands the personality to such a degree that I certainly don't want to go back to reality. . . . Then I fall asleep. Then I wake up, terrifically depressed.

The summary of the *TAT* analysis, done with knowledge only of the "face data," caught his spirit well:

> There is a Pagliacci-like tone about S's *TAT* stories. Beneath an exterior which makes him out to be a lighthearted, out-going individual who knows all about life, there is a tense, frustrated, anxious, and unhappy individual who is quite ego-involved in most of his pursuits and who has developed a role for himself in order to keep people from learning of his weaknesses.

His Communist attitudes, we shall see, were of great help to him in coping with his underlying tendencies toward personal desperation.

Basic Strivings

The pathological cast to much of Sullivan's history points clearly to deep-seated conflicts. One cluster of his needs that we inferred from his interviews and fantasy productions centered around security and affection, including needs for dependence, friendship, and recognition. These needs were in partial conflict with aggressive tendencies and strivings toward autonomy.

In evaluating his childhood, Sullivan told us disjunctively that he would like to have had "a home where the semblance of security . . . a mother who gave me some affection . . . and where there was some serenity, which there wasn't." On the one hand, he often described his whole life as a quest for minimal security; on the other, security remained a dream that he had only rarely pursued effectively. Short of full security of relationship, he was wont to seek emotional response from his fellows with somewhat more success. So highly dependent was he on response from people that, as we have seen, he would clown, against his ideal conception of himself, to get it. More stable sources of security in a well-composed pattern of life had eluded him, and he had, indeed, so contrived his life as to achieve the opposite result.

Two probable reasons suggest themselves as to why he had done so. His bereavements and frustrations, to begin with, had led him to define security defensively in the minimal terms of the "hamburg standard." He may have learned in the thorny bosom of his family that the fruits of a responsible quest for security would be taken away from him; only immediate pleasures were safe. And as he had found, it was easier to do something about his life when he was at rock-bottom. The less complicated a structure he built, the smaller distance he had to fall. Much of his life may thus be seen as a kind of flight into insecurity, a defense by willing the inevitable.

> . . . I never had security, so why should I miss something I never had? I have no sense of insecurity; I never had it.

Besides his need for defining security in minimal terms—a need that may have found symbolic expression in his persistent phobia of literally falling—there seems to have been a self-destructive element in the chaotic middle years of his history. We detect in his escapades something of self-punishment as well as of flight from an intolerable burden of guilt that was very likely the by-product of the intense hatred of his early years.

His ideology and attitudes partly resolved this conflict around security. First the Catholic Church, then the church of Communism, provided him with havens of security not to be found in his mundane affairs. Sullivan well could echo Luther's sentiment, *"Ein' feste Burg ist unser Gott."* It is interesting in this connection to note that to Russia, the tangible guarantee of his faith, he attributed the same total perfection that he ascribed to his father, the only solace of his turbulent childhood. Both had been too important to him, and his inner resources had been too precarious, for him to admit the slightest flaw. To the seemingly unfair attacks on Russia in the mass media, he reacted just as he had learned to respond to his mother's attempted defamation of his father, with utter denial of the criticism.

Among the tendencies that conflicted with Sullivan's drives toward security and friendship was considerable aggressiveness. His paradoxical humor, directed at others and at himself, had hostile overtones. With the average person whose views he did not respect, he would veer between trying to shock and condescending agreement.

> I shock them, then I retreat. All they want to talk about is what a great man . . . oh, Taft, is. "He's wonderful. Wonderful man." And I could go right out and shoot the ass off of him. See? But I agree and they think I'm wonderful. If they say, "Today is Wednesday," I say, "I guess you're right. It is Wednesday. I just didn't happen to look at the calendar."

Both these tactics had an aggressive flavor. The sequence of frustrations in his life gave reason for much resentment, of which that against his mother became explicit.

His Communist attitudes served these aggressive tendencies in at least two ways. On the one hand, their extreme nonconformity gave him a way of shocking people and disturbing their complacency. That he was strongly moved to do so is indicated by the fact that he did it against his wife's remonstrance and his own better judgment. But his ideology also provided an acceptable rationale for his aggressive feelings, so that he could tolerate them without undue disturbance. Several times he stressed that "revolution is not fun and people will get hurt," and he saw the new day arising from the total ruin of the old order. As a revolutionary in fantasy, Sullivan cast himself in a Samson's role; self as well as contemporaries were to go down in ruin together.

His strong need for autonomy seemed related to his security needs in a more complex way. We infer its existence from such facts as his insistence on defining on his own terms the relationships that he entered at the Clinic, his choice of a free-lance occupation, the loosely integrated nature of his marriage, his preference for an inefficient but *laissez-faire* employer in comparison with a just but authoritarian one on the *Argument Completion Test,* and his hatred of bureaucratic organization when it impinged on his own life. Seeking autonomy may appear like a polar opposite of seeking dependent security, yet we must probably conceive Sullivan's stress on autonomy as primarily a defense against what he had found to be the dangers and frustrations of staking much on dependence. It was a way out of the trap. In his daydreams, he imagined a solution that would give him both: his ideological mentor, Scott Nearing, again provided the model for his reveries of a farm that would leave him secure to pursue his beliefs independent of economic and social pressure. But what a different dream farm this was from Chatwell's! There was none of Chatwell's stress on productivity; none of the realism that led Chatwell to investigate the dollars-and-cents considerations in bringing his fantasy to life. Both in conception and in psychological function, Sullivan's farm was even more clearly a refuge of escape. His simultaneous desires for autonomy and security, as our analysis of his daydream suggests, entailed the evasion of mature responsibility that had been a salient fact through most of Sullivan's history.

Being a Communist also served his need for autonomy. His espousal of an unpopular ideology was as much a declaration of independence as it was an act of covertly aggressive nose-thumbing. Moreover, he was not actually a Party member. Very likely the rigorous demands of Party discipline would have conflicted too strongly with his autonomous needs, and required of him a degree of responsibility that he was unable to accept. His Communism seemed to gratify simultaneously both his needs for autonomy and for security: security by aligning himself with a world movement that he believed to be the wave of the future, and autonomy because his beliefs gave him a vantage point detached from society on the one hand and uncommitted to Party discipline on the other. In this respect, too, the independent radical Scott Nearing represented his ideal.

There are a number of indications from test procedures and personal history that sex created problems for Sullivan. Overtly, his sexual life had been normal though not particularly active. The exact nature of his psychosexual problems, while important to a full account of his personality, makes little difference here. We can safely assume that their only bearing on his attitudes toward Russia was through their possible contribution to his burden of insecurity, guilt, and anxiety.

Finally, Sullivan's strong need to understand should be noted. Following his father's example though probably for complex reasons, Sullivan early developed a strong intellectual curiosity, a desire to know the inside story. Marxist philosophy furnished a particularly inclusive pattern according to which he could interpret the world.

Adjustive Strategies

The succession of bereavements and frustrating experiences that had been his lot, his conflicts about security, and his considerable anxiety demanded of Sullivan a well-furnished armory of adjustive or defensive techniques. In broad outline, they involved a twofold strategy. In the realm of his personal life, the scope of his preoccupations, hopes, and fears was narrowed to exclude his immediate and seemingly insoluble problems from awareness. Balancing this impoverishment was his highly developed world-view in the realm of safely impersonal ideology. In his personal life he often seemed to blunder rather desperately against odds that he felt were stacked against him. Although it was scarcely possible for him to imagine an encouraging future for himself, his broad ideological perspective seems to have provided a substitute for personal aspirations.

Sullivan characteristically did not attempt to solve his problems by long-range planning. Having little faith in the arrival of future goods, he was unwilling to renounce present benefits for their sake.

If I had butter, I'd use a lot, then eat plain bread for a while.

Only when these benefits had totally vanished as he hit rock-bottom was he able to bestir himself effectively to cope with his problems. More typically he avoided awareness of them. In the past drink had helped him to evade some of his critical difficulties; he currently appeared to use passivity and sleep to the same end. Frequently spending an entire day lounging in his pajamas with a newspaper, he would also retire very early in the evening. His restriction of awareness did not actually protect him from dangerous situations, of course. It was as if he had been forced to admit defeat beforehand, but shielded his eyes from the blow as a stop-gap measure to preserve his psychological integrity.

His restriction of goals to excessively modest ones was akin to this strategy of avoidance. To minimize frustration, he lowered his level of aspiration drastically, often directing his sense of humor at himself to aid in the process. One might describe this pattern as a defense in depth: he tried to be ready for the worst. Although he spoke of "hedging," his preparation was mainly psychological; he seemed to feel that there was little he could do to prevent the worst from happening.

There can be little doubt that Sullivan had *repressed* a great deal. His childhood memories began late, at the time he started school. The idealization we have observed in the portraits he formed of his father and of himself could only have been attained through repression. In an early session Sullivan informed the interviewer with great emphasis: *"I have been a Socialist since I reached the age of reason."* When the results of probing in later interviews made this statement incredible, he showed considerable disturbance in readjusting his account.

To make up for this defensive limitation of his personal life, there was his highly elaborated Communist ideology. One of its important strategic functions may be described as the *intellectualization* of his personal problems. The "pattern" of historic processes, for example, helped to absolve him from personal responsibility for his actions and their outcome. Foreseeing capitalist breakdown as inevitable, he could put his personally fearful expectations in a context in which they appeared as part of an unavoidable process—hence depersonalized, less threatening, and something to be accepted rather than struggled against futilely. His ideology thus protected him from catastrophic reaction without making impossible demands on him for actual solution of his immediate problems. His philosophy of flux, change, and the pursuit of the unknown, which we shall shortly examine, helped to justify the disorderly and unknown in his own life.

Finally, his ideology permitted him to *identify* with a source of vicarious strength—the Communist movement and Russia. His ideological sources of dependent security were less vulnerable than his personal ones.

A precarious stance such as Sullivan's required much *rationalization* to shore it up. He was too insecure, and his consciously formulated picture of himself and the world played too vital a role in his security system, for him to tolerate discrepant features in his images of self and world. We are familiar with his propensity to explain away all of Russia's possible limitations. This characteristic he showed in other realms, as on the *Argument Completion Test*, where his arguments were the most one-sided of all our subjects.

In this description of Sullivan's principal defenses, we have so far ignored the considerable degree of *effective restriving* with which, as we have suggested, he was most likely to respond when he felt that his back was against the wall. Particularly after his divorce, he set about deliberately and effectively to build a new life. That was the time that he managed to give up alcohol once and for all. Quite without the benefit of Alcoholics Anonymous or of religious or moral scruples, he held himself to abstinence, although we have no reason to assume that the problems originally setting him to pathological drinking had been solved. In all respects he managed to pursue a wavering but on the whole by no means unsuccessful course of life in spite of a bad start and more than his share of body blows on the way.

Nevertheless, it is fair to say of his principal adjustive strategies that while they had the merit of preparing him to accept the worst, they did not equip him to do much to forestall it. How to avoid "going to pieces" in the face of ill fortune—not how to achieve good fortune—had been his primary concern. Nor were his defenses very efficient: his impulses broke through, his repressions leaked, and his anxiety lurked near the surface. Yet he seemed to have stabilized his conflicts at a low level of security. His strategies did work at the level of his unambitious demands.

Opinion Maintenance and Furtherance

When opinions are as deeply embedded in important functions of personality as were Sullivan's on Russia and Communism, it should be no surprise that he guarded them carefully from internal contradiction and from the buffetings of the outside world. His well-developed procedures for maintenance made it especially difficult to investigate the development of his opinions. To questions about the evolution of his views, his first reaction was that he had always had them. Only relatively late in the course of our interviews and with difficulty was he able to say that he had once thought differently. He then became hypersensitive lest we interpret his Communism as a simple equivalent for his earlier adherence to Catholicism. He was never able to point with any certainty to the time when most of his present views took form. Repression and rationalization had created a picture of himself as a consistent Socialist, endowing his present beliefs with apparent timelessness, stability, and validity.

Not only did he iron out temporal inconsistency, but as we have seen, he also ruled out internal conflict in his present opinions by creating a mental picture of Russia that was uniformly favorable. This achievement was such a *tour de force* that we can assume that the mere possibility of conflict within his attitudes toward Russia was intolerable.

As a Marxist, Sullivan was sophisticated enough to discount readily the more reactionary sources of outside challenge to his opinions. As we have seen, he could move comfortably among Republicans, with little showing save an unruly tendency to shock them. His closer friends, it is true, put no challenge to his attitudes, since he had selected them in terms of their political and social beliefs, but he by no means limited his selection of news sources to ones that were favorable to his attitudes.

The maintenance of his attitudes, then, depended on his interpretation of experience, not on pre-selection of the experience to which he exposed himself.

He had a variety of ways of dealing with experience that appeared to challenge his attitudes. Some of these were apparent in his justification of Russia as a temporary police state that we quoted earlier. When he could attribute the attack to manifestly reactionary sources, he could deny or discredit it without even feeling a challenge. Such "shrugging off" was typical of his reaction to the more virulently anti-Russian cartoons of the *Cartoon Stereotype Test*. A good example is his response to a Burris Jenkins cartoon showing the United States as Little Red Riding Hood being duped of her basket of atomic bomb secrets by the Communist wolf.

> Well, this is jingoism. It's against One World but very subtly—no, not subtly, but pretty good. I know Burris Jenkins. He used to be a sports cartoonist. The United States shouldn't give away the bomb secrets and shouldn't engage in disarmament conferences and give up some of its sovereignty. The hostile nation is Russia. Well, let's see. The little girl dressed to represent America has a basket of atom bomb secrets, in the position of Little Red Riding Hood—blithely and naively going to her doom, with the big bear waiting. That, my friend, is a lot of bullshit. The more I see of them the more I lose my veneer of so-called civilization. But Burris Jenkins—you can't blame him. Burris Jenkins is a member of the middle class, tied to the bourgeoisie. I'd do the same probably, if I had his job. If you're a newspaperman, you have to chop up your rationalism. Like Walter Lippmann. One of the Harvard boys. He sees chaos so he takes his axe and chops up his powers of rationalism . . . rationalization.

His ability to discredit sources of challenge stood him in good stead when the challenge itself was more serious than those provided by Hearst cartoons. He used this as merely the first of a much larger defensive repertory in response to the sixth item of the *Information Apperception Test: "Russians have been arrested from time to time without knowing what their crime was."*

> Of course, I don't know who made this statement. And . . . the conditions might exist. I have no evidence to the contrary. I believe that when you're arrested, that you should be told what you're arrested for. But . . . and let me put the BUT in caps . . . law enforcement officers very rarely tell you why they are arresting you. That's true in this country or in any country. According to the law, a United States law enforcement officer is supposed

to tell you "I arrest you for a specific crime." They do not do that. My authority for that is their own word. Ask the next cop you see. If you know the law, you say, "No, I won't go." But . . . I would say that the condition probably did exist in Russia. I don't know one way or the other. It probably does exist because when you have a revolution and defend it against a counter-revolution . . . then you have to resort to a police state for a while until you make things secure. After the revolution is secure and the state is secure, then the . . . there is a relaxation of the police methods and civil liberties as we know them are restored. The liberties are given back to the people. That is the intent of the Russian . . . the Union of Soviet Socialist Republics. If their constitution is to be believed. [Does this item interest you?] The item doesn't interest me any more than it's a condition that exists because of this pattern of revolution and counter-revolution. Now, would I care to be arrested without being told? No. Would I like to see someone else arrested? No.

The quotation bears testimony, of course, to Sullivan's mastery of two other defensive measures: pointing to similar defects in the United States (the so-called "mote-beam" technique) and minimizing the importance of Russian faults by denying their typicality or relevance.

Elsewhere he managed to transform challenging information even to support his position. In the *Stress Interview*, further, he sometimes "played possum," pleading ignorance and refusing to argue when hard pressed. It is less notable that he used these techniques than that he used them so successfully, digesting all information that reached him to a form that agreed with his attitudes. So armed, he could be little disturbed by outside events. From the Russo-German pact to the Truman Doctrine, events were carefully fitted into their place in his ideology with little modification in its fundamental structure.

So much for Sullivan's campaigns in defense of his opinions. What of his behavior on the opinion offensive? Mostly, one gathers, it consisted of verbal exchange among the faithful. As *Weltanschauung*, Sullivan's Communism served its many adjustive functions without involving him in the unwelcome responsibilities and constraints of Party membership. One has the feeling that his need for action, to the extent that he had it, arose from his wish to maintain a self-image worthy of his own respect. Two considerations excused him from taking such feelings seriously. First, a literal interpretation of Communist doctrine assured him that the American Communist Party was bound to be futile during the inevitable stage of Fascism. Beyond that, he could down any nascent urges toward martyrdom by applying economic determinism (the compulsions of the "pattern") to his own case. Full integrity, he concluded, was only for the Nearings, while much "venality" would be forgiven the Sullivans.

While Sullivan may not have conducted as vigorous a campaign in behalf of his views as their salience might have led one to expect, he was as active as any of our subjects in the search for information on which to nourish them. We have seen how much time and attention he devoted to working out the current implications of his views in critical reading, thinking, and discussion. In spite of the stability of his basic ideology in recent years, he characteristically told an interviewer who inquired, "What have you learned that you'd like to pass on—that has been most important to you?": "Gee, I don't know. I'm always learning."

What could we predict for Sullivan's attitudes toward Russia in the eventualities with which we have speculatively confronted our previous two subjects? Outright war between the United States and Russia, we thought, would simply augment the detachment with which he was wont to survey the contemporary scene. While we would not expect him to lose his faith in Russia or to become swept up in any tide of patriotism, we think that he would not be a bad security risk. Forced to be more discreet than would come easily to him, he would, as far as possible, cultivate his garden and wait for the inevitable to unfold. These adjustments would involve a greater compromise in the direction of "venality" than he was making at the time of the study, and would probably require considerable renunciation of his favorite roles. Remaining, and crucial to his psychological integrity, would be his Cassandra-like perspective. There is little different to be said about his probable reaction to a prolonged armed stalemate, except to note that he would most likely show a marked defeatism. As the worst approaches, he will have accepted it already.

A Functional Summing-Up

Let us, finally, pull together the strands of our analysis of why Russia came to mean so much to Hilary Sullivan and why his opinions assumed their present form. First consider their *expressive nature*. We have seen how his high intelligence and his proneness to careless generalization were essential conditions for an awareness of Russia that was at once so complex and so grossly one-sided. His intense, impulsive temperamental endowment was a necessary though not sufficient condition for the colorful intensity of his opinions.

From the standpoint of their adjustive functions, his opinions had complex roots. For our other subjects, Russia was something peripheral, intersected here and there, to be sure, by the personal values in terms of which it was seen and judged. Not so with Sullivan, whose attitudes toward Russia were central to his ideology. Our first question must be concerned with how this broader system of values and interpretations of the world entered his psychological economy.

From the standpoint of *object appraisal*, Sullivan's Marxist world view served only the most general function of sorting out the flux of events into a personally meaningful order. Object appraisal as we analytically distinguish the function fuses in his case with externalization. The all-encompassing order that he rigidly imposed on events had its source in what we can only interpret as a severely neurotic inner predicament. Given his ideology, however, his opinions appraise Russia in terms of his values. The Russia that he saw, the embodiment of all that was new and hopeful, was furthering his values of justice, progress, and social welfare. The uniform, enthusiastic outcome of his evaluation is evidence that object appraisal was dominated for Sullivan by the use to which he put it in the service of externalization. His powers of discriminating judgment had been sacrificed. Yet Sullivan rarely falsified; he interpreted. His attitudes were therefore not very vulnerable.

Russia as an actual fact today and tomorrow had very little relevance to Sullivan's personal needs and interests. Only when involved in the prospect of war did Russia seem to impinge on his current enterprises; precisely here his opinions became incoherent. Russia touched his ideology, not his daily life.

The function of his attitudes in *social adjustment* was also complex. On the one hand, he shared the universal desire for approval. Life had taught him to be modest in this regard, however, and the approval that he sought for his opinions was limited to the rather small group of friends whose judgment he respected. More generally, he wanted response from people, and his non-conforming attitudes led admirably to this result. For those who did not share his deviant views, his opinions laid bait for a reaction that was gratifying in at least two ways: they would take notice of him and respond to him as a consequential person, and, moreover, if they let themselves be shocked, he could feel himself superior. In the role that his attitudes played in his social adjustment, then, non-conformity appears considerably more important than conformity.

It is in the *externalization* of Sullivan's very difficult inner problems, however, that his opinions and Communist ideology played their most essential role in his adjustment, a role that did not require him to be a political activist. These attitudes put his aggressive tendencies in a guise that was acceptable to himself, as well as affording some opportunity for their direct expression. Having espoused a movement of protest, he could both contemplate the final day of reckoning with its settling of scores and enjoy shocking the complacency of his contemporaries.

More than this, his attitudes enabled him to maintain an image of himself that added to his resources for coping with his difficulties. As a Communist, Sullivan became, to his own eyes, a person with "savvy," sophisticated in the back-stage deals by which the world operates, scornful of the euphemistic Pollyannaism of bourgeois respectability. Security and support came, moreover, from his identification with a strong world movement.

Most important of all, it was through his attitudes toward Russia and Communism that he was able to work out, in a comprehensive world view, a strategy which though not a solution to his inner problems at least served to keep them tolerable. In this sense, they became major bastions of ego defense. They helped him construct a world in which his life prospects did not appear catastrophic. They placed his immediate frustration and hopelessness in the impersonal context of historic necessity, and on this solidly pessimistic foundation—a foundation less vulnerable than his Catholicism had been—offered him hope and confidence in the well-elaborated time perspective of ideology. His uncertain personal prospects were submerged in the inevitable pattern of an historic future.

NOTE

1. For pertinent evidence on the characteristics of American, British, French, and Italian Communists, *see* G. A. Almond, *The appeals of Communism*, Princeton, Princeton University Press, 1954.

Chapter Eight

What It Means to Be Human

At the core of the answer to the oldest, most central question known to human self-consciousness, "What does it mean to be human?" must be that it means being the sort of creature that can frame such a question about itself.

In the dawn of self-consciousness in individual infancy and, presumably, in the evolution of our species, self and interpreted world emerge together. Questions about human origins, human nature, and human fate have always been linked indissolubly with questions about the human significance of the world in which people live their lives. Or rather, the content of human symbolic culture—the rich web of myth and ritual and folklore, then of religion and philosophy and the "humanities" and, just very recently, of the natural, social, and psychological sciences—has "always" provided *answers* to these two kinds of questions of meaning. The questions themselves must have remained largely implicit until urbanized civilizations created the conditions for a degree of cognitive complexity to emerge in which traditional answers could no longer be taken for granted: when the culturally available answers become open to choice or doubt, the questions themselves become salient as, in our Western tradition, they did in pre-Socratic Greece, and as, with new force, they have become especially salient for us today.

Our present position is both unprecedentedly privileged and exceptionally vulnerable.

Privileged: as never before, we have ever-increasing stretches of the historical and cross-cultural record spread before us. As Malraux put it dramatically for the realm of art,[1] a remarkably wide range of visions of human meaning is now available to those of us who are educated to look, a truly unprecedented situation. We are potentially at the edge of freedom from the otherwise universal human condition of being culture-bound.

But vulnerable: such freedom entails heavy costs and frightens us, as

Kierkegaard put it most poignantly[2] and Erich Fromm[3] and Rollo May[4] have reminded us in more recent contexts. The thoughtful, analytic, mostly academic representatives of our privileged culture share in the general plight, in which the plethora of meanings often seems to add up to meaninglessness. So many meanings! How is one to choose among them? By what charter can any particular answer to the perennial questions be taken as more persuasive, more valid, than the others? From this perspective, there is little to choose between the absurdism of the existentialist posture and Lévi-Strauss's sometime view of his own structuralism as just another modern myth on all fours with the traditional ones. It only aggravates our predicament that the scientific view—our recent invention that is our most distinctive asset but is also (through its technological by-products) deeply implicated in our distinctive peril— has mostly been a strong corrosive of the older anthropocentric meanings cast in an appropriately human scale, but has not provided a satisfying or perhaps a satisfactory replacement. It is hard when the new answers to questions about the world dethrone humankind; it is worse when scientific accounts of human nature reduce it to terms no longer "anthropomorphic."

Under these circumstances, to attempt any sort of answer to the big old question requires some blend of foolhardiness and *chutzpah*. Yet we need to keep facing it, to keep talking about it as intelligently as we can. It is not good to duck problems of meaning by burying ourselves in "value-free" specialization or technological-applied work—following the predominant American trend in psychology and the social sciences— thus contributing by default (sometimes by assault)[5] to the spread of meaninglessness. It is not good to leave problems of meaning to "countercultural" irrationalism and occultism[6] or even to philosophical specialists.

Our privileged-vulnerable position of cross-historical, cross-cultural sophistication contains at least the possibility of transcending the demoralizing relativism and attrition of meaning that it breeds. By facing the historical, cultural nature of human nature squarely, we might be able to arrive at a processual, contextual view of what it means to be human, rather than a static view that fits a particular time and place but is bound to be wrong if we take it as a timeless, universal account. (Yet we also need to worry about what it means to be human in *our* time and place!)

We have become sharply aware of the empirical fact that human beings, wherever and whenever we find them, seek meaning and create it, individually and collectively. To be human is to be engaged in a life infused with meaning. In the long eons of human prehistory spent in hunting-gathering bands and in the dozen millenia of village or pastoral life, slowly evolving systems of cultural meaning provided unquestioned frames that endowed individual lives with significance—that made them humanly livable in the face of unpredictable adversity and inevitable death. It is the shattering of these traditional frames of meaning and the transience, weak authority, and human inadequacy of their successors in the brief episode of modernity which raises the problem of meaningless-ness as a persisting feature of cultural crisis. Collectively, we now know about meaninglessness and we know that it is dehumanizing. So our hard-earned knowledge can provide the starting point for an attempted answer to our central question. If we take seriously the fact that people are intrinsically seekers and creators of meaning, we must regard "the meaning of being human" as intrinsically open, an unfolding, creative human project. In Clifford Geertz's happy phrase, man is the "unfinished animal."[7] In culture and in history humankind participates in giving form to its human nature in a variety of ways.

The perspectives we have recently gained on human evolution make both the boundary between the prehuman animal and the truly human more ambiguous for us, and the distinctive features of humanness more remarkable. We have pushed our divergence from our closest primate cousins back some five million years or more. We have learned that our Pliocene ancestors could already walk bipedally and were first using, then making, crude tools long before they developed the big brains which underlie our present complexity of experience and behavior. This greatly expanded time frame for human evolution is a matter of fact. On it we have built the speculative construction[8] that manipulation, tool use and tool making—phenomena of incipient "material culture"—gave important selective advantage to the genes that govern brain size and neural complexity. According to this now plausible view, material cul-ture and distinctive human biology evolved in tandem and interactively.

Such speculations about the causal processes involving one feature of distinctive humanness—our technology—rest on the factual basis of dated sequences of bones and hearths and artifacts we have unearthed. The evolution of language and symbolic culture unfortunately leaves no such traces until very late in the course of human emergence, in Nean-derthal burial sites dating from about the time our own subspecies of *Homo sapiens* appeared. Burial in graves lined with flowers surely attests to well-elaborated cultural beliefs in an afterlife. But 50,000 years ago for the flower-lined graves[9] and 70,000 for other evidence of deliberate burial[10] is only yesterday in the evolutionary time span that has recently opened out behind us.

Primitive communication to coordinate the hunt must have been just as selectively advantageous as manipulative cleverness and tool use to those bands of protohuman hunters on the East African savannahs who excelled at it. Natural selection for communicative capacity also seems likely to be involved in the rapid increase in brain size in later Pleistocene times. What is certain is that the capacity to learn the elaborate structures of human speech is built into the human brain in intricate and fundamental ways which would seem to have required long eons to evolve—ways that differ radically from the cerebral basis of communication in other primates. It is also clear that the universal pattern of all existing human languages has no parallel in the communication of other primates. This is a two-stage, immensely flexible coding system. First, the continuously varying sounds that are the acoustic products of vocal articulation are coded into a limited set of discrete and arbitrary "phonemes." Then meaning units composed of these phonemes—words—are combined creatively in open syntactical structures. Not even the fascinating apes who have recently learned under human tutelage to manipulate symbols in quasihuman ways come near this achievement; indeed the breakthrough in their training was to bypass the problem of articulation and therefore the entire stage of phonemic coding.[11]

Linguists are fond of emphasizing that every known human language is completely adequate to the lives of the human communities which share it. Everything "significant" has a name, and everything that needs to be said can be said. No language is a closed system; it can accommodate and express endless novelty. We may never know just when in prehistory the slow evolution of human communicative capacity arrived at this state of affairs.

However, contemporary conjecture suggests a remarkably late date for this crucial attainment—maybe about 50,000 years ago among members of our own subspecies equipped genetically as we are today.[12] A date that recent does fit the sudden efflorescence and diversification of Late Paleolithic culture beginning about then. For more than a million years[13] the Acheulian culture, identified by its simple tool kit of crudely flaked stones, had persisted whenever early human beings were found. Something extraordinary happened around fifty millenia ago to launch a process of cultural innovation, population expansion, and artistic-aesthetic objectification of human experience. Within this brief span the "new worlds" of Australia and the Americas were colonized across formidable geographic barriers. By 19,000 years ago the Magdalenian cave paintings displayed a fully developed high art. In comparison with the cultural stability of Acheulian times, a new dynamic history began that sweeps to our own historic present in its headlong trajectory.

The late date of the "take off" in human cultural development is a matter of fact, though the link to language is conjectural. If we accept the explanation that the take off occurred when humankind passed a critical point in the attainment of true language, we are left with extremely difficult puzzles as to how the neural bases of language could have evolved over the million years in which little change is apparent in material culture. (New puzzles continually replace old ones in the search for human origins!) However, one can imagine that the attainment of true language by a few intercommunicating bands of hunter-gatherers must have struck the speakers as a quantum leap, akin to that experienced by Helen Keller when it dawned on her that things have names—*everything* has a name and can be talked about. Whenever and however it occurred—and occur it did—humanness as we know it was essentially established.

I have begun with this account of the new perspectives on human origins because I don't think the news has spread sufficiently to psychologists, social scientists, and social theorists who are more philosophically inclined. Certainly we have yet to digest its import. For the facts we must rely on our anthropological colleagues. The implication of the new facts is something for all the rest of us to work out, from many perspectives.

Let us consider the emergent situation of people newly possessed of true language. For more than a million years, the Acheulian bands of hunter-gatherers had been poised at the juncture of Nature and Culture. They had been part of Nature. Their slowly evolving culture of tools and fire and, at the boundaries of the last glaciation, of clothing and constructed shelter—also of social organization and protolinguistic communication—fed back to give a selective biological advantage to those whose bigger and more complex brains made them more adept first at using, then at inventing culture. But this insecure, partly cultural adaptation within Nature was stable. Proto-people depended more than other animals on learning, but hardly on innovation. Their tool-making

culture had a universal sameness which approached the stereotyped behavior traits of other animal species.

The attainment of language gave its speakers immense practical advantages. They could co-ordinate the activities of the band in more
complex and effective ways than had hitherto been possible. They could
pass on to the young a more complex heritage of skills, knowledge, and
belief, taking fuller advantage of the long developmental period of infancy and childhood for *socializing* the young to evolving humanness.
They could build on to the biological facts of family relatedness and
simple primate social organization the elaborate structures of kinship
which until recently provided the universal supportive social context for
human life. And, very much more effectively than before, they could
think, thanks to the culturally transmitted symbol system of language
which provided the framework and tools for thought.

Thinking mediated by language gave people new powers of "time-
binding" in Korzybski's apt phrase.[14] Forethought and afterthought became possible and a distinctive human attribute (think of the myth of
Prometheus and Epimetheus)—again an immense practical advantage in
the struggle for existence that assured the selective survival and propagation of language speakers. People could now make plans, undertake
commitments, and recognize and correct errors—all essential adaptive
ingredients of human social life as we know it.

But there were inherent consequences of becoming a speaking, thinking creature that provided no such obvious evolutionary advantage yet
are central to the situation of being human and our experience of it. One
is an aspect of the elaborated experience of selfhood. Though it has
recently been shown that chimpanzees are capable of responding appropriately to themselves as social objects in ways not demonstrated for
other mammals,[15] G. H. Mead was surely right in emphasizing the *reflexiveness* of language as centrally involved in the human capacity and
propensity to take the self as object, figuratively to look at the self as if
through the eyes of others.[16] When we speak, we understand ourselves
as if from the perspective of our hearers. We are part of our own
audience, sharing meanings in terms of a common symbol system. *Self-
consciousness*, the sense of *me*-ness, arises in the course of "symbolic
interaction" (the label given to the school of thought carried forward in
social psychology by Mead's followers).

Mead argued persuasively that the development of reflexive selfhood
is crucially "functional," in that the implicated ability to "take the role

of the other" is essential for our participation in the coordinated activities of organized social life. So it surely is. Yet there are heavy costs in the side effects. Human self-consciousness breaks the unity of Man and Nature and, when forethought and afterthought are added as gifts of language, the ingredients of the human existential predicament emerge. As speaking self-conscious human beings, we and our forebears for more than 50,000 years have faced the cognitive puzzle of whence we came into the world, why we are here, and what happens when we die. But as we all know, this is no matter of mere curiosity released by the fact that our language permits us to ask questions. (We have that too!) Primarily through language, we have become *persons*, linked to other persons whom we love and care for in a web of "intersubjective" meaning.[17] The inevitability of the eventual death of self and loved ones and the arbitrary unpredictability of death from famine, disease, accident, predation, or human assault becomes the occasion not for momentary animal terror but for what is potentially unremitting human anguish. So the quest for meaning, for meanings compatible with a human life of self-conscious mortality, becomes a matter of life and death urgency. I don't think Ernest Becker exaggerated the importance of this theme in the history of human culture.[18]

Of course, this mainly familiar account is wrong in one obvious respect. Contrary to the old myth, our forebears cannot have been cast out of Nature's Garden of Eden in one sudden tragic event of "birth trauma." Perhaps, from the time perspective of the whole span of human evolution, the final full attainment of language competence worked itself out very rapidly once the basic structural-generative principles of truly human language had been hit upon. Intrinsic potentialities for organized complexity inherent in the new symbolic structures may have guided the latter stages of the process toward rapid completion. All the same, self-conscious selfhood, with its peremptory challenge to find supportive meaning in the face of creature mortality, must have been a gradual emergent.

If so, the symbolic resources of language-bearing human communities could meet the need for meaning as it arose. Thus emerged the many cultural worlds of myth, ritual, and religion, which provided the traditional answers to the question of what it means to be human. They were good answers, proclaiming to each communicating tribal group its value as The People; legitimizing the group's way of life as ordained by their ancestors; giving intelligible meaning to the exigencies of life and death;

providing appropriate ways in which individual and community could participate in the encouragement of auspicious outcomes and the avoidance of ominous ones. These traditional mythic answers could not fully eliminate occasions for anguish and terror, but they could give intelligible shape to formless terror; and they could make the blows of fate more bearable to the victim and certainly more endurable to the fellow members of the victim's kindred and community. They allowed life to go on quite satisfactorily between emergencies.

Students of myth and folklore found recurrent themes and motifs wherever they turned among the world's traditional peoples. This was surely to be expected, given the universal focal events in the life cycle, in human relationships, and in dealings with the natural world, and given large commonalities in the respective dramas of hunter-gatherer, pastoral, or peasant life. They also found a universally applicable distinction between the commonplace objects and meanings of everyday life and *sacred* objects and meanings of transcendent power and value. The commonplace and everyday seemed to be sustained in its human meaning by its contact with and participation in a realm of the sacred and numinous. In all times and places, from the emergence of meaning-seeking humanity until the very recent immediate past, the core meaning of being human was contained in conceived relationships of human life to a more-than-human order, which was nevertheless infused with value and purpose imagined in very human terms.

I have stressed what was common among these cultural systems of meaning, but in fact we know that their accounts of the meaning of being human, and the ways of life to which they lent significance and support, were enormously various. For millenia each self-enclosed system provided a secure, unchallenged interpretation of human life. Each system was open to such novelty and change as altered circumstances of life might call for, yet was conservative of tradition—which, from our vantage point, was the source of its authority. The wide divergences among these different cultural worlds occasioned no problem. The Babel of language differentiation helped to isolate the meaning systems of tribal groups whose cultures, after all, were very locally based. And when significant contact did occur, each cultural group had the natural ethnocentric self-confidence to reject foreign conceptions and life-ways as barbarous or subhuman. (Though particular attractive cultural features were often borrowed and transmitted, and one cultural group sometimes engulfed or dominated others, with some cultural merging.)

Over the millenia what can only be described in retrospect by the unfashionable terms *progress* and *cultural evolution* manifestly occurred. As we know, a first landmark that altered the condition and meaning of being human was the invention of agriculture. First in the Middle East, then in India and China, and then again in Middle and South America, hunter-gatherers began to domesticate plants and animals and became peasant farmers, producing a surplus of food which allowed the species to multiply rapidly. In Old World and New, the parallels in the urban civilizations which soon emerged rightly continue to amaze us; and though a few continue to cling to the straws of diffusionist theories, I think we have to accommodate as part of *our* understanding of the meaning of being human the surprising fact that we are a culture-bearing species which repeatedly reinvents urban ways of life (in a word, civilizations) whenever we gain the resources to do so.

With civilizations and their attendant states and empires came the competing world religions with their now more fully elaborated conceptions of the meaning of human life. These persist until today for most of the world's people. With states and empires also came a new *political* life: first a politics of crude domination, legitimized by religious sanctions (the old myths transformed and put to new uses) and restrained mainly by the interests of what McNeill[19] has aptly called the human "macro-parasites" (the exploitative rulers) in the survival and productiveness of their peasant hosts. In our own Western tradition, the vision that eventually developed among the dominating class in ancient Attica, of a free political life as the condition in which truly human status can be fully realized, certainly does *not* describe the meaning of being human to most human beings then or now. However, the Aristotelian ideal of humankind as the political animal set forth—and the actual politics of Periclean Athens partly exemplified—a valued possibility for the meaning of human life that continues to provide us with a standard for appraising the quality of social life we have been able to attain in our urban communities. It is noteworthy that this important ideal of human social existence was formulated in the same burst of reflective inquiry that, seemingly for the first time in the proliferation of human culture, was shaking human consciousness free of purely traditional—mythic—answers to the central questions concerning humankind's being-in-the-world. It was accompanied, as we know, by a flowering of remarkable artistic and poetic creativeness.

There *was* progress, I suggest, in the rapid and convergent invention (from our present perspective) of agriculture, urban life and civilization in the course of a quickly countable number of millenia, after the "take-off" we speculatively attribute to our attainment of true language competence. However, the *idea* of progress[20] as a source of transcendent meaning belongs to the penultimate episode of our recent past; before that, like most of the world's peoples, our ancestors were more likely to conceive of eternal cycles of recurrence or to honor their ancestors by some version of the myth of a Golden Age.

In our mounting disillusionment following our experience of the horrors of two world wars, the human costs of totalitarian utopianism, the Holocaust, the preview of nuclear catastrophe at Hiroshima and Nagasaki, the foreshadowing of a closed, exhausted, polluted planet, and the cheapening of traditional values in commercial mass society, the idea of progress is understandably in ill repute. But if we are to formulate for ourselves a version of the "meaning of being human" adequate to our own time and situation, we need to appreciate what, in this recent episode, compelled people to believe in progress and how this stage in the unfolding of the nature of "the unfinished animal" conditions, potentiates, and limits the possibilities of meaning that are now open to us.

As we look back on the last half millenium of Western history—a phase of history that began parochially but came to engulf the whole human world—there was indeed dramatic progress in the standards of value shared by the people who were the major actors in the course of events. (To be sure, other peoples and their ways of life were regarded as expendable and fell disastrously by the wayside. The vanishing American Indians, the enslaved Africans, the uprooted peasants in mushrooming urban shantytowns had no good reason to speak of progress.) Knowledge increased, first in the recovery of the texts of the Ancients and in printing for the many, then in the new "takeoff" of scientific discovery—which was really a metadiscovery, a cultural mutation akin to the agricultural revolution of ten millenia ago—setting in motion a social process that (in spite of Kuhn)[21] kept leading inexorably to an ever more comprehensive grasp of the workings of the world in which humankind is planted. Technology developed first in its own independent trajectory, then increasingly as a by-product, and then again as an explicit goal of progress in science; it continually extended and replaced "manpower," resulting in new and eventually frightening capacities to transform the world and affect the condition and quality of human life for better or worse. Communication and commerce expanded to include the whole globe, and the globe shrank as "life space" for humankind. Older ills of infancy and childhood and plagues of adulthood that in times past had checked the growth of human populations were brought under control[22] with the result that population growth leapt out of control, especially in the parts of the world that were last touched by "modernity." Our very success as a biological species raised doubts of impending failure.

In spite of cavernous divisions between "haves" and "have-nots," the era of progress left humankind involved in a common worldwide predicament, sharing as never before a common fate. Cultures that had existed in proud and isolated independence were independent no longer; some ceased to be proud and others just ceased. The old sheltered plural worlds of cultureboundedness seemed to be fading away in every quarter; indeed, if *variety* in possible directions of human meaning is itself a value (permitting the species the adaptive advantage of a multiplicity of routes toward the realization of human potentialities), deliberate planning now seemed to be required if aspects of variety in human values were to be preserved—so strongly did the "materialistic" values of the new worldwide technological culture corrode older sources of meaning.

But I am running ahead of our common story in noting features of the predicament with which the era of progress has left us. While we were still caught up in its momentum and before our modern doubts arose to preoccupy reflective people, progress seemed factual; progress seemed the firmest justification of hope. And while progress did indeed undermine the parochial, timeless certainties—the traditional mythic and religious worlds—humankind's symbolic creativeness once more provided a reconstructed and livable world which kept the human enterprise significant and satisfying.

In the era of progress, traditional religious world views were "progressively" secularized, a process that was by no means played out by the time modern twentieth-century doubts about progress arose, so there remain enclaves of mythic conception and large sweeps of inconsistent and partly modernized popular thinking. That is, with the exceptions just noted, the old humanly universal distinction was fading between the secular and the sacred, the everyday and the numinous. People who were caught up in progress lost touch with the sacred. But for the time being they hardly needed it. What they needed (I tentatively suggest as a conclusion from our synoptic review of human history and prehistory) was a source of *transcendent* meaning taken for granted: a source of meaning beyond the desperate trivialities of everyday life and death and disappointment.

The sacred world traditionally provided those meanings. Worldly life gained significance through its culturally orchestrated participation in the other-worldly drama. But as progress in its scientific-technological-skeptical guise eroded the foundations of the old and humanly satisfying mythic world view, it also provided a transcendent basis for significance in individual and social life. In this new view "Man" is not just what is but rather, and more significantly, what is to be, and in the era of progress whether the "wave of the future" were interpreted grandly (as by Hegel and Marx) or more crassly (in terms of economic growth and "the bigger the better") the future justified the present as well as the past. We were producers of "Whig History"—the story of "onward and upward"—and participants in it.

At the level of individual people and their families, we could share a faith that the future would be a continually better one for our offspring and for theirs in turn. The tribulations of individual lives gained significance in this larger frame. It may not have been so satisfyingly transcendent as the religious frame that it displaced (viz. the tortured reexaminations of the human condition that abound in nineteenth-century literature) but it *was* transcendent. Human life acquired meaning in terms of the greater perfection of human potentiality toward which it was understood to be tending.

We now have enough distance to see in clearly outlined perspective the drama of this recent scene in the development of what it means to be human, in the nineteenth century of our Western tradition that has now pervaded the world. The new era of progress had been en route for quite some time, but the century of reason and the Enlightenment had been bemused by the reversible clockwork order of the Newtonian universe, and its deistic view of cosmos did not bring change and development or history into self-conscious focus. It took the disruptions of the French and Industrial Revolutions to make the reflective denizens of the world of progress aware of change and development as its distinctive mark. The idea of history (which of course underlies the whole approach of this essay) emerged only then as a major approach for accounting for "what it means to be human."

Hegel, Marx and Darwin—as we look back, the century's major intellectual lights as interpreters of the human condition—all participated in giving form to this new transcendent perspective on the meaning of human life. Early in the century, Hegel wedded the idea of progress to deistic religion. His view of human history as the dialectical unfolding of Absolute Spirit in self-objectification included enduring insights into ways in which humankind participate in the creation of their "unfinished" human nature; it was welcomed because it seemed to salvage the mythic, anthropomorphic sacred world as a grounding of everyday human life. The Hegelian vision incorporated the idea of progress into the old sacred world, but in closer connection to historical human life than before. Hegel inspired the more intellectual among the romantics, who did not like the manifestations of progress in the uncontrolled, antihuman dirtiness of the early Industrial Revolution.

In the next generation Marx disavowed the mythic and "turned Hegel on his head." He espoused science, but borrowed from Hegel a scheme for the dynamic of progress that was still transcendental—the dialectic of "historical materialism." He, too, provided a transcendent scheme of meaning in which our lives (within the limitations of "unfinished" human nature and imperfect society) gain significance in their contribution to a progressive future. Many people today continue to nourish themselves on this meaning.

Darwin's contribution to our present understanding of the meaning of being human is the most paradoxical and interesting of all. A child of the century, the idea of development and evolution was in his bones. But Darwin was in tune, as Hegel was not–and he was certainly more closely in tune than Marx—with the spirit of the new post-Newtonian science which ripened in chemistry, thermodynamics, and biology during the century: a mechanistic science in non-Newtonian domains that arrayed itself against the vitalistic, intrinsically purposive conceptions which appealed to the romantics and made contact with the old anthropomorphic world people could feel at home in.

What Darwin achieved with his principle of natural selection can be stated as a truly Hegelian synthesis, between Hegel's conception of humanity's emergent self-creation in history and the powerful physicalist conception of a colorless, unintentional world of blind cause and effect. Natural selection, through random (meaningless or mechanical) variation and selective survival and propagation of variants that happened to fit environmental specifications, provided an intelligible account of our actual biological world of manifest adaptiveness—without requiring a designer. Subsequently elaborated by modern genetics and molecular biology, the Darwinian synthesis allows us to recognize an actual world of purposive creatures, including ourselves, without needing to believe in an exterior source of prior purpose built into the scheme of things. Hitherto, we have always depended on such external, sacred support for our own purposes, so the "transcendence" available in Darwinian evolution has been small comfort. Yet even as the Darwinian perspective dethroned humankind as a chosen people of special cosmic concern, it has its own glory as an account of the emergence of meaning in an otherwise meaningless universe. My attempt at a processual, historical interpretation of the meaning of being human would be inconceivable without the new way of thinking bequeathed by Darwin.

If we continue to look to our immediate past for meanings of being human—which seems almost presumptuously out of balance in the light of what we now know about the temporal scope of human history—we must also take into account the human meaning of a further step in the nineteenth-century progress of the physical sciences: the Second Law of Thermodynamics. Entropy, disorder, and chaos must always increase. For people who had taken progress in the physical sciences as a model and guarantee for progress in human affairs, the Second Law was shakingly paradoxical. Attending to abstract problems produced by the practical need to understand the steam-powered basis of the Industrial Revolution, physical science came forth with a principle that decreed the end of progress. Things fall apart. In the long run, progress is a perturbation within a cosmic decline.

This news threw Henry Adams into his phase of nostalgic pessimism.[23] With the harder news of the First World War, it probably predisposed Freud to propound a death instinct (Thanatos) as a second principle paralleling his conception of the libido economy. (Freud's two "metapsychological" principles seem more closely linked to the two laws of thermodynamics as models than they are to his clinical observations.)

During the recent epoch of technological advance, progress thus provided an evaluative frame within which people could find transcendent meaning—the only sort of meaning that makes self-conscious mortal human life worth the candle. At best, progress was never a wholly satisfactory replacement for sacred transcendence. In our own century the shock of entropy was followed by gruesome facts of current events that further undermined our faith in progress. To satisfy existential needs which have been with us since we became self-conscious mortals, human meaning has to be transcendent of our own immediate self-interested situations. The idea of progress, on which we relied as the older mythic meanings lost conviction, no longer gives us dependable help. Once more humankind has arrived at unprecedented and unique predicaments—in our search for meaning and in our placement in a newly vulnerable ecological niche on the small planet we have come to dominate and may be near the point of destroying.

What it means to be human has been an open venture, a developing human project. But the meaning of being human is by no means unconstrained in the present, nor was it ever in the past. The many meanings of being human that have been actualized historically have been formulated and lived by people in relation to the social and biological realities and requirements of their particular historical situations. Because, as we like to say, we now live in a "global village"—a bad term because we have lost community, and our human setting is no longer village-like— we press one another toward common, consensual meanings of being human. We may value cultural pluralism sentimentally or politically but we know now, as we did not know before, that we live in one world, of which we embrace competing interpretations and in which we pursue competing interests. For the first time we are becoming aware of our objective involvement in a common fate, all of us constrained by the visibly fearsome consequences of letting the course of history run along present trends without our deliberate intervention. For "unfinished animals" of our generation, the meaning of being human in our world today has to take our novel human situation sharply into account. We had better take it into account, or our fate will surely be that of just one more *finished* animal, a successor in the parade of extinction.

The core of what it has continually meant to be human, then, is processual. It lies in the endless human quest for meaning and its creation in symbolic culture. Meanings that have sustained people in the self-awareness of their mortal condition have hitherto transcended the mundane. People have attributed their sources of meaning to a sacred realm of human values and purposes read into the supposed general scheme of things. With the fading of the traditional mythic world under pressure from the enormously "successful" strategy of science and technology (which has transformed our common sense), even the idea of progress in its various forms has failed us as a source of hope, a secular basis for transcendence. So, with all our historical burden of symbolic sophistication and technical competence, we find ourselves back in the original position of First People contemplating their mortality, facing a new set of dangers and opportunities, to be sure, and also fortunately blessed with new resources for understanding and coping.

In this predicament, our social scientists and humanists and prophets of popular culture would variously lead us in all possible directions, urging upon us a cacophony of competing meanings. Some, like B. F. Skinner, deify the natural sciences. According to Skinner[24] our time-honored interpretation of our own humanness in terms of a life of intention, purpose, commitment, and virtue or their lack, a drama of good and evil and human responsibility—the comedy and tragedy of life, in effect—is just as mythical as our former vision of the environing natural world in these human terms. To gird ourselves for survival, he says, we must conquer these illusions and analyze and program our own behavior with the same dispassionate intelligence that Skinnerians apply to the training of animals. But this is extravagant and unwarranted mythocide; in calling upon us to move "beyond freedom and dignity," Skinner would have us give up the very qualities in our self-conception that many of us have come to value most in our humanness. There is nothing in the scientific strategy, even applied to ourselves, that forces this denial of meaning upon us. To the extent that Skinner's dehuman-ized reinterpretation of human nature gains acceptance, this reductionist version—a nonhuman meaning of being human—contributes to our cultural crisis of meaninglessness rather than to its solution.

Others, especially the young and well-to-do in the aftermath of the so-called counterculture of the 1960s, would pick and choose as con-noisseurs in the supermarket of alternative transcendental meanings.[25] A little yoga, a workshop on primal scream, some transcendental medita-tion, a Zen retreat: one can experiment with many meanings in the half-world between religion and therapy, drawing upon the most disparate cultural sources, just as one can experiment with a variety of mind-altering drugs. There have been many seekers, we know, who are fol-lowing that route, and there are leaders in the humanistic psychology movement who set the example and give them encouragement.[26] But such desultory experimentation with meaning is superficial and undisci-plined, and rather reflects the dis-ease of meaninglessness than offers a solid cure. Meanings have to be taken more seriously if they are to matter to us.

In the recent proliferation of cults and the occult, and in the spread of Pentecostalism—the "charismatic movement" in the established churches—we can readily see equivalents of the Ghost Dance of the

Plains Indians at the end of their cultural tether or the cargo cults of the beleaguered Pacific Islanders: messianic bursts of nativistic revival, desperately reasserting traditional meanings that are rightly felt to be in mortal danger. To the nonbeliever, these too smack more of symptoms than of cure, though we should remember that our Christian era began with the emergent predominance of just one such messianic cult among many competitors in the faltering days of the late Classical world. We cannot exclude the possibility—indeed it fits the historical record all too well—that people's unsatisfied need for transcendent meaning may be becoming so urgent that only the literalness of old-style religion will satisfy it. From the perspective of enlightenment values still cherished in the intellectual and academic community, we may indeed be at the outset of a new Dark Age. Heilbroner's grim analysis of "the human prospect"[27] leaves this as a possibility we cannot readily dismiss.

From the standpoint of some social critics in the humanistic camp as well, not only modern technology but also the very enterprise of civilization itself has to be viewed as a disease.[28] For reasons that do not persuade me, Freud in his latter years came to see neurosis and human misery as inherent costs of civilization[29] but that did not lead him to throw in with the cause of the savage. Post-Freudian romantics have found less satisfaction in Freud's stoic posture. For many there is a strong appeal to the regressive route. Humankind is out of touch with Nature, and our life of reason even at its best leads us toward destruction of the texture of natural life. We should retreat from the city and the machine, retreat from our delusory self-consciousness and trust the animal life of instinct. The theme has been familiar since D. H. Lawrence, and he surely had his predecessors.

But just where, in this view of the human episode, did people get off the track? The point of view developed early in this essay sees a dynamism in human transactions with Nature ever since Paleolithic times, when we began talking to each other and ourselves. The dawn of language *was* a portentous, risky break with Nature, and the myth of Original Sin does symbolize something deeply problematic about our footing in the world. However, looking through the far end of the temporal telescope we see no further Rubicon, once we crossed the boundary of language, at which humankind can be said to have gone astray. (Cogent arguments have been advanced that atomic energy and genetic engineering in our own day may constitute such Rubicons.) Our very nature as "incomplete animals" requires culture for our viability, let alone for our fulfillment. Once we set out on our remarkable course, agriculture, villages, cities, civilization, industry, and science all seem steps in a trajectory toward greater power in the world and greater understanding of our place in it. It is clear that even if we would turn back from this adventure in humanness not many of us or our offspring could survive the trip. After our recent brushes with apocalypse, apocalyptic thinking has become all too understandable, but in spite of Norman O. Brown[30] I see no reason to cheer for human defeat.

If we do not let ourselves become derailed by the difficulty and complexity of our awesome problems as a species, their challenge honestly faced could provide a frame of meaning more than sufficient. The story of human life thus far reads like a long picaresque novel. Now the plot thickens, and it is hard not to believe we are moving toward a denouement. However, this time we cannot count on progress; our fate depends, and more and more of us know it, upon our own human actions, intelligent and compassionate, or the contrary. Surely it was such a reading that led the biophysicist—and polymath and prophet—John Platt to call the title essay of a recent book "The Step to Man."[31] He argues that *if* we manage to solve the interrelated ecological and human problems defined by exponential trends that seem to be carrying us to catastrophe, we will have transformed our human nature as we know it in the process. He seeks to engage our transcendent commitment to this high task—not in fulfillment of a fated progress, but in response to a momentous challenge in which the stakes are very high. To meet the challenge would indeed be a giant step toward the adult, responsible conduct of our lives in the world.

My understanding of the open-ended meaning of what it is to be human is in good accord with Platt's rallying cry. Human beings *have* formed their own human nature very substantially in the course of coping symbolically, as well as technically, with their world and with themselves and their fellows as increasingly salient components of that world. Though we are seriously at risk in new ways by the very success of the strategy our unique species hit upon, the forming of human nature is not finished—nor would it be should we accomplish Platt's devoutly-to-be-hoped-for Step to Man. The meanings of being human that served us so long and so well—the mythic and religious ones handed down to us by tradition—formulate important emergent truths of human life, but they no longer give us good guidance or dependable support in the world we must deal with today. The problems of the real world should now yield sufficient high drama to engage and make meaningful the lives of those whose imaginations can be aroused by them.

If we are to give ourselves a chance to respond adequately to this challenge, however, we need to conserve and re-form our *human* resources, and deploy our scientific resources with all the intelligence and wisdom we can muster. Our ways of life shape who we are; and our self-conceptions of what it means to be human participate in constituting our actual human nature. We need to reknit our ravelled human relationships in family and community life: part of the enduring meaning of what it has been to be human is our mutual support in loving care of one another, which has suffered in a time of exaggerated individualism. We need also to reknit our connection to historical continuity, badly strained everywhere by the headlong rapidity of culture change. We need to practice caring more deeply than has become customary about our posterity and the future, if we are to become capable of doing the hard things that preserving a human future now requires of us. We need to take nourishment in our "natural" joy in the world's beauties and in our kinship with all living things. We need to raise our sights in the standards of our political discourse and controversy, because it is in the political world that we can take steps toward coping with our species-wide problems—and it is in the political world that we can pursue our narrow interests until it is too late.

In the social, psychological, or behavioral sciences, we need to find or restore a language caring and respectful of people, and a formulation of our enterprises that feeds information and insight back to people to increase their competence and satisfaction in relating to one another and dealing cooperatively with their common problems. The last thing we need from the sciences of people is the mistaken and self-diminishing message that people are just programmable mechanisms, not really people after all.

In this new challenge to critical self-conscious social and personal reconstruction, we should take heart in some remarkable recent changes in how we conceive of our humanness that are still in an early stage of being worked out in actual social life: gains in the recognized humanness of women, minorities, and Third World peoples, both in the humanity they claim and espouse for themselves and in the humanity they are accorded by others in what had been the mainstream of progress. We must remember that the project of being human traditionally left women in a limited, secondary position,[32] and that the other face of progress for the dominant classes of the industrialized West was imperialism, colonialism, and exploitation—the white man's privilege that was implicit in the "white man's burden." We are far from having earned the right to complacency about actual results of the struggle for justice toward women, minorities, and "have-not" peoples: the actual gap between "haves" and "have-nots" is even increasing. But we have certainly gained the basis for *hope* in the remarkable advance in our conception of what justice requires.

I say "our" conception, but to understand the real basis for our new hope—in turn the basis for commitment and action that can redefine what it means to be human in the relations of our daily life—requires us to penetrate the ambiguity of "our." In times past "we" were the more or less enlightened passengers on the train of progress, who sometimes exhorted one another toward more inclusive definitions of fellow humanity. But today "we" also include those who were formerly "others," who are now making their own claims and, in gaining their own self-respect, are earning the respect of the rest of us.

A profound revision of the meaning of being human would seem to be in progress. We have become the people we are by a long hard road which in the reconstructed "scientific" account is just as miraculous and awe inspiring as the accounts of Creation in religious myth. The tragedy and comedy, the pathos and glory of our earthly life includes the fact that our common human project of self-understanding is also one of collective self-development and social creation and reconstruction. The meaning of being human is not a given, not a stable constant. We have encountered many reasons for believing our own time to be a critical one in which to have a part in re-creating it. Let us get on with this important agenda!

NOTES

1. André Malraux, *The Voices of Silence*, trans. Stuart Gilbert, Doubleday, Garden City, New York, 1953.

2. Søren Kierkegaard, *The Concept of Dread*, trans. Walter Lowrie, Princeton University Press, Princeton, New Jersey, 1944.

3. Erich Fromm, *Escape from Freedom*, Farrar and Rinehart, New York, 1941.

4. Rollo May, *The Meaning of Anxiety* (revised edition), W. W. Norton, New York, 1977.

5. B. F. Skinner, *Beyond Freedom and Dignity*, Alfred A. Knopf, New York, 1971.

6. M. Brewster Smith, "Encounter groups and humanistic psychology," in *In Search of Community*, ed. K. Back, American Association for Advancement of Science—Westview Press, Washington, D.C., and Boulder, Colorado, 1977.

7. Clifford Geertz, *The Interpretation of Cultures*, Basic Books, New York, 1973.

8. See Sherwood L. Washburn, "Speculations on the interrelations of the history of tools and biological evolution," in *The Evolution of Man's Capacity for Culture,* ed. J. N. Spuhler, Wayne State University Press, Detroit, Michigan, 1959; also S. L. Washburn, "Human behavior and the behavior of other animals," *American Psychologist*, 1978, 33, 405–418 (1978).

9. See Alexander Marshak, "Implications of the paleolithic symbolic evidence for the origin of language," *American Scientist*, 64, 136–145 (1976).

10. Karl W. Butzer, "Environment, culture, and human evolution," *American Scientist*, 65, 572–584 (1977).

11. See *Origins and Evolution of Language and Speech*, ed. Stevan R. Harnad, Horst D. Steklis and Jane Lancaster, *Annals of the New York Academy of Sciences*, 280 (1976); also Washburn (1978), op. cit.

12. See *Origins and Evolution of Language and Speech*, loc. cit.

13. Butzer, op. cit.

14. Alfred Korzybski, *Science and Sanity: An Introduction to Non-Aristotelian Systems and General Semantics* (second edition), International Non-Aristotelian Library, New York, 1941.

15. See Gordon G. Gallup, Jr, "Self-recognition in primates: A comparative approach to the bidirectional properties of consciousness," *American Psychologist*, 32, 329–338 (1977).

16. George Herbert Mead, *Mind, Self, and Society*, University of Chicago Press, Chicago, 1934.

17. See Alfred Schutz, *The Phenomenology of the Social World*, trans. George Walsh and Frederick Lehnert, Northwestern University Press, Evanston, Illinois, 1967; Peter L. Berger and Thomas Luckmann, *The Social Construction of Reality*, Doubleday, Garden City, New York, 1966.

18. Ernest Becker, *The Denial of Death*, The Free Press, New York, 1973.

19. William H. McNeill, *Plagues and Peoples*, Doubleday-Anchor, Garden City, New York, 1976.

20. John B. Bury, *The Idea of Progress: An Inquiry into Its Origin and Growth*, Macmillan, London, 1920.

21. Thomas S. Kuhn, *The Structure of Scientific Revolutions*, University of Chicago Press, Chicago, 1962.

22. McNeill, op. cit.

23. Henry Adams, *The Education of Henry Adams*, Houghton Mifflin, Boston and New York, 1918.

24. B. F. Skinner, op. cit.

25. See Christopher Lasch, "The narcissistic society," *New York Review of Books*, 23 (No. 15, September 30, 1976), 5–13; Peter Marin, "The new narcissism," *Harpers*, October, 1975.

26. See M. Brewster Smith, op. cit.

27. Robert L. Heilbroner, *An Inquiry into the Human Prospect*, W. W. Norton, New York, 1974.

28. Thus, Lewis Mumford, *The Myth of the Machine*, Vol. 1, *Tecnics and Human Development*, Vol. 2, *The Pentagon of Power*, Harcourt Brace Jovanovich, New York, 1967–1970; Norman O. Brown, *Life Against Death: The Psychoanalytical Meaning of History*, Viking, New York, 1959; *Closing Time*, Random House, New York, 1973.

29. Sigmund Freud, *Civilization and Its Discontents*, trans. James Strachey, standard edition, Hogarth Press, London, 1961.

30. Norman O. Brown, op. cit.

31. John R. Platt, *The Step to Man*, Wiley, New York, 1966.

32. Simone de Beauvoir, *The Second Sex*, trans. H. M. Parshley, Alfred A. Knopf, New York, 1953.

_____

Chapter Nine

Selfhood at Risk
Postmodern Perils and the Perils of Postmodernism

Ever since I was exposed to the heady atmosphere of Murray's Harvard Psychological Clinic in the prewar years just after Murray had published *Explorations in Personality* (Murray et al., 1938), I have identified with his holistic and dynamic personological tradition. My empirical contributions to that tradition came a long time ago (Smith, 1966; Smith, Bruner, & White, 1956). More recently, my attempts to reconcile scientific and humanistic approaches to personality (Smith, 1974, 1991b) have sensitized me to ways in which Murray was actively devoted to the same task. I will therefore invoke the memory of Henry Murray by drawing on his Harvard Phi Beta Kappa address, "Beyond Yesterday's Idealisms" (Shneidman, 1981), for a text. Talking to the Harvard honors graduates of 1959, with Emerson's address of 1837 on a similar occasion in mind, Murray observed,

> Certainly most of the best poets, playwrights, and novelists, together with many psychoanalysts, behavioral psychologists, social philosophers, existentialists, and some angry others, seem to be conspiring, with peculiar unanimity, to reduce or decompose, to humiliate so far as they can do it, man's image of himself. In one way or another, the impression is conveyed that, in the realm of spirit, all of us are baffled Beats, Beatniks, or deadbeats, unable to cope as persons with the existential situation.
>
> The sensitive, alienated portions of our society—artists, would-be artists, and their followers— . . . [reflect the] want of a kindling and heartening mythology to feel, think, live, and write by. Our eyes and ears are incessantly bombarded by a mythology which breeds greed, envy, pride, lust, and violence, the mythology of our mass media. . . . But a mythology that is sufficient to the claim of head and heart is as absent from the American scene as symbolism is absent from the new straight-edged, barefaced glass buildings of New York.

An emotional deficiency disease, a paralysis of the creative imagination, an addiction to superficials—this is the physician's diagnosis I would offer to account for the greater part of the widespread desperation of our time. (pp. 607–608)

Remember, Murray was saying this in 1959—before the assassinations of Martin Luther King and the Kennedys, who embodied the nation's hopes, before the disillusionment of the Vietnam War, before Watergate, before the corruption and cynicism of the Reagan-Bush years. Since the appearance of Forrest Robinson's (1992) extraordinary biography of Murray, with its account of his *folie á deux* with his lover and collaborator, Christiana Morgan, and of Claire Douglas's (1993) complementary and just as extraordinary biography of Morgan, we know more about the kind of mythology Murray had in mind but could hardly expound for his Harvard audience. Murray was indeed a great romantic. I will not be concerned here with Henry and Christiana's bizarre mythology—or with alternative mythologies that might fill the need. Rather, I will begin with the cultural plight and "emotional deficiency disease" that troubled Murray, selectively consider some of the speculations that psychologists and others have offered regarding the perils involved for personal well-being, and turn to ways in which I think emerging styles of metatheory that are spreading to psychology and other social sciences from the humanities reflect this plight without giving us adequate help to cope with it. I conclude with my best effort to communicate a constructive and livable stance for like-minded psychologists, especially personality and social psychologists, a combination that I identify with, who seem to be an endangered breed.

When I gave my APA presidential address, "Perspectives on Selfhood" (Smith, 1978), I had the thrill of being an unwitting surfer: The big wave of psychological concern with "the self" was still mostly to come, and I was riding on its incipient crest (which I had nothing to do with causing). The subsequent flood of publications about self and selfhood may well reflect the especially problematic status of selfhood in our time. In the United States, the decade and a half since 1978 also saw the peaking of just plain selfishness during the greedy, me-first years of the Reagan and Bush presidencies. Now I sense what may be quite a different tone in the literature of social criticism and, falteringly, in the political arena. As I returned to "the scene of the crime" after 15 years, I set myself the challenge to take this new note into account, to reflect on the perils to selfhood at a point that may just possibly warrant a little more hope.

Postmodern Perils vs. Survival Problems

There has been so much commentary about the perils to selfhood in our time that I can evoke only a few of the themes with which all of us are too familiar; I feel no constraint to be original. As a middle-class intellectual, like most other social critics, I am most alert to features of our own middle-class life world that threaten our morale—the prevalent cynicism about politics, indeed, about most social institutions; the shallowness of the mass media and the chaos of contemporary attempts at high art and literature; the inescapable climate of sensationalism focused on sex and violence; the unnegotiable clash between fundamentalism and absolutism on the one hand and nihilistic relativism on the other; the uncertainty about all standards, whether they concern knowledge, art, or morals—or the utter rejection of standards; and the *fin de siècle* sense of drift and doom. It is the experience of the Euro-American elite that is evoked when we apply the label "postmodern" to our present predicament.

To maintain perspective, however, it is essential to remember that for the great majority of people, the existential perils that trouble the elite are eclipsed by real perils of survival and damage control. We had no sooner put away the unthinkable Cold War terror of nuclear holocaust (by no means disposed of for keeps) when we entered the present regime of ethnic and nationalistic hatred and slaughter. The impoverished world of Africa, of South America, and much of Asia seethes with booming population in desperate circumstances, in contrast to the industrial and postindustrial North, whose multinational corporations continue to profit from Third World resources. In our own privileged society, people who are disadvantaged by race, class, and gender face daunting barriers that undermine hope, barriers that must be dealt with realistically before the less tangible sources of middle-class demoralization become relevant. If we are to allow ourselves the luxury of deploring empty selves, or saturated selves, or fragmented selves, we had better remember the plight of children growing up in central city poverty and in fractured families, of HIV-infected people around the world facing the prospect of AIDS, of impoverished multitudes crowding against immigration barriers and sometimes leaking through them.

All the same, we do not need to apologize for concern with the civilized discontents reflected in the disarray of high culture and the speculations of psychologists and social critics about the predicament of selfhood in our time. To be so concerned is not just a matter of elitist self-interest. In spite of the recent trend to disparage the cultural tradition of dead White European men, the products of that tradition—and of parallel traditions of the East—embody unique realizations of human potentiality. Pop culture and folk arts, which seem to be given equal status with the greats in contemporary academic "cultural studies," cannot replace them as creations of human value. We should remember, too, that people who are stuck in the ways of life of impoverished Third World countries, of our internal third world of disparaged minorities, owe their position more to exclusion than to their own choice. The appeal of opulent Euro-American lifestyles is universal, unattainable as their present opulence must necessarily be for the world as a whole and for us too in the long run. Failure of nerve, demoralization among the well-to-do, is thus a matter of general human consequence. To the extent that the "real" barriers to hope and grounds for despair that affect disadvantaged categories of people are ameliorated, these people will encounter the same threats to integral selfhood that now affect the affluent. I will therefore pursue my topic, which bears mainly on the psychological plight of the Western middle class, with a clear conscience.

In my sketch of approaches to selfhood 15 years ago (Smith, 1978), I noted that the historical and cross-cultural approaches are very similar in conceptual features. Whether we look back to the less individualistic Middle Ages or across cultures to Japan, India, or the remnants of unlettered societies, our natural tendency to take our own present perspective on self and world as the only right and true perspective is challenged. Both approaches raise the challenge of relativism, although somehow my students turn out to be extreme cultural relativists without the slightest sense of historical relativism: They forgive the Buga-Buga everything, except maybe infanticide and clitoridectomy, but they hold their forebears morally responsible for extreme benightedness.

It is now well established that the Euro-American sense of strong individuality that we take for granted is a historical emergent and that more collectivist orientations remain the norm elsewhere (Marsella, De Vos, & Hsu, 1985; Triandis, 1990; Triandis et al., 1993). There have recently been a number of useful, complementary accounts of the development of selfhood in modern history (e.g., Baumeister, 1986, 1991; Broughton, 1986; Cushman, 1990; Taylor, 1989), so I can forgo the task of retracing that story, only noting the common agreement that the systems of self-representation (Gregg, 1991) with which I am concerned are social constructions that have emerged historically.

Modern versions of selfhood took shape in the intellectual context of the Enlightenment and the Romantic movement (Taylor, 1989) and the social context of capitalism and the industrial and political revolutions of the 18th and 19th centuries (Baumeister, 1986). The cultural focus during the present century on the autonomous, self-contained individual with a rich conscious and even unconscious inner life may be partly responsible for the popularity and proliferation of psychology as a science and profession and of personality and clinical psychology among its subfields. If, as seems to be an emerging consensus, this individualistic ideal and the related ideal of self-actualization are in considerable trouble as the century draws to a close, these doubts touch our discipline and profession to the quick (cf. Sampson, 1977, for an early indication). In choosing my title, I have acceded to current usage in labeling the current context as postmodern, but I prefer Giddens's (1991) term *late modern*, which avoids commitment to the interpretations of our plight as purveyed by intellectuals from the humanities who have enthusiastically appropriated postmodernism. (More of this later on.)

Competing Interpretations

What seems to have gone wrong? Prevalent interpretations of our troubles involve metaphors of both expansion and depletion, which are not as incompatible as that sounds. On the side of expansion are views (see, especially, Baumeister, 1986, 1991) that, with the fading of the religious interpretation of life as the foundation of moral values and of life purposes and goals, self-actualization and self-commitment as a replacement for objectively given standards of morality place a heavier burden on selfhood than it can satisfactorily sustain. Human lives seem most meaningful and satisfying when they are devoted to projects and guided by values that transcend the self. Lives organized around self-actualization and the pursuit of gratification are particularly vulnerable to the threat of death, for which religion provided the traditional solace. Among the most articulate current critics supporting an essentially religious orientation is the philosopher Charles Taylor (1989), although his underlying religious commitment is not obvious on the surface of his historical analysis. His scholarly *Sources of the Self: The Making of the Modern Identity* deplores the inadequate basis for our existing moral consensus on benevolence and justice that the prevalent a-theistic naturalism provides. The inflated pretensions to selfhood that we inherit from the Romantics and Existentialists are basically unworkable as a frame for living our lives, according to this set of views.

On the side of depletion are critics who wrote of the "empty self" (Cushman, 1990) or the "minimal self" (Lasch, 1984). Cushman (1990) put the case most succinctly:

> Many authors have described how the bounded, masterful self has slowly and unevenly emerged in Western history. This is a self that has specific psychological boundaries, an internal locus of control, and a wish to manipulate the external world for its own personal ends. I believe that in the post–World War II era in the United States, there are indications that the present configuration of the bounded, masterful self is the empty self. By this I mean that our terrain has shaped a self that experiences a significant absence of community, tradition, and shared meaning. It experiences these social absences and their consequences "interiorly" as a lack of personal conviction and worth, and it embodies the absences as a chronic, undifferentiated emotional hunger. The post–World War II self thus yearns to acquire and consume as an unconscious way of compensation for what it has lost: it is empty. (p. 600)

In *The Culture of Narcissism*, Christopher Lasch (1979) provided astute cultural criticism along similar lines—impaired by his commitment to the concept of narcissism, which I see as a fundamentally unsatisfactory relic of Freudian metapsychology, although it deals with important psychological phenomena. *The Minimal Self: Psychic Survival in Troubled Times* (Lasch, 1984), which he wrote at the height of Cold War anxieties, retained the narcissistic conceptualization but emphasized a new note: how failure of hope leads our preoccupation with self to focus defensively on mere survival. Here I strongly agree (Smith, 1991b). For me, failure of hope is at the crux of our late-modern predicament. When religious concern with salvation and damnation declined as sources of life's meaning, religious hope was replaced by faith in progress, whether of a Hegelian, Darwinian, Marxist, or bourgeois democratic variety. Things will surely get better in the long run. That served to put our own inherently petty individual lives in the context of the future and posterity, a better life on earth if not in heaven. World wars, the Holocaust, the population problem, environmental pollution and depletion, assassinations and scandals at home, and the failure of international order abroad have seriously undermined our hopefulness, even though the end of the Cold War gave respite to our fears of impending nuclear war. There is much evidence that hope is an essential ingredient of a good life and of a democratic society. The increasingly plausible case for despair seems to me the most serious threat to selfhood in the present age.

It is emptiness and hopelessness that make people vulnerable to false prophets, cult leaders, or would-be führers, who help them become true believers (Hofer, 1951) again, secure in the comfort of new absolutisms. Given the cynicism about government and most established institutions that is prominent in contemporary hopelessness, I regard this vulnerability as a serious threat.

Kenneth Gergen's (1991) recent proposals about the saturated self partake of both expansion and depletion. He tells us that in modern life, we are continually bombarded with new information, new social encounters, new role models, so that we are overwhelmed by the overload— a case almost the opposite of Cushman's (1990) empty self, yet there is underlying congruence between their views. Gergen wrote:

> It is my central thesis that . . . [increasing immersion in the social world] is propelling us toward a new self-consciousness: the post-modern. The emerging commonplaces of communication . . . are critical to understanding the passing of both the romantic and the modern views of self. What I call the technologies of social saturation are central to the contemporary erasure of individual self. . . . As we become increasingly conjoined with our social surroundings, we come to reflect those surroundings. There is a population of the self, reflecting the infusion of partial identities through social saturation. And there is the onset of a multiphrenic condition, in which one begins to experience the vertigo of unlimited multiplicity. Both the populating of the self and the multiphrenic condition are significant preludes to post-modern consciousness. (p. 49)

Gergen's (1991) examples suggest that he may be unduly focused on the experiences of the academic and corporate jet set to which he belongs. He certainly makes a good case for influences that have augmented the threat to integral selfhood identified long ago by David Riesman (1950) in his concept of other-directedness. Indeed the multiplicity of social input probably does tend to unroot people from the comforting support of a stable social context. But I would argue that the demise of progress, the undermining of hopes that we used to take for granted, is by far the more serious ingredient of our present predicament.

Gergen's Promotion of Postmodernism

As my quotation shows, Gergen (1991) explicitly linked his diagnosis of social saturation with the emergence of what he identified as the postmodern stance toward self and the world, to which I turn next. For Gergen, who drew on poststructuralist movements in the humanities, such as deconstructionism in literary criticism and anti-foundationism in epistemology and ethics (the abandonment of hope to find a secure foundation for beliefs and values), the postmodern stance is one of radical relativism, rejecting the claims of science to a privileged perspective, rejecting the conception of truth as an approachable ideal. The postmodern orientation, as Gergen characterized it, is dizzy and disoriented. What may surprise the reader of Gergen's account is that he did not present this topsy-turvy *weltanschauung* as the pathological result of social saturation—or of other troubles of late modern selfhood, even though he proposed a causal linkage; he spent an entire chapter, "Truth in Trouble," expounding this increasingly fashionable perspective as intrinsically valid.

I cannot summarize or sample systematically Gergen's (1991) generally apt account of postmodernism here, but I will illustrate where it leads psychology. After introducing Richard Rorty's (1979) philosophical argument that rejected the "problem of knowledge" by regarding the conception that knowledge represents external reality as merely optional, he went on to write,

> And so also is the concept of the individual self. For if it makes no sense to ask, as a matter of serious concern, how the objective world makes its imprint on the subjective world, how the individual mind comprehends external reality, why continue to grant honorific status to the distinction between subject and object at all? Why must we take seriously the presumption that there are individual minds about which we must gain knowledge? And what, after all, should we mean by knowledge in such a case? To eradicate the distinction between world and mind, object and subject, is to remove both from the field of existing essences. "World" and "mind" become entries in the discursive practices of the culture. (p. 103)

The flow of discourse leaves us bereft of anchors to stabilize a view of self and world. This version of postmodernism certainly challenges the discourses of psychology, let alone the science and profession of psychology. Is psychology, like life in Gergen's (1991) partial view, just a matter of fun and games?

> Life itself may become a form of play, in which one transforms ventures into adventures, purpose into performance, and desire into drama. Culture seems a carnival with a never-ending array of sideshows. It is in this way that we shall avoid the confining qualities of singular and ingurgitating realities. [I should rather say, distract ourselves from the depths of despair.] It is also in this way that we stand maximally open to the multiplicity of surrounding voices. For there is no need to defend one's reigning reality against the disagreeable clamor from without, "to persecute the infidels." Their realities, one sees, also possess an internal validity, and one may even be enriched by playing in their tents. (p. 193)

I am not being entirely fair to Gergen (1991), because he goes on to say that "serious play" as well as ironic drollery has a place in postmodern consciousness, and throughout his provocative discussion of contemporary attitudes and practices, I sense ambivalence between Gergen the tendentious advocate of postmodern liberation—libertinism, it sounds more like—and Gergen the astute social critic. But advocacy has the upper hand.

A Reasoned Stance toward Postmodernism

I am giving this much attention to Gergen's (1991) popular book because I am alarmed by the extent to which just such an extreme version of antiscientific relativism is gaining prominence at the margins of mainstream psychology. Psychologists on the softer, more humanistically oriented side of psychology can rightly applaud the demise of logical positivism as a constraining, proscriptive philosophy of science that was a disastrous choice for the psychological enterprise. They can welcome social constructionism—the recognition that people actively construct their worlds of experience and behavior in a social process that carries the momentum of culturally transmitted fabrics of symbol and metaphor. They can recognize that people's ideas about selfhood are social constructions that have real consequences for the constitution of personality. They can accept the contextualist criticism that many of the claims of Euro-American psychology are probably history and culture bound. They can even agree that when psychology is concerned with people, who are creatures of meaning and value, it needs to work in an interpretative, hermeneutic framework as well as in the causal-explanatory one customary in natural science. All of this is constructive and helps to correct the damage done in the half century dominated by behaviorism (cf. Smith, 1991a, 1991b). What I see as most unfortunate, however, is the tendency abetted by Gergen, to give up the conception of science—natural or human, historical or ahistorical—as an evidential, public, self-critical social enterprise, an enterprise that has successfully sought progressively more adequate and comprehensive understanding of the phenomena in its domain—an enterprise committed to an ideal of truth, the approach to which can be evaluated pragmatically. I find little justification in the postmodernist literature for the claim that scientific constructions, fallible as they are and always subject to disconfirmation and revision, are simply optional myths on all fours with religious or political dogmas and ideologies.

Postmodernism as a movement is spreading from the humanities to the social sciences. It has no foothold in the natural sciences, which nevertheless are beginning to take note of it as a cloud on their horizon (Nicholson, 1993). Physical and biological scientists may worry about the decline in the growth curve of their financial support and see postmodernism as an external threat, but their excitement of discovery has not diminished with the demise of the logical positivist account of their success. Postmodernism flourished in the humanities because of their attunement to the cultural crisis of late modernity that has been our present concern. It took an explicitly antiscientific direction, not only because technology as a product of science is at the crux of so many late-modern problems but also, I think, because professors of the humanistic disciplines have sat at the far end of the table of academic support, while their colleagues in the sciences ate high on the hog. There is an ingredient of resentful envy in the postmodern stance.

The social sciences and psychology, particularly the more distinctively human aspects of psychology that include personality, developmental, and social psychology, stand between the natural sciences and the humanities and understandably share in the orientations and problems of each. To a substantial extent they are historical and cultural sciences, concerned with understanding relationships specific to particular historical and cultural contexts as well as with more universal features of human experience and behavior. They are properly much concerned with the phenomena of late modernity that I am examining here. They are also vulnerable to the postmodernist attitudes that I have been deploring.

In the face of the postmodern challenges, the crux of the matter is whether it is still possible to retain some toehold to sustain the old human struggle toward truth, goodness, and beauty as meaningful ideals. Putting it this way sounds very old-fashioned, but the shock these words evoke is evidence of the degree to which nihilistic relativism has permeated our perspective. So far as truth is concerned, I am moderately optimistic. The position taken by Gergen (1991) and the more dramatic postmodernists is clearly extreme and is not followed by many in psychology and in the social sciences who take the constructionist, contextualist, and yes, feminist critiques very seriously. Truth claims cannot be reduced to rhetoric and politics, even when we become more alert to the role of rhetoric and politics in our would-be scientific discourse.

I am not going to consider beauty, but the collapse of traditions and standards in the aesthetic realm obviously raises issues much like those about truth and goodness. With the good, I think we are in deeper trouble than with truth, inasmuch as there has been no cultural invention in ethics parallel to the 17th century creation of science as a social enterprise. The rapidity of change in values in our own culture and our exposure to the values of other cultures around the world free us from the previously universal state of being culture bound, but the process can be literally de-moralizing.

Religious solutions to demoralization are in considerable revival in the United States and abroad. That may be the turn human history takes, one that carries the risk of reinforcing ethnocentric intolerance, because those who reject religious truth belong to the devil's party. I would hope, rather, that the human sciences can help us look a little beyond the self-interest of our individual lives, beyond the ethnocentric interests of our tribes and nations that seem so prominent in the post–Cold War world (Smith, 1992). We can start with our own provisionally held versions of humanistic values and contribute to the analysis of threats to those values in our present historical situation. We can examine the options that are historically open to us in relation to the resources and limitations that bear on our political and social choices. Such an orientation is what I find attractive in so-called critical theory (Held, 1980), once its dogmatically Marxian assumptions are discounted.

Giddens on Self and Modernity

My attempt to sketch an alternative to postmodernism, to communicate my own way of regaining foothold and balance in the vertiginous world that Gergen (1991) has evoked for us, has led me rather far from the consideration of selfhood. I now return to consider a different treatment of contemporary selfhood, one in which I encountered more good ideas that were new to me, or were presented in new relationships, than in any other piece of recent reading: the British sociologist Anthony Giddens's (1991) *Modernity and Self-Identity: Self and Society in the Late Modern Age*. Giddens's subtle, culturally based analysis of present challenges to identity is much too complex for me to summarize here. I recommend the careful reading that it requires (especially because he likes to invent his own sociological jargon), but I will draw from it selectively because, more than the psychological accounts that I have leaned on thus far, Giddens identified positive options as well as negative threats in a way that is congruent with my argument.

Giddens (1991) called to our attention pervasive novelties of our lives that provide them with significant context, although we take them for granted—for instance, that we, essentially all people now, enact our lives in a world perspective in standard (or daylight saving) time and a universal dating system—in great contrast with the local embeddedness of traditional lives. With rapid change in values and agenda from one generation to the next, we cannot depend on traditional rites of passage to ease us through transitions in individual lives; "in settings of modernity . . . the altered self has to be explored and constructed as part of a reflexive [self-referential] process of connecting personal and social change" (Giddens, p. 33). We grow up increasingly dependent on the advice of experts, on pediatricians and educators, rather than on the direct initiation of one generation by another. What Giddens called *abstract expert systems* play an increasing part in constituting the fabric of our lives. He saw the rise and prominence of counseling and psychotherapy more in this context than as support for empty and alienated selves:

Self-identity becomes problematic in modernity in a way which contrasts with self-society relations in more traditional contexts; yet this is not only a situation of loss, and it does not imply either that anxiety levels necessarily increase. Therapy is not simply a means of coping with novel anxieties, but an expression of the reflexivity of the self—a phenomenon which, on the level of the individual, like the broader institutions of modernity, balances opportunity and potential catastrophe in equal measure. (p. 34)

Giddens (1991) highlighted the prominence of uncertainty and risk in the culture of late modernity, a theme that has also been emphasized by the psychological futurist Donald Michael (e.g., 1993). In spite of the salience of "high risk consequences" such as nuclear war or ecological collapse, it is not that life is riskier than before for the advantaged Western middle classes. Rather, ordinary people and specialized experts organize their social world in terms of risk assessment. My treatment of selfhood at risk participates in this feature of late modernity.

Giddens's (1991) analysis culminates in a provocative discussion of how what he called *life politics* has emerged out of the "emancipatory politics" that was stimulated by the emergence of modern institutions. From early modern times through the present, concerns with justice, equality, and participation—with people's life chances—have inspired a politics of emancipation. Now that a certain level of emancipation has been reached, political issues of "how we should live" arise, which "flow from processes of self-actualization in post-traditional contexts, where globalizing influences intrude deeply into the reflexive project of the self, and conversely where processes of self-realization influence global strategies" (p. 214). Life politics is a politics of life decisions concerning lifestyles. Issues like those concerning human responsibilities to nature, the rights of the unborn, the ethics of genetic engineering, limits on technological innovation, the value of gender differences, and animal rights emerge.

Giddens (1991) wrote,

Life politics brings back to prominence precisely those moral and existential questions repressed by the core institutions of modernity. Here we see the limitations of accounts of "post-modernity" developed under the aegis of post-structuralism [the postmodernism that I have used Kenneth Gergen to castigate]. According to such views, moral questions become completely denuded of meaning or relevance in current social circumstances. But while this perspective accurately reflects aspects of the internally referential systems of modernity, it cannot explain why moral issues return to the centre of the agenda of life politics. Life–political issues cannot be debated outside the scope of abstract systems: information drawn from various kinds of expertise is central to their definition. Yet because they centre on questions of how we should live our lives in emancipated social circumstances they cannot but bring to the fore problems and questions of a moral and existential type. . . . They call for a remoralising of social life and they demand a new sensitivity to questions that the institutions of modernity systematically dissolve. (pp. 223–224)

As he observed, the agenda of feminism cuts squarely across the distinction between emancipatory and life politics.

The picture that Giddens (1991) painted for us is by no means one of rosy optimism. The issues around which the new politics revolve do not find us in consensus, and the strong and uncompromising feelings that they evoke pose serious problems for political leadership. Without pressing the details of Giddens's analysis, however, one can note that the "remoralisation" that he proclaimed is in the sharpest contrast to the meaninglessness that Gergen's (1991) variety of postmodernism accepts as inevitable and partly tries to revel in. It also provides a context in which a value-relevant science and profession of psychology can make sense.[1]

Beyond Individualism, Toward Hope

Underlying the new politics is an emerging consensus that rejects the problematic individualism that was an early focus of this article. The women's movement has played a major part in questioning the preeminent values of instrumentalism and macho autonomy. Largely because of women's strong voices, we are seeing a change in our value assumptions in psychology. Bakan's (1966) old principles of agency and communion, or individuality and interpersonal relatedness, emerge in dialectical conjunction as pillars of human life, no longer linked so stereotypically to the genders (see, especially, Guisinger & Blatt, 1994). The welcoming response to *Habits of the Heart: Individualism and Commitment in American Life*, the best-seller by the Berkeley sociologist Robert Bellah and his collaborators (Bellah, Madsen, Sullivan, Swidler, & Tipton, 1985), indicated the way the wind was blowing. Etzioni's (1993) manifesto of "communitarianism" carries the message forward.

But psychologists as well as sociologists are giving voice to similar concerns, to commitment to a reorientation of psychology's contribution to society. I think immediately of Sarason's (1981, 1988) lifetime contributions, of the valiant efforts of Michael and Lisa Wallach (1983, 1990) to counteract psychology's promotion of selfishness and revive a concern with goodness, and of the recent volume edited by Staub and Green (1992) that assembles contributions of psychologists toward facing global challenges. This name-dropping is unfair to a good many others equally deserving of mention.

The point with which I therefore conclude is that psychologists do not need to follow in the footsteps of alienated writers from the humanities and contribute to *fin de siècle* gloom and ineffectualness or withdraw to fun and games. Our late modern times do indeed shake our accustomed assumptions about self and world. They also provide us with challenges that are more than ample to provide meaning for our lives and those of our offspring and successors. As psychologists, and as students of selfhood, we can contribute to hope rather than undermine it. We can do so not by any subterfuge of positive thinking but by using our competencies to cope with humanity's many challenges as best we can. In our endeavor, we must include in our scope the realm of meanings and values that distinguishes human science from the other sciences. But we abdicate any distinctive or useful role as science and profession if we give up either the aims and strategies of science toward approximating an ideal of truth or the aspirations of ethics toward approximating ideals of the good. I think Harry Murray would have agreed.

NOTE

1. Giddens's reappraisal of contemporary risks to selfhood is nicely complemented by Arlene Skolnik's (1991) balanced assessment of the "crisis" in the American family. Equally critical of gloomy diagnoses such as Lasch's (1979), Skolnik challenged prevalent romantic idealizations of the earlier family as a context for selfhood and put our present challenges in a perspective that is conducive to constructive political and social action.

References

Bakan, D. (1966). *The duality of human existence.* Chicago: Rand McNally.
Baumeister, R. F. (1986). *Identity: Cultural change and the struggle for self.* New York: Oxford University Press.

Baumeister, R. F. (1991). *Meanings of life.* New York: Guilford.

Bellah, R. N., Madsen, R., Sullivan, W. M., Swidler, A., & Tipton, S. M. (1985). *Habits of the heart: Individualism and commitment in American life.* Berkeley: University of California Press.

Broughton, J. M. (1986). The psychology, history, and ideology of the self. In K. S. Larsen (Ed.), *Dialectics and ideology in psychology* (pp. 129–164). Norwood, NJ: Ablex.

Cushman, P. (1990). Why the self is empty: Toward a historically situated psychology. *American Psychologist, 45,* 599–611.

Douglas, C. (1993). *Translate this darkness: The life of Christiana Morgan.* New York: Simon & Schuster.

Etzioni, A. (1993). *Spirit of community: Rights, responsibilities, and the communitarian agenda.* New York: Crown.

Gergen, K. J. (1991). *The saturated self: Dilemmas of identity in contemporary life.* New York: Basic Books.

Giddens, A. (1991). *Modernity and identity: Self and society in the late modern age.* Stanford, CA: Stanford University Press.

Gregg, G. S. (1991). *Self-representation: Life narrative studies in identity and ideology.* New York: Greenwood.

Guisinger, S., & Blatt, S. J. (1994). Dialectics of individuality and interpersonal relatedness: An evolutionary perspective. *American Psychologists, 49,* 104–111.

Held, D. (1980). *Introduction to critical theory: Horkheimer to Habermas.* Berkeley: University of California Press.

Hofer, E. (1951). *The true believer.* New York: Harper.

Lasch, C. (1979). *The culture of narcissism.* New York: Norton.

Lasch, C. (1984). *The minimal self: Psychic survival in troubled times.* New York: Norton.

Marsella, A. J., DeVos, G., & Hsu, F.L.K. (Eds.). (1985). *Culture and self.* New York: Tavistock.

Michael, D. N. (1993). Governing by learning: Boundaries, myths and metaphors. *Futures, 25*(1), 81–89.

Murray, H. A., et al. (1938). *Explorations in personality.* New York: Oxford University Press.

Nicholson, R. S. (1993). Editorial: Postmodernism. *Science, 261,* 143.

Riesman, D. (with R. Denny & N. Glazer). (1950). *The lonely crowd.* New Haven, CT: Yale University Press.

Robinson, F. G. (1992). *Love's story told: A life of Henry A. Murray.* Cambridge, MA: Harvard University Press.

Rorty, R. (1979). *Philosophy and the mirror of nature.* Princeton, NJ: Princeton University Press.

Sampson, E. E. (1977). Psychology and the American ideal. *Journal of Personality and Social Psychology, 35,* 767–782.

Sarason, S. B., (1981). *Psychology misdirected.* New York: Free Press.

Sarason, S. B. (1988). *The making of an American psychologist: An autobiography.* San Francisco: Jossey-Bass.

Shneidman, E. S. (Ed.). (1981). *Endeavors in psychology: Selections from the personology of Henry A. Murray.* New York: Harper.

Skolnick A. (1991). *Embattled paradise: The American family in an age of uncertainty.* New York: Basic Books.

Smith, M. B. (1966). Explorations in competence: A study of Peace Corps teachers in Ghana. *American Psychologist, 21,* 555–566.

Smith, M. B. (1974). *Humanizing social psychology.* San Francisco: Jossey-Bass.

Smith, M. B. (1978). Perspectives on selfhood. *American Psychologist, 33,* 1053–1063.

Smith, M. B. (1991a). Psychology and the decline of positivism. In R. Jessor (Ed.), *Perspectives on behavioral science: The Colorado lectures* (pp. 53–69). Boulder, CO: Westview.

Smith, M. B. (1991b). *Values, self, and society: Toward a humanist social psychology.* New Brunswick, NJ: Transaction.

Smith, M. B. (1992). Nationalism, ethnocentrism, and the new world order. *Journal of Humanistic Psychology, 32*(4), 76–91.

Smith, M. B., Bruner, J. S., & White; R. W. (1956). *Opinions and personality.* New York: Wiley.

Staub, S., & Green, P. (Eds.). (1992). *Psychology and social responsibility: Facing global challenges.* New York: New York University Press.

Taylor, C. (1989). *Sources of the self: The making of the modern identity.* Cambridge, MA: Harvard University Press.

Triandis, H. C. (1990). *Cross-cultural studies of individualism and collectivism: Nebraska Symposium on Motivation, 1989.* Lincoln: University of Nebraska Press.

Triandis, H. C., Betancourt, H., Iwav, S., Leung, K., Salazar, J. M., Setiadi, B., Sinha, J.B.P., Touzard, H., & Zaleski, Z. (1993). An etic-emic analysis of individualism and collectivism. *Journal of Cross-Cultural Psychology, 24,* 366–383.

Wallach, M. A., & Wallach, L. (1983). *Psychology's sanction for selfishness: The error of egoism in theory and therapy.* New York: Freeman.

Wallach, M. A., & Wallach, L. (1990). *Rethinking goodness.* Albany: State University of New York Press.

Chapter Ten

Self and Identity in Historical/Sociocultural Context
"Perspectives on Selfhood" Revisited

I am an oldtimer identified with the older conception of personality and social psychology, who at present identifies more with personality than with contemporary cognitive social psychology—already I have to speak of identity! So I cannot aspire to be in close touch with the forefront: of treatment of self and identity in current social psychology. In this chapter I try to make a virtue of these limitations by bringing my oldtimer's perspective to bear on issues in the field. I am concerned with how our social psychological conceptions of selfhood may be enriched from a perspective that is mainly rooted in personality psychology.

My baseline consists of three papers I wrote a quarter century ago (Smith, 1978a, 1978b, 1980). These papers came rather early in the continuing surge of psychological interest in self and identity. Sober judgment leads me to conclude that they have had virtually no influence on what subsequently got published—metaphorically, I was a relatively early surfer on the tide of self and identity but didn't make or shape the waves. I am pleased that some of the ideas I thought were good then continue to be interesting—and that some deserve to be revived. I refer to these papers in the light of subsequent developments.

A Bit of History

Another role I can play, as a personality-oriented oldtimer, is to reinstate some relevant history that I think gets neglected from the current cognitive-social perspective. Everyone interested in self and identity is well aware of James's (1890) treatment of "The Consciousness of Self," with its distinction between *I* and *Me*—and many will remember its positivistically resolute reduction of the I to the passing thought that integrates recollection of the person's past and anticipation of the person's future. The title of his chapter as I have quoted it from his full-length *Psychology* fits his basically phenomenological approach better than "The Self," as he captioned the corresponding chapter in his *Briefer Course* (1892). We are also likely to cite G. H. Mead (1934), although not always with as full acquaintance, for his emphasis on the social origins of reflexive self-consciousness, its dependence on symbolic communication, and its importance for *Mind Self, and Society*. But we are likely to neglect Helen Lynd's (1958) *On Shame and the Search for Identity*, which connects better with current thought now that we are less frozen on the psychoanalytic formulations of shame and guilt. We may also need to be reminded how Erich Fromm's (1941) *Escape from Freedom* gave a powerful account of the burdens imposed on selfhood in modern times by liberation from feudal social connectedness.

Most psychologists have completely forgotten the contribution of Gardner Murphy, a leading psychologist at midcentury and coauthor of the early text *Experimental Social Psychology* (Murphy & Murphy, 1931; Murphy, Murphy, & Newcomb, 1937), which featured socialization research, not experimentation. Murphy (1947) devoted a major section of his remarkably comprehensive postwar textbook on personality to the self as a thing perceived and conceived, giving an account of its origins and development and making the self the focus of his treatment of psychoanalytic defense mechanisms. For Murphy, "a large part of the behavior that constitutes personality is self-oriented behavior" (p. 479). He stands close to the origin of the tide of self psychology in which we are immersed.

And there is Erikson (e.g., 1959), whose symphonic treatment of identity resists cleanly defined conceptualization but has been very influential on the present intellectual climate concerning self and identity. In his recent definitive biography, the historian Lawrence Friedman (1999) examined the retrievable details of Erikson's life with psychologically sophisticated concern for their relevance to his developing ideas. It became very clear that Erikson had dramatic lifelong unresolved problems about his own identity. Erik Homberger was conceived out of wedlock and raised as the son of a Danish Jewish mother and a German Jewish stepfather, who were not honest with him about his origins. He fantasized that his biological father was from Danish gentility, nobility, or artistic circles, and he managed not to pursue his true parentage to a conclusion until the people who might have been able to inform him were deceased. Living with ambiguities as to whether he was or was not a Jew and whether he was inside or outside the Freudian inner circle, he adopted the name Erikson, making himself symbolically his own progenitor when he resolved another identity problem by becoming an American citizen. His conceptualization of identity may be symphonic and fuzzy, but his own problems with it seem to have concerned very basic uncertainties and ambivalences.

Other contributors to theorizing about selfhood from a psychodynamic standpoint should not be entirely neglected by social psychologists. There was Harry Stack Sullivan (1953), whose view of the "self system" was entirely defensive, and Heinz Kohut (1971), whose version of psychoanalysis as "self psychology" increasingly converged on positions similar to those of the emphatically nonpsychoanalytic Carl Rogers (1961).

Another bit of history to be noted, this time for its conspicuous lack of central relevance to today's concerns, is Wylie's (1961, 1974, 1979) thorough reviews of the major literature on the self-concept. At the time of her reviews, which then were central to psychological treatment of selfhood, empirical research on the self-concept was mainly concerned with the measurement of self-esteem, which seemed to have important links with psychodynamic views of personality then in fashion. Neither the self-concept nor its evaluation as self-esteem is lost in the dustbin of faded concepts and issues, of course, but it is clearly a gain from cognitive social psychology that our present conceptions of self-cognition are much more complex, and that, to a considerable extent, measures of self-efficacy (Bandura, 1997) appropriately get more attention than pencil-and-paper measures of self-esteem, which have always seemed to me very vulnerable to effects of self-presentation to self and others.

Some Matters of Definition

Because their use in common speech touches central human interests to the quick, the terms *self* and *identity* give rise to substantial definitional problems as psychologists and others employ them in theoretical discourse. I don't think there is much point in fussing about definitions as long as we try individually to make as clear as we can what we intend by our terms—definitions have to follow our gains in understanding. All the same, I'd like to try once more to promote a convention that I proposed in 1980. I take *selfhood* as labeling criterial features of the human condition that center on reflexive self-awareness—a historical, cultural, creative project in symbolization. For me, selfhood involves much the same features that Sedikides and Skowronski (1997) ascribed to symbolic self-awareness, although I would add some additional ones that seem to me to have important existential implications (which I discuss later).

> There are a number of terms in the domain of selfhood that give me no trouble, or seem potentially useful. There is the *person*, the actual, concrete participant in symbolically construed and governed social relations. There is *personality*, the psychologist's formulation or construction of the person, a construction of organized processes, states, and dispositions. . . . There is Erikson's (1959) rich but slippery concept of *identity*—some trouble, here, to disentangle and pin down the meanings. There is a set of terms in the reflexive mode—*self-perceptions, self-attributions, self-concepts, self-theories* (Epstein, 1973)—in which the prefix *self-* implies reflexive reference but does not imply a surgically or conceptually separable object of reference, other than *the person*. People—persons—may reify "I" and "Me," but psychologists shouldn't, except as they recognize the causal/functional importance of people's own reifications. . . . I don't see a place for *the self* in such a list. It is not a term that designates an entity or agency, except in usages that treat it as synonymous with the *person* in which case one or the other term is superfluous.
>
> Yet there are contexts in which *self* is employed in near synonymy with person that seem to me more justifiable. We may talk about transformations of the Greek self from Homer to Euripides, or of the Western self from Shakespeare to Proust, Pynchon, or R. D. Laing. When we use such locutions, we are emphasizing the symbolic *self-referential* aspect of being a person (with the reflexive prefix having its usual sense as interpreted above), with the implied reminder that self-referential features in which we are interested are somehow constitutive of the person as social actor. We are not talking about an entity, conceptual or otherwise, that is distinguishable from the person. If it makes sense to talk about a fragmented or divided self, the fragmentation or division is a metaphor of metaphors: a characteristic of the metaphoric symbol system that partly constitutes us as persons. (Smith, 1980, pp. 69–70)

The *person*, that is, has aspects of both *I* and *Me*, of both agent and self-object, but it seems to me confusing to use the term *self* to refer to both. The deepest problem, how the reflexive structures of meaning that make up the *Me* or "symbolic self" participate in constituting the person's structures of motivation, intention, and agency, is obscured if we simply say that they are input and output aspects of the same Self. As I see it, it is a problem for personality theory—of psychological conceptualization of the organization and functioning of the human person, now seen more clearly in sociocultural context, a problem to which the considerable resources of cognitive social psychology can be expected to contribute.

Perspectives on Selfhood Then and Now

A quarter century ago, I sorted out three major perspectives on selfhood: the evolutionary phylogenetic perspective, the cross-cultural or transhistorical perspective, and the developmental or ontogenetic perspective. I felt some originality in asserting that historical change and cross-cultural variation pose the same conceptual and methodological problems for our formulations of selfhood.

The Evolutionary Perspective

My attempt to speculate responsibly about the emergence of selfhood in human evolution could have benefited substantially from the more recent information about human origins interpreted by Sedikides and Skowronski (1997), but I think it continues to stand up pretty well. It included a further speculative idea that seems to me to go beyond their evolutionary account in a way that is very consequential. As they proposed, the symbolic selfhood that emerged with the attainment of fully elaborated language competence had obvious adaptive features that favored human survival and proliferation, especially in regard to planful and socially coordinated intentional behavior and the cultural retention and transmission of problem-solving tactics. But it also had side effects that could only create problems for people as I wrote for an Australian publication (see Chapter 8):

> Yet there are heavy costs in the side-effects of attaining symbolic selfhood. Human self-consciousness breaks the unity of Man [*sic*] and Nature and, when forethought and afterthought are added as gifts of language, the ingredients of the human existential predicament emerge. As speaking self-

conscious human beings, we and our forebears for more than 50,000 years have faced the cognitive puzzle of whence we came into the world, why we are here and what happens when we die. . . . Primarily through language, we have become *persons*, linked to other persons whom we love and care for in a web of "inter-subjective" meaning (Schutz, 1967). The inevitability of the eventual death of self and loved ones and the arbitrary unpredictability of death from famine, disease, accident, predation or human assault become the occasion not for momentary animal terror but for what is potentially unremitting human anguish. So the quest for meaning, for meanings compatible with a human life of self-conscious mortality, becomes a matter of life and death urgency. I don't think Ernest Becker (1973) exaggerated the importance of this theme in the history of human culture. (Greenberg, Pyszczynski, and Solomon [1986] and Solomon, Greenberg, and Pyszczynski [1991] recently resurrected Becker's ideas in their theory of terror management.)

Of course, this mainly familiar account is wrong in one obvious respect. Contrary to the old myth, our forebears cannot have been cast out of Nature's Garden of Eden in one sudden tragic event of "birth trauma." . . . Self-conscious selfhood, with its peremptory challenge to find supportive meaning in the face of creature mortality, must have been a gradual emergent.

If so, the symbolic resources of language-bearing human communities could meet the need for meaning as it arose. Thus emerged the many cultural worlds of myth, ritual and religion, which provided the traditional answers to the question of what it means to be human. They were good answers, proclaiming to each communicating tribal group its value as The People; legitimizing the group's way of life as ordained by their ancestors; giving intelligible meaning to the exigencies of life and death; providing appropriate ways in which individual and community could participate in the encouragement of auspicious outcomes and the avoidance of ominous ones. These traditional mythic answers could not fully eliminate occasions for anguish and terror, but they could give intelligible shape to formless terror; and they could make the blows of fate more bearable to the victim and certainly more endurable to the fellow members of the victim's kindred and community. (Smith, 1978a, pp. 9–11)

It is important to our enterprise, I think, to see cultural evolution in close connection with biological evolution in some such way. Donald Campbell (1991) has made a similar suggestion in regard to the emergence of culturally established moral sanctions, especially religious ones, against selfish, socially destructive behaviors that biological evolution may have selected, a consideration that is relevant to current concerns about sociocultural challenges to moral values as constitutive ingredients of selfhood.

The Cross-Cultural and Transhistorical Perspectives

These two perspectives raise essentially the same serious problem for the culture-bound views of selfhood that had been prevalent in the United States and Western Europe. Once this contextual point is grasped, we are still left with the question whether the underlying psychological processes are appropriately regarded as human universals with the "content" provided historically and culturally, or whether aspects of even these processes are subject to historical and cultural influence. The perspectives are similar in their conceptual and methodological significance, but they point in different directions in regard to the research required to give them substance.

For an historical approach to selfhood, I relied on humanistic scholarship such as that of Snell (1953) and Onians (1951/1973) on the emergence of the self-conscious European mind in the centuries that followed the Homeric epics, and of Lionel Trilling's *Sincerity and Authenticity* (1972) for apparent transformations of selfhood revealed in the European literature of modern times. Baumeister (1986) meanwhile provided us with a well-focused treatment of the historical vicissitudes of Euro-American selfhood since the Middle Ages. From immersal in the philosophical history of ideas, Taylor (1989) gave us a rich account of "the making of the modern identity." The British sociologist Giddens (1991) carried historical analysis forward to challenging conceptual vistas in his treatment of "self and society in the late modern age." It seems to me that the case for major historical changes in the content and organization of selfhood in the Western tradition has been made beyond reasonable doubt. Because of the nature of historical data and historical scholarship, however, we cannot expect to understand these changes with much scientific firmness or precision—and of course, Euro-American psychologists have not explored whatever literature may be relevant to changes in selfhood in other historical traditions.

The situation is different with the cross-cultural approach, because in spite of the homogenizing effect of global communication, living examples of considerably diverse cultures can be studied by our most sophisticated ethnographic and psychological methods, and the multicultural network of psychologists interested in such research and competent to do it keeps expanding. Two decades ago I relied heavily on the work of Geertz (1973, 1975) to make the now obvious point that culture matters to selfhood. More recently, I was captured by the "anthropology of the self" presented by Heelas and Lock (1981), which also served mainly to illustrate the variety of cultural influence. And I got glimmerings of the processes involved in how culture enters the constitution of selfhood in Lakoff and Johnson's *Metaphors We Live By* (Lakoff & Johnson, 1980; see also Lakoff, 1987; Smith, 1985). The recent ground-breaking work by Kitayama, Markus, and their collaborators (Kitayama, Markus, Matsumoto, & Norasakkunkit, 1997; Markus & Kitayama, 1991) seems to me to open a new era. It is no longer important just to illustrate the obvious fact that culture affects selfhood. We can now accept the challenge to understand what is invariant transculturally and what is culture specific in selfhood, and to understand the processes by which environing symbolic culture has its influence. This ambitious objective is beyond the resources of a narrowly conceived cognitive social psychology. Affect and emotion, motivation, and action are involved. Cognitive social psychology needs not only interdisciplinary collaboration as with anthropology and sociology, which it is ready to accept, but also collaboration with other subdisciplines of psychology, which may be more difficult.

The recent substantive focus on individualism and collectivism as cultural orientations (e.g., Triandis, 1989) has special relevance to the psychology of self and identity, because the very emphasis on self and identity as interesting topics may be a reflection of Euro-American individualism. Bandura's (1997) masterwork on self-efficacy is certainly a comprehensive exploration of the agency pole of Bakan's (1966) dimension of agency vs. communion, where agency is the conventionally individualistic (and also masculine) pole. Perhaps we may be ready to go beyond the controversies involved in these polarities. I am impressed that Kağitçibasi (1996), in her recent examination of early child development from a "majority world" perspective influenced by her pathbreaking Turkish research, suggested that developing countries might well reaffirm their commitment to values of relatedness while adopting the Western value of autonomy. Her position goes beyond the conventional relativism of multiculturalism at the same time that it rejects the necessity of cultural choice in terms of the polarity.

The Ontogenetic or Developmental Perspective

A quarter century ago I was able to take note of the emerging empirical work on early child development that was refining and partly replacing G. H. Mead's (1934) schematic account of the development of reflexive self-reference and its accompaniments. Developmental psychologists have continued to contribute to an enriched picture of the roots of selfhood in individual development, which social psychological theorizing must take into account. Higgins (1996) provides a coherent version for social psychologists in his "self-digest" theory of self-knowledge. The present challenge is whether this individually focused theory can be made to deal adequately with the self-constituting role of participation in cultural symbol systems and practices, and in the stratification and role differentiation of the social order.

In the 1970s, developmental psychologists were still mainly responding to the Piagetian challenge. In the recent decades, the social-historical school with roots in the Marxist work of Lev Vygotsky has gained in visibility and importance, linked with the increasing prominence of "cultural psychology" (Cole, 1996) as a metatheoretical alternative to cross-cultural psychology that takes a more fluid dialectical or transactional approach to the development of selfhood in the context of social participation. Rogoff's (1990) work *Apprenticeship in Thinking* is an especially challenging recent example.

Why the Surge of Interest in Selfhood and Identity?

It may be productive to consider possible reasons that underlie the recent surge of interest in self and identity and why social psychologists in particular have joined in it enthusiastically. The long-term tide of general interests has sources that have been much discussed by Baumeister (1986), Giddens (1991), and many others. Modern society with its geographical and social mobility and loosened social bonds highlights individual choice in the lives of its more fortunate members, and both the goals intentionally chosen and the anxieties exposed by the waning of traditional social supports make self-conscious selfhood salient. The diminishing role of traditional religion in a society featuring science and technology is a special case of waning sociocultural support, felt so

keenly by many that religious fundamentalism is on the rise. My speculations earlier about the cultural-evolutionary basis of religion suggest
grounds for taking this loss seriously. In earlier modern times, faith in
earthly progress (Nisbet, 1980) compensated for the fading prospect of
heavenly reward (and punishment)—whether via the ascending dialectics of Hegel's romantic view of history or of Marx's materialistic equivalent or via the mundane progressivism of modern bourgeois democracies. The century's calamities have shaken belief in progress and led to
skepticism about the prospect that science and technology can solve the
looming, potentially catastrophic problems. Rather than *fin-de-siècle*
malaise, also, we were recently experiencing end-of-the-millenium heeby-
jeebies. This unease makes people, at least people in the Western individualistic tradition, more saliently aware of their vulnerably exposed
selfhood.

I return shortly to considering some features of the immediate scene
that make selfhood especially problematic and therefore of research interest, but I first note a matter of subdisciplinary politics that seems to
me to have played a part in social psychologists' special interest in
identity and selfhood in recent years. The partnership of personality and
social psychology reflected in Division 8 of the American Psychological
Association (now the Society for Personality and Social Psychology) and
embodied in the dual leadership roles of pioneers like Gardner Murphy
and Gordon Allport came under great strain in the expansive days of
post-Festingerian experimental social psychology. In my own department at the University of California at Santa Cruz, for example, I found
it desirable to maneuver to link our graduate program in personality
with developmental psychology, not with social as in the original
arrangement—the tendency of my social psychological colleagues was
so strong to regard any reference to personality as exemplifying Lee
Ross's (1977) "fundamental attribution error." Under these circumstances, selfhood and identity became attractive emblems under which
social psychology could establish its own claims to territory otherwise
occupied by a personality psychology that it had come to regard as
hardly legitimate.

Reinforcing this attraction was the amenability of self-related concepts to treatment in cultural and historical context, with which we have
been centrally concerned. One could address *Culture and Self* (Marsella,
DeVos, & Hsu, 1985) without being encumbered by the mistakes and
blind alleys of the failed culture-and-personality movement. "Culture

and self" allowed a fresh start, with the option of salvaging much that remained valuable in the earlier tradition.

I would not put much stress on these by-products of academic intellectual politics. More important, it seems to me, are some recent historical developments that inherently focus attention on selfhood and identity, and give human urgency to the attempt to bring social psychology to bear on them. I highlight two: disorientation with respect to moral values as anchors of identity (Baumeister, 1986), which I will label De-Moralization, and heightened in-group identification (Us vs. Them), as involved in the current plague of ethnic, tribal, religious, or national conflict. Having these concrete sets of human problems in mind should reduce the danger that our theoretical examinations of selfhood and identity remain at a level of empty abstractions.

De-Moralization

The firm anchoring of traditional moral values in consensual religious belief has been under attack in Western societies for a long time. But there have been recent changes that must be quite disorienting, especially to the young. With worldwide intercommunication and worldwide sharing of the pop culture of which the United States is a leader and primary source, the changes are by no means limited to the United States or Western Europe. I am thinking about the results of lifting the old moral taboos about sexuality after the "sexual revolution" of the 1960s, the prevalence of corrosive relativism in academic/intellectual circles and its ethical promotion in the name of multiculturalism, the inescapable invitation to recreational sex in the mass media of entertainment, the pervasive cynicism about government and purported idealistic motivation, the weakening of ties that hold families together—this is beginning to sound like a litany of those of the Religious Right who feel they have a monopoly on "Family Values." I would be among the first to recognize that there have been major human gains in getting beyond the stifling restrictions of Main Street. But it seems indubitable to me that insofar as moral values have been a stabilizing anchor in personal identity and a link binding people together in a livable society, we are in trouble.

The immediacy of our problem was brought home to me by Mary Pipher's (1994) popular best-seller, *Reviving Ophelia*. Her account displays the predicament of adolescent girls in school settings characterized by the pervasive presence of alcohol and drugs, sexual pressures from boys, gender-linked academic expectations, peer pressures, and cultural pressures from immersion in the synthetic youth culture of the mass media, including its stress on physical beauty of a biologically improbable kind. These current features of the early adolescent world combine with the biological stirrings of puberty and its sequels to make the adolescent passage of teenage girls riskier and more disturbing to their selfhood and identity than girls of earlier generations mostly experienced. Similar qualitative accounts about other segments of the population would enrich our consideration of selfhood in historical context.

As an old Liberal, I am troubled that I am troubled about the lifting of older cultural constraints. But we are becoming aware of human costs in the reformulations of human nature partly brought about by Sigmund Freud's campaign against Victorian restrictiveness. The Superego, such a cruel bugbear to the Freudian generations, is no longer much of a problem. Indeed, the cases that seem to get the most psychoanalytic attention today, "borderline" states and the like, draw therapists to the self-and-other intricacies of self-psychology and object relations theory, rather than to the compromises negotiated by a coherent Ego between Id and Superego that Freudians used to be concerned with.

One current response to our loss of the old anchors—not only loss of moral values but, more generally, loss of our previous conviction that truthful conceptions of the nature of reality and of people's place in it are at least approachable if not finally attainable, and can help people make a better life—is the fashion of "postmodernism" originating in the humanities and spreading in the softer side of psychology and the social sciences. Gergen (1991) has been a conspicuous spokesperson for the postmodern position in regard to the conceptualization of contemporary selfhood. I am not persuaded by his argument that the coherence of our symbolic selfhood is challenged primarily by relational overload, resulting in what he calls the "saturated self": It seems to me that the loss of anchors just noted and warranted loss of hope are more important factors. I agree with him that the integral selfhood that Romantic and early Modern thought could regard as a worthy human achievement is in deep trouble. I do not share his sense of playful delight in the new freedom he values in the postmodern situation.

Our present historical/cultural situation strikes me as pathological, and because of the existential strains produced by the withdrawal of traditional sources of meaning (Baumeister, 1991), I think it is intrinsically unstable and cannot last for long. Because the religious answers that pull many toward a new fundamentalism make no sense to me, I look ahead with doubt and misgiving. Perhaps the "communitarians" (Etzioni, 2001) have a sense of direction that is relevant to our common predicament. In any case, a social psychology of selfhood and identity should be attending to these problems, which are now embedded in a worldwide multicultural context.

Problematic Ingroup Identification: Us Versus Them

Social psychologists shared in the general surprise and dismay that the end of Cold War polarization and latent terror about a prospective nuclear Doomsday has been followed not by peace but by a state of world affairs featuring tribal, ethnic, and religious conflict with little regard for national boundaries. In Ireland, the Middle East, Rwanda and the Congo, and the countries of the former Soviet Union, virulent internal conflicts erupted, seen by each side as between virtuous Us and diabolical Them, thus having genocidal potential (see Smith, 1999). Within the United States and several European countries, racial or ethnic antagonisms were also conspicuous. Multiculturalism became a widespread ideal replacing that of the "melting pot." These developments made salient the phenomena of ingroup identification and its role in intergroup conflict.

Fortunately, Tajfel (1978) and Turner (1987) provided social psychology with conceptual tools to deal with such conflicts in their social identity and self-categorization theories, to which Brewer (1991) and Deaux (1993) contributed, along with various others. These need to be elaborated in relation to processes by which historical/cultural factors enter into the constitution of social identity. I see an interesting possibility in the plausible interrelation between the challenges to selfhood already considered under De-Moralization and the pathological exaggeration of ingroup identification just noted. Sensed meaninglessness or hopeless impotence—intolerable states of selfhood—may be dispelled by identification with a group and commitment to its cause. The correlation between right-wing authoritarianism and both religious fundamentalism and trigger-happy superpatriotism (cf. Altemeyer, 1996) is in accord with this suggestion.

Some Considerations of Conceptual Strategy

To be adequate to the problems I have just been calling attention to, I think a systems/process view of selfhood is required, one that takes into account the whole person in his or her embeddedness in culture and social relationships. In the terminology borrowed from Dewey and Bentley (1949), the approach should be transactional, not just interactional or unidirectionally causal. People construct their social and cultural worlds at the same time that they themselves are being shaped by them. As social psychologists, we cannot be content with a conceptual world populated by independent and dependent variables.

Because reflexive self-reference, which is the central feature of selfhood, is a matter of the attribution or creation of meanings, I find the recent approaches that draw on self-narratives (McAdams, 1996; Sarbin, 1986) or multivocal dialogue (Hermans, 1996; Hermans & Kempen, 1993) especially attractive. But, given what I think we now know about the historical/cultural malleability of how self-reference as well as its contents are organized, whatever conceptualization we employ should not assume the privileged status of particular historically or culturally given models of selfhood. Thus, I wondered whether Hermans's view of selfhood as dispersed multivocal dialogue might not be viewed as a good metaphor for people's present response to the predicaments of "postmodern" times rather than as a general, transhistorical and pancultural model.

Meanings and values are at the heart of the humanities, the *Geisteswissenschaften* in Dilthey's old distinction between interpretative and explanatory (*Naturwissenschaftlich*) scholarship (Rickman, 1979). Advocates of a narrative approach to selfhood, especially those identified with the postmodern revolt against "positivism," often take a stand opposed to scientific concern with causal explanation. I think that is a mistake. It has long seemed to me that reflexive self-reference and self-awareness—that is, human selfhood—is the one natural phenomenon that requires by its very nature both causal and interpretative analysis. We can work productively on either side of this street, but it seems to me the most interesting challenge is how to coordinate explanatory and interpretative approaches. Modern experimental social psychology has been committed to the causal/explanatory vein, but it should be recognized that the research tradition beginning with Rotter's (1966) research on locus of control and including Seligman's work on explanatory styles (1990) is an excellent example of successful causal analysis of the attribution of meaning in regard to matters very relevant to self-conception. Bandura's (1997) impressive treatment of self-efficacy is a closely related example. I look forward to further developments in this scientific/humanistic pursuit of human self-understanding.

References

Altemeyer, B. (1996). *The authoritarian spector*, Cambridge, MA: Harvard University Press.

Bakan, D. (1966). *The duality of human existence*. Chicago: Rand McNally.

Bandura, A. (1997). *Self-efficacy: The exercise of control*. New York: Freeman.

Baumeister, R. F. (1986). *Identity: Culture change and the struggle for self*. New York: Oxford University Press.

Baumeister, R. F. (1991). *Meanings of life*. New York: Guilford.

Becker, E. (1973). *The denial of death*. New York: Free Press.

Brewer, M. B. (1991). The social self: On being the same and different at the same time. *Personality and Social Psychology Bulletin, 17,* 475–482.

Campbell, D. T. (1991). A naturalistic theory of archaic moral orders. *Zygon, 26,* 91–114.

Cole, M. (1996). *Cultural psychology: A once and future discipline*. Cambridge, MA: Belknap/Harvard University Press.

Dewey, J., & Bentley, A. F. (1949). *Knowing and the known*. Boston: Beacon.

Deaux, K: (1993). Reconstructing social identity. *Personality and Social Psychology Bulletin, 19,* 4–12.

Epstein, S. (1973). The self-concept revisited: Or a theory of a theory. *American Psychologist, 28,* 404–416.

Erikson, E. H. (1959). Identity and the life cycle. *Psychological Issues, 1*(1).

Etzioni, A. (2001). *Next: The road to the good society*. New York: Basic Books.

Friedman, L. J. (1999). *Identity's architect: A biography of Erik H. Erikson*. New York: Scribner.

Fromm, E. (1941). *Escape from freedom*. New York: Farrar & Rinehart.

Geertz, C. (1973). *The interpretation of cultures*. New York: Basic Books.

Geertz, C. (1975). On the nature of anthropological understanding. *American Scientist, 63,* 47–53.

Gergen, K. J. (1991). *The saturated self: Dilemmas of identity in contemporary life*. New York: Basic Books.

Giddens, A. (1991), *Modernity and self-identity: Self and society in the late modern age*. Stanford, CA: Stanford University Press.

Greenberg, J., Pyszczynski, T., & Solomon, S. (1986). A terror management theory of the role of the need for self-esteem in social behavior. In R. F. Baumeister (Ed.), *Public self and private self* New York: Springer Verlag.

Heelas, P.L.F., & Lock, A. J. (Eds.). (1981). *Indigenous psychologies: The anthropology of the self*. New York: Academic Press.

Hermans, H.J.M. (1996). Voicing the self: From information processing to dialogical interchange. *Psychological Bulletin, 119,* 31–50.

Hermans, H.J.M., & Kempen, H.J.G. (1993). *The dialogical self: Meaning as movement*. San Diego, GA: Academic Press.

Higgins, E. T. (1996). The "self-digest": Self-knowledge serving self-regulating functions. *Journal of Personality and Social Psychology, 71,* 1062–1083.

James, W. (1890). The consciousness of self. In *Principles of psychology, Vol. 1.* New York: Holt.

James, W. (1892). *Psychology: Briefer course*. New York: Holt.

Kağitçibasi, C. (1996). The autonomous-relational self: A new synthesis. *European Psychologist, 1,* 180–186.

Kitayama, S., Markus, H. R., Matsumoto, H., & Norasakkunkit, V. (1997). Individual and collective processes in the construction of self: Self-enhancement in the United States and self-criticisms in Japan. *Journal of Personality and Social Psychology, 72,* 1245–1267.

Kohut, H. (1971). *The analysis of self*. New York: International Universities Press.

Lakoff, G. (1987). *Women, fire, and dangerous things: What categories reveal about the mind*. Chicago: University of Chicago Press.

Lakoff, G., & Johnson, M. (1980). *Metaphors we live by*. Chicago: University of Chicago Press.

Lynd, H. M. (1958). *On shame and the search for identity*. New York: Harcourt Brace.

Markus, H. R., & Kitayama, S. (1991). Culture and the self: Implications for cognition, emotion, and motivation. *Psychological Review, 98,* 224–253.

Marsella, A. J., DeVos, G., & Hsu, F.L.K. (Eds.). (1985). *Culture and self: Asian and western perspectives*. New York: Tavistock.

McAdams, D. P. (1996). Personality, modernity, and the storied self. *Psychological Inquiry, 7,* 295–321.

Mead, G. H. (1934). *Mind, self, and society*. Chicago: University of Chicago Press.

Murphy, G. (1947). *Personality: A biosocial approach to origins and structure*. New York: Harper.

Murphy, G., & Murphy, L. B. (1931). *Experimental social psychology*. New York: Harper.

Murphy, G., Murphy, L. B., & Newcomb, T. M. (1937). *Experimental social psychology* (rev. ed.). New York: Harper.

Nisbet, R. (1980). *History of the idea of progress*. New York: Basic Books.

Onians, R. B. (1973). *The origins of European thought.* New York: Arno. (Original work published 1951).

Pipher, M. (1994). *Reviving Ophelia: Saving the selves of adolescent girls.* New York: Putnam.

Rickman, H. P. (1979). *Wilhelm Dilthey: Pioneer of the human studies.* Berkeley, CA: University of California Press.

Rogers, C. (1961). *On becoming a person.* Boston: Houghton-Mifflin.

Rogoff, B. (1990). *Apprenticeship in thinking: Cognitive development in social context.* New York: Oxford University Press.

Ross, L. (1977). The intuitive psychologist and his shortcomings: Distortions in the attribution process. In L. Berkowitz (Ed.), *Advances in experimental social psychology* (pp. 173–220). New York: Academic Press.

Rotter, J. R. (1966). Generalized expectations for internal versus external control of reinforcement. *Psychological Monographs 80* (1, Whole No. 609).

Sarbin, T. (Ed.) (1986). *Narrative psychology: The storied nature of human conduct.* New York: Praeger.

Schutz, A. (1967). *The phenomenology of the social world.* Evanston, IL: Northwestern University Press.

Sedikides, C.,& Skowronski, J. J. (1997). The symbolic self in evolutionary context. *Personality and Social Psychology Review, 1,* 80–102.

Seligman, M. E. P. (1990). *Learned optimism.* New York: Knopf.

Smith, M. B. (1978a). Essay 1. In R. Fitzgerald (Ed.), *What it means to be human: Essays in philosophical anthropology, political philosophy, and social psychology* (pp. 3–24). Rushcutters Bay, New South Wales: Pergamon.

Smith, M. B. (1978b). Perspectives on selfhood. *American Psychologist, 33,* 1053–1063. [Reprinted in M. B. Smith (1991). *Values, self, and society.* New Brunswick, NJ: Transaction.]

Smith, M. B. (1980). Attitudes, values, and selfhood. In H. E. Howe & M. M. Page (Eds.), *Nebraska Symposium on Motivation 1979* (pp. 305–350). Lincoln: University of Nebraska Press. [Reprinted in M. B. Smith (1991). *Values, self, and society.* New Brunswick, NJ: Transaction.]

Smith, M. B. (1985). The metaphorical basis of selfhood. In A. J. Marsella, G. DeVos, & F.L.K. Hsu (Eds.), *Culture and self: Asian and western perspectives* (pp. 56–88). New York: Tavistock. [Reprinted in M. B. Smith. (1991). *Values, self, and society.* New Brunswick, NJ: Transaction.]

Smith, M. B. (1999). Political psychology and peace: A half century perspective. *Peace and Conflict: Journal of Peace Psychology, 5,* 1–16.

Snell, B. (1953). *The discovery of mind: The Greek origins of European thought.* Oxford: Blackwell.

Solomon, S., Greenberg, J., & Pyszczynski, T. (1991). A terror management theory of social behavior: The psychological functions of self-esteem and cultural world views. *Advances in Experimental Social Psychology, 34,* 93–159.

Sullivan, H. S. (1953). *Conceptions of modern psychiatry.* New York: Norton.

Tajfel, H. (1978). *Differentiation between social groups: Studies in the social psychology of intergroup relations.* London: Academic Press.

Taylor, C. (1989). *Sources of the self: The making of modern identity.* Cambridge, MA: Harvard University Press.

Triandis, H. C. (1989). The self and social behavior in differing cultural contexts. *Psychological Review, 96,* 506–520.

Trilling, L. (1972). *Sincerity and authenticity.* Cambridge, MA: Harvard University Press.

Turner, J. C. (1987). *Rediscovering the social group: A self-categorization theory.* Oxford: Blackwell.

Wylie, R. C. (1961). *The self-concept.* Lincoln: University of Nebraska Press.

Wylie, R. C. (1974). *The self-concept* (Vol. 1). Lincoln: University of Nebraska Press.

Wylie, R. C. (1979). *The self-concept* (Vol. 2). Lincoln: University of Nebraska Press.

Part III

Toward an Emancipatory Human Science

Commentary

In SPSSI (the Society for the Psychological Study of Social Issues), it has been traditional to talk of the three P's as foci of concern: Poverty, Prejudice, and Peace. I regret to say that I have not been involved in research or policy on poverty. Neither have many other socially concerned psychologists, though the combination of income and education indexing socioeconomic status (SES) recurrently appears as a strong correlate of individual and social pathology—or at the other pole, of achievement and life satisfaction. But I have been continually concerned with Prejudice and Peace. The chapters in this section reflect these involvements. In their present relevance, these chapters examine the nature of the value conflicts that inevitably accompany involvement in controversial social issues. They consider changes in the problems that psychologists faced and in psychological responses to them over the half century in which I have been a participant-observer. They recount and celebrate an occasion when social psychology indeed "made a difference." And they bring my concerns with the psychology of war and peace almost up-to-date with an entry written after the George W. Bush administration had been crowing about its foray in Afghanistan and was beginning to threaten expansion of its War on Terrorism to the new terrain of Iraq.

In chapter 11, "McCarthyism: A Personal Account," with which the part begins, the account of my own experience as a target of the authoritarian attack on American civil liberties also puts on record aspects of my own political background that are relevant context for my various advocacies displayed in this book. The continuation of McCarthyite policies in the federal government long after Senator Joseph McCarthy vanished from the scene may be surprising to new readers. I have come to terms long since with my very unheroic response to the McCarthyite challenge, but my putting it on record previously and here is an act of penance.

Chapter 12, "Value Dilemmas in Public Health: A Psychologist's Perspective," is also introductory to the controversial issues with which the rest of the section is concerned. Addressing an audience of public health educators and professionals in memory of a fine psychologist colleague, Andie Knutson, I used his research on professionals' attitudes toward abortion to illustrate how value clashes amount to collisions of assumptive worlds (Frank, 1973), and proposed that if the attractive option of coercion is ruled out, what remains is the possibility of negotiated compromise, in which the findings of psychological research can play a part. Here I tease at one of my continuing obsessions, essentially one of moral philosophy—I believe in my own values; I want to respect other people who hold different, maybe opposing values; yet I don't believe, relativistically, that all value claims are equivalently valid or empty. What sort of process might favor the prevalence of outcomes that are humanly more desirable? Yet in posing this question, I have already taken a humanistic position rather than one with a religious basis.

Chapter 13, "The Psychology of Prejudice," is a retrospective review of two landmark books that appeared near midcentury: Allport's *The Nature of Prejudice* (1954) and Adorno, Frenkel-Brunswik, Levinson, and Sanford's *The Authoritarian Personality* (1950). My comparative discussion still gives a useful view of the issues as they appeared by 1978. There have been some major developments in the quarter century since. I had already noted the trend to focus more on racism, a matter of consequential injustice, than on prejudice, one of feelings and attitudes. That shift in emphasis continued. With the emergence of social norms condemning the overt expression of prejudice, prejudice and racism took modern, less obvious forms, identified by David Sears (Sears et al., 1979) as "symbolic racism." And the measurement and theory of authoritarianism was put on a new and more solid footing by Bob Altemeyer (e.g., 1996) in his program of research on right-wing authoritarianism (RWA). His measure of RWA captured the essence of the important personality dimension inefficiently indexed by the much-criticized F-scale (F for fascism) of *The Authoritarian Personality* (Adorno et al., 1950), and also facilitated exploration of its empirical relations to important social and political phenomena without requiring commitment to a psychoanalytic explanatory framework. Still more recently, Pratto, Sidanius, and others have introduced a measure of social dominance orientation (Pratto et al., 1994), which appears to complement RWA in predicting antidemocratic attitudes. I believe that social psychology has made real progress in its study of prejudice, discrimination, and antidemocratic attitudes and behavior.

In chapter 14, "The Social Scientists' Role in *Brown v. Board of Education*: A Non-revisionist Appraisal," my retrospections also come in quarter-century segments. The chapter was my contribution to a symposium commemorating the 25th anniversary of the celebrated Supreme Court decision that ended legally imposed school segregation. Now, almost a quarter century later, it is still necessary to remind ourselves that we can be proud of the psychological contribution in that case. Since I continue to be proud of my minor part in it, I want to confute the neoconservatives among us who belittle and disparage it. The chapter also takes note of psychological participation in a more recent controversial case involving racial justice, the "Larry P" case in California about the use of I.Q. tests to place black children in classes for the educable mentally retarded (EMR). This case involved complex issues, without as much value consensus in our science and profession as supported our participation in *Brown v. Board of Education*. The value issues I raised in chapter 12 recur.

Chapter 14, "Racism, Education, and Student Protest," was based on a talk I gave at the Conference on Racism and Education at Chicago State College in 1969. Chicago State had recently experienced disruptive protest from its black students. I was invited from the neighboring University of Chicago, but I had recently come from the University of California at Berkeley, where I had done some research on participants in the Free Speech movement that initiated the national and partly international wave of student protests (Smith, Haan, & Block, 1969). In retrospect, I think the chapter does rather well in giving present reality to the value conflicts that faculties and administrations faced in those protests, and in clarifying the concept of institutional racism, which they brought into prominence.

The issues of war and peace have been prominent throughout my life as a psychologist—extending from the threats posed by Naziism and Fascism before World War II, World War II itself, the Cold War with its prospect of nuclear annihilation, and most recently the period of ethnonationalistic conflict that, after September 11, 2001, has enmeshed the

United States in a "War on Terrorism," which, as I write, may evolve to a war on much else. I have been much concerned to enlist the resources of psychology in the cause of peace, though I would not regard myself as a traditional pacifist.

Chapter 16, "Political Psychology and Peace: A Half Century Perspective," was my presidential address to the Division of Political Psychology of the International Association of Applied Psychology. Like chapter 1, it uses my own personal involvement as a portal of entry for a selective examination of what the field of psychology has been doing, this time in the cause of peace. Given the scale of danger to humankind and life that characterized the Cold War, I was puzzled that most psychologists were content to pursue "business as usual."

I confess to a degree of chutzpah in including chapter 17, "The Metaphor (and Fact) of War," which I revised in final form in April, 2002, in deep concern about the "War on Terrorism" with which President Bush responded to the attacks of September 11, about his war in Afghanistan, and about the emerging prospect of war against Iraq. The chapter is rooted in a brief historical moment, which is likely to be superseded before this book is published. I include it all the same because my discussion of the prevalent war metaphor has more general relevance. At a time when one could sense dampers on the free expression of dissident views in the name of patriotism, also, I felt an obligation to speak out. In the months since, fortunately, criticism is more widely visible.

I have linked these chapters to SPSSI's three P's. The values of justice and beneficence that underlie them involve other important foci of concern that have provided agenda for psychologists during the past half century—especially gender, including women's and gay and lesbian rights, aging, and disability. My participation in psychology during this time of substantial social change, together with my life experience in human relationships, has changed my own psychological perspective on these matters. I believe psychology is playing an emancipatory role on them, but I have not written chapters to advance it.

References

Adorno, T. W., Frenkel-Brunswik, E., Levinson, D. J., & Sanford, R. N. (1950). *The authoritarian personality.* New York: Harper.
Allport, G. W. (1954). *The nature of prejudice.* Cambridge, MA: Addison-Wesley.

Altemeyer, B. (1996). *The authoritarian specter*. Cambridge, MA: Harvard University Press.

Frank, J. D. (1973). *Persuasion and healing: A comparative study of psychotherapy* (rev. ed.). Baltimore, MD: Johns Hopkins University Press.

Pratto, F., Sidanius, J., Stallworth, L. M., & Malle B. F. (1994). Social dominance orientation: A personality variable predicting social and political attitudes. *Journal of Personality and Social Psychology, 67,* 741–763.

Sears, D. O., Hensler, C. P., & Speer, L. K. (1979). White opposition to "busing": Self-interest or symbolic politics? *American Political Science Review,* 73, 369–384.

Smith, M. B., Haan, N., & Block, J. H. (1969). Social-psychological aspects of student activism. In B. Rubinstein & M. Levin (Eds.), *Rebels and the campus revolt*. Englewood Cliffs, NJ: Prentice-Hall.

Chapter Eleven

McCarthyism
A Personal Account

In pulling together and documenting my memories of the wretched episode called McCarthyism, I was amazed to discover their state of disarray, considering how central the issues had been in my life. It *is* hard to keep the past straight! Maybe the review that was useful to me can also help my contemporaries and juniors get that period in perspective. I draw especially on my own minor part in the events, as my best way of giving the events the immediacy that may make them relevant to our situation today. These were events and issues in which SPSSI and SPSSI members were deeply involved—issues that tore lives and careers apart, and that are still with us.

What Was McCarthyism?

The phenomenon of McCarthyism is much broader than the meteoric career of Senator Joseph McCarthy, from his first publicized charges, in 1950, of Communists in the State Department to his downfall, in 1954, with the Army—McCarthy hearings—which the new medium of television allowed many of us to watch with fascination. It has often been observed that McCarthy was basically nihilistic, a destroying angel who fortunately built no party and left no antidemocratic organization behind him. Whereas his personal style was spectacular, McCarthyism as a historical phenomenon began before McCarthy and lasted long after his collapse.

We can begin with the spring of 1947. Then-President Harry Truman heralded the cold war with his Truman Doctrine calling for aid to the anti-Communist forces in Greece and Turkey; on the domestic front, he instituted the infamous Attorney General's list of dubious organizations implicated in communist, fascist, totalitarian, or otherwise "subversive" activities. Initially developed for internal governmental use in screening prospective government employees for more intensive investigation, the list soon was made public and became a multipurpose instrument of intimidation.

In the new cold war climate, the House Un-American Activities Committee (HUAC), which as the "Dies committee" had had a long history of harassing New Deal liberals and leftists, rolled into high gear. With young Congressman Nixon playing a prominent role, the committee's first big quarry was Alger Hiss, who was indicted for perjury at the end of 1948 and convicted after a second trial in the beginning of 1950. In 1949, the Regents of the University of California voted to impose a special anti-Communist oath on all faculty, initiating the Loyalty Oath controversy that lasted into 1952. (Edward Tolman, a SPSSI president, led the nonsigners who immediately forfeited their jobs; Nevitt Sanford, also a SPSSI president, was a nonsigner too, along with Hugh Coffey.) In 1950, as we have noted, McCarthy made his initial charges; in 1953 he acquired the chairmanship of the Senate Permanent Investigating Committee, which gave him large resources. In 1951, Julius and Ethel Rosenberg were condemned to death for espionage. By 1953, J. Robert Oppenheimer was suspended by the Atomic Energy Commission as a security risk. And on March 2 in the same year (on a ridiculously different scale, though it hardly seemed so to me at the time), I testified under subpoena before the Senate Internal Security Subcommittee — the so-called "Jenner committee" that was the Senate's counterpart to HUAC.

The immediately significant context for this crescendo of domestic preoccupation with loyalty and internal security, of course, was the inability of the United States, the great victor of World War II, to have its way in the postwar world, in which the Soviet Union had already established control over Eastern Europe. (Our wartime alliance with the Soviet Union seemed by then a brief aberration from our usual distrustful antagonism.) The forces of Chairman Mao, then a Soviet ally, conquered China in 1949, and when the Soviets exploded a fission bomb of their own in 1949 our atomic monopoly was ended. The Korean War began in June 1950. In spite of Oppenheimer's opposition, we tried out our first hydrogen bomb in 1952, and were taken aback when the Soviet Union came forth with its first fusion bomb the following year; treachery was suspected. Given this rapid set of developments, it is also hard to remember that the court fight against legally enforced racial segregation in the schools, another matter in which SPSSI was deeply involved, was coming to a climax at about the same time.

My Encounter with the Jenner Committee

My 1953 appearance before the Jenner committee was neither heroic nor really dastardly. It felt unique to me, but I now suspect my experience was more typical than I could recognize at the time. It left me feeling very bad about myself, so I have almost never talked about it since. With the help of the Freedom of Information Act, I recently obtained the transcript of my testimony. When it arrived, I hardly dared look at it—not only from general repugnance, I now realize, but because I had actually revised my memory of the events in a self-serving way and was afraid of the truth.

I need to give a little background first. Fifty years ago [in 1936], as a student at Reed College, I had become first a "fellow traveler" in the large chapter of the American Student Union (ASU), a Popular Front organization including major old-Socialist components, and had later become a pretty good Stalinist in the much smaller covert chapter of the Young Communist League (YCL) that provided the ASU leadership. With most of my friends I soon came to see things very differently, after the Moscow trials that purged the Old Bolsheviks and the Nazi-Soviet pact. But by the time of McCarthyism, I felt—and I still feel—very much as Lillian Hellman (1976) expressed it in *Scoundrel Time*, the account of her encounter with HUAC. As a former "fellow traveler" but not a Party member, Hellman wrote,

> . . . I am still angry that the anti-Communist writers' and intellectuals' reason for disagreeing with McCarthy was too often his crude methods. . . . Such people would have a right to say that I, and many like me, took too long to see what was going on in the Soviet Union. But whatever our mistakes, I do not believe we did our country any harm. And I think they did. They went to too many respectable conferences that turned out not to be under respectable auspices, contributed to and published too many CIA magazines. The step from such capers was straight into the Vietnam War and the days of Nixon. (pp. 154–155)

I did not want to join the anti-Communist hue-and-cry, and particularly, I did not want to "name names," the crucial symbolic act demanded of those subpoenaed to testify.

When I received the subpoena, I had just joined the staff of the Social Science Research Council (SSRC) after having chaired the psychology department at Vassar. Self-analyses of motives are always dubious, but I think mine included principled opposition to the committee's witch-hunt (then focused on "Reds" in education), together with selfish reluctance to jeopardize my career and family. The top foundation lawyer whom the SSRC made available to me agreed with my strategy to cooperate with the committee to the extent of naming the publicly identified members who were our organizer-leaders, letting my memory for events 15 years earlier stop at that point. Here are some extracts from my testimony:

> *Mr. Morris [counsel to the committee]:* Were you ever invited to join the Young Communist League?
>
> *Mr. Smith:* I belonged to it.
>
> *Mr. Morris:* Would you be willing to tell this committee the names of the people who were members of that union *[sic]?*
>
> *Mr. Smith:* I would be very reluctant to do it.
>
> *Mr. Morris:* You are talking here in Executive Session.
>
> *The Chairman [Senator Jenner]:* This is not for publication.
>
> *Mr. Smith:* I would still be very reluctant, but I know that the law is the law. I would prefer to answer in general terms first and then leave it to your discretion whether to put further questions to me, because, for myself, I have no feeling of particular regret or shame at having belonged at that point way back in my student career, and I think it was, if anything, a healthy sign rather than a bad one. It certainly didn't make an adult Communist out of me . . . I would say this, however: that of the people that I knew in connection with the Young Communists' League there at Reed, none of them are important people today, and we had no official tie with any faculty group. So I have no guilty knowledge in that respect, and the persons that I have been in touch with since have all completely changed their point of view, as I have. . . . So I will answer your questions if you insist on putting it to me, but I very much hope you won't feel the need to.
>
> *Mr. Morris:* Mr. Chairman, we would like, for purposes of investigation, just to determine whether or not the reasons given by the former professor are true, namely, whether or not those people who were once

active in the Communist organization are any longer active, to have the names.

The Chairman: It would be a big help to the committee if you would do it. We have to find out the facts and have information. This is an executive session. The record will not be divulged. It will not be made public. Even the fact that you are testifying will not be made public. It will give us a basis of facts to go on.

Mr. Smith: I understand, and it is really my conscience that I am struggling with, not merely a point of law. [*Why* did I feel the need to share that scruple with *them?*]

Mr. Chairman: We would appreciate it if you would give us the names. (Subcommittee, 1953, pp. 49–52)

And I gave names—the ones I had originally planned who were public in their recruiting role, but to my shame—and as I had really managed to "forget," also a couple of others—people I knew well and could swear were no longer at all sympathetic to Communism. I had not intended to but I did, and that still leaves me deeply ashamed.

There were some ridiculous aspects to the transcript:

Senator Welker: . . . In these little meetings in the lounge that you had, you had some literature furnished to you?

Mr. Smith: Often we bought it ourselves, at whatever the Communist bookstore was called, downtown. . . .

Senator Welker: You mean that in Portland they had a Communist bookstore?

Mr. Smith: Certainly, sir. (pp. 57–58)

The committee was interested in things I had signed:

Mr. Morris: Do you know an organization called the Bill of Rights Conference, in New York, in 1949?

Mr. Smith: I have some dim memories of it. It doesn't mean anything very concrete to me.

Mr. Morris: Were you active in that organization?

Mr. Smith: No, I wasn't active.

Mr. Morris: Did you sign a statement on behalf of that organization?

Mr. Smith: I may have done that, sir. What happened, if I can just expand a little bit, is that during the course of a year about a dozen pieces of mail would come in and ask for me to sign this, that, or the other thing. I tossed ten or eleven of them into the wastebasket because I feel that these groups for the most part are Communist inspired. By the time I have tossed the tenth one in, when the thing that is on paper in front of me is a thing I deeply believe in, regardless of whether it is Communist supported or not, I get feeling sufficiently badly about the thing that I sign it.

I think the things I have signed are a somewhat random selection of the things that come in my mail and don't have anything significant of themselves, except in the case of the Civil Rights Congress or whatever it was. I am very firmly in favor of civil rights. (pp. 54–55)

In retrospect, I was addressing the wrong audience with my talk about scruples and my rationale for signing statements. The committee members could not have cared less. By politely letting me go on talking like a professor, they probably lured me into going beyond my original uncourageous but defensible intention. That I did so left me feeling demeaned and wretched. I had violated my basic values, though as I look back on it, I do not believe I actually hurt anybody else. But what I said *could* have hurt them. I remember slinking back to my small room in the old Willard Hotel feeling physically sick. Maybe people felt better who took the Fifth Amendment or who, like my former colleague Lloyd Barenblatt, went to federal prison for taking the First Amendment. But Lillian Hellman, who made her refusal to give names to HUAC stick on her own terms, writes about how wretched she felt. Such an inquisition is a chilling experience.

My Security Problems at NIMH

My other encounter testifies to the long-lasting effects of the acute episode of McCarthyism. It became known in the early 1960s that the National Institute of Mental Health (NIMH), and indeed, the Department of Health, Education and Welfare (HEW) to which it belonged screened prospective members of scientific advisory ("peer review") panels for suitability on security grounds. People who were turned down mostly never heard about it, and were never given the chance to learn what derogatory information was involved or to respond to it. I had learned through the grapevine that I was on such a blacklist, though I had been a consultant to the Veterans Administration (VA) beginning in 1957 and to the National Science Foundation (NSF) in 1962, having listed my YCL membership on the government personnel form in both cases.

Recently I obtained from the Department of Health and Human Services a copy of a report dated June 26, 1957, concerning a security check made on me in connection with my proposed appointment to the "Mental Health Study Section of the National Institute of Health." (I had not known until now that I had been considered at that early date.) The report quotes my account of ASU and YCL membership on the personnel forms in connection with my VA appointment. It mentions my presence at the head table of a fund-raising dinner for the Spanish Refugee Appeal in Boston in 1948 (I remember being proud of sitting next to the then famous music critic Olin Downs), and signing a protest in the Harvard *Crimson* against the Mundt-Nixon anti-Communist bill, also in 1948. I was also noted to have joined a Communist-front protest against the discharge of three professors from the University of Washington for alleged Communist involvement. (One of them was Ralph Gundlach, who was active in SPSSI.) To my amazement, the report also said,

> The records of the Civil Service Commission contain information indicating that the Department of the Army advised the Civil Service Commission that it had a file . . . indicating that one M. B. Smith, Room 82, Perkins Hall, Oxford Street, Cambridge, Massachusetts [yes, me as a beginning graduate student at Harvard before the war] was an alleged Nazi *[sic]*. Military records were checked during the course of the investigation and no information regarding the information allegedly furnished by the Army to the Civil Service Commission was found. It is not believed that this material is of any significance. (Department of Health and Human Services, 1986, p. 3)

The substantive part of the report ended,

> In general, the Subject's associates, neighbors, and co-workers commented most favorably regarding his loyalty to this country. [Good!]

In its conclusions, the report stated:

> If the Subject is believed, his interest in Communism was the result of youthful immaturity and was shortlived. If such was the case, it is not felt that his membership in the American Student Union or the Young Communist League would be a bar to his appointment to the Mental Health Study Section. However, some information has been developed indicating that possibly the Subject in the late 1940's was connected in some fashion with Communist organizations. [Here the items quoted above are summarized. There is a funny reference to my appearing at the Spanish Refugee Appeal dinner]. . . . It is not known whether the Subject is identical

with the M. Brewster Smith who reportedly attended the meeting in question. However, the Subject is rather generally referred to as M. Brewster Smith rather than as Mahlon Brewster Smith. It is felt that this fact increases the likelihood that the M. Brewster Smith who reportedly attended a meeting of the Spanish Refugee Appeal of the Joint Anti-Fascist Refugee Committee is identical with the Subject. . . .

While it cannot be stated that the activities of the Subject previously mentioned are necessarily reflective of pro-Communist sympathy on his part, it is certainly obvious that these activities in view of his previous Communist connections raises [sic] a very grave doubt as to the Subject's present attitude regarding Communism. In order to reach a security determination in this case, it is believed the comments of the Subject regarding his reported activities in the late 1940's would be essential. (Department of Health, 1986, p. 4)

The document was initialled 6/28/57, with a handwritten addition similarly initialled:

Advise PHS [Public Health Service] that it would be necessary to obtain further information including a possible confrontation of derogatory information to Dr. Smith, before we can reach a security decision. . . .

Of course, I was not so confronted—nobody was in those days.

It was only on my rereading the full account in *Science* of the HEW blacklisting, still persisting in 1969, that I was reminded how I got off the blacklist in the mid-1960s—"by the somewhat accidental intervention of a senator important to the welfare of HEW" (Nelson, 1969, pp. 1501–1502). (It must have been Senator Morse of Oregon, since one of his senior staff was an old friend of mine.) I was immediately appointed to the Psychology Training Committee of NIMH as soon as I became available—in 1967, ten years, as I now learn, after I was initially proposed by NIMH staff.

The same article lists other psychologists turned down by HEW on security grounds—Theodore Newcomb and Stuart Cook, both SPSSI presidents, and Stephan Chorover of the Massachusetts Institute of Technology. According to *Science*:

One university professor interviewed by *Science*, who said that he knew that he had been refused clearance for participation on an NIMH panel, said that he had surreptitiously been given a list of people who also were not eligible for NIMH advising. This list, a copy of which is now in the possession of *Science*, has 37 names marked "Currently ineligible" and 11 additional names marked "not nominated recently but ineligible in the past." The professor noted that many of the names on the list were older, established psychologists who are active in the Society for the Psychological Study of Social Issues (SPSSI). An NIMH official also speculated that activity in SPSSI might have been a factor in keeping some people from being cleared. There are, however, some SPSSI leaders who are members of HEW panels. Many of the nation's leading social psychologists are active in SPSSI, a group founded to facilitate application of the findings of the social sciences to the solution of social problems. (Nelson, 1969, p. 1501)

This was written in 1969—almost two decades after the height of the McCarthy blight.

The *Science* article describes how in July 1968, under the leadership of the American Orthopsychiatric Association (*not* of SPSSI), representatives of eight scientific and professional associations (including the American Psychological Association) addressed a letter to then-HEW Secretary Wilbur Cohen and met with him, asking for abolition of security checks for nonsensitive advisory positions or, at the least, an opportunity for scientists to know and challenge the information being used against them. To quote *Science*:

Participants in the meeting said that Cohen appeared sympathetic to their requests but worried that a lapse in HEW investigating rigor might lead congressmen to try to cut HEW funds. . . . After receiving Cohen's reply, Dane G. Prugh [president of Ortho] wrote the interested organizations that Cohen's "answer must be read as a rejection of the position taken in our letter. . . . Individuals denied clearance still have no opportunity to confront the 'record' against them. There are still no stated standards for determining whether an appointee is clearable." (Nelson, 1969, p. 1500)

Of course, Secretary Cohen, the "father of Social Security," was a strong New Deal liberal. His pragmatic justification of the security clearance system in terms of HEW funding illustrates, as did my Jenner Committee testimony, the inadequacy of good liberal intentions.

SPSSI's Involvement with McCarthyism

In the 50th anniversary number of the *Journal of Social Issues*, Sargent and Harris (1986) provide us with a fuller account of the involvement of SPSSI in civil liberties and academic freedom, especially in the cases of prominent psychologists like Ralph Gundlach and Bernard Riess who lost their jobs because of Red-baiting. Neither SPSSI nor the APA, which was also involved, could be really effective in dealing with such cases. Understandably, Gundlach and Riess (1954) were not happy with the quite academic treatment of academic freedom in the number of the *Journal of Social Issues* on "Academic Freedom in a Climate of Insecurity" (Melby & Smith, 1953) for which I was partly responsible. They wanted a more resounding statement of position, and they objected with real justification to gestures toward anti-Communism in the introductory essay by E. O. Melby, then Dean of Education at New York University, which had an institutional record that was by no means unblemished.

Psychologists and SPSSI were involved with McCarthyism by being victimized, and by resisting victimization or accommodating to it. Another characteristic SPSSI response is to do research on the problem so as to gain a better understanding of it. Here our record is rather slim. Nevitt Sanford (1953) gave us a sophisticated participant-observer's account of the University of California Oath controversy (see also Gardner, 1967; Stewart, 1950). But the most substantial work was that undertaken by Marie Jahoda and Stuart Cook, both former SPSSI presidents and Lewin Award winners, on the impact of the loyalty-security program on federal employees and of the effect of "blacklisting" in radio and television (Jahoda, 1956a, 1956b; Jahoda & Cook, 1952, 1954). Cook (1986) has recently summarized the outcome of these qualitative studies:

> In spite of being familiar with . . . group mechanisms [such as pressures toward conformity under conditions of external threat], the investigators were still not prepared for the extent to which people were adjusting their behavior to avoid *exposure* to pressure to conform. Individuals did not wait for their behavior to be questioned. Their knowledge that certain categories of behavior were under surveillance was sufficient to lead them to make anticipatory behavioral changes. (p. 70)

At an institutional level, we saw Secretary Cohen anticipating sanctions from Congress in much the same way, in maintaining security procedures that he did not personally like, without, one gathers, any overt pressure from Congress.

And Now —

As far as I am aware, the conservative atmosphere of the Reagan administration with its strong anti-Communist rhetoric has still not produced anything like the constraint against free consideration of policy alternatives that was felt in the McCarthy era. We cannot take this state of affairs smugly for granted, as we are reminded by the existence of neoconservative campus groups that have set themselves up to spy on the teaching of liberal or radical professors. In human terms, I have recently been involved with a more serious case in which the Immigration and Naturalization Service, under instruction from the State Department, incarcerated on what appear political grounds an advanced graduate student in psychology—a foreign student—on his return from an international psychological meeting. On the morning of the SPSSI occasion, the *New York Times* (August 21, 1986) carried the account of Choichiro Yatani's release from detention after six weeks—a victory for justice and I hope a precedent for the future. But six weeks in jail after nine years of responsible conduct in the United States is wrong. The *Times* later cited his case in its lead editorial of November 13, 1986, under the headline, "Why Fear Foreigners' Free Speech?"

McCarthyism is a piece of history, but American history in a larger perspective includes repeated episodes of Know-Nothingism. The experience of the 1950s will not be our last, granting that our history *has* a long continuation.

References

Cook, S. W. (1986). Research on anticipatory ideological compliance: Comment on Sargent and Harris. *Journal of Social Issues, 42*(1), 69–73.

Department of Health and Human Services. (1986). *Subject*: Mahlon Brewster Smith, June 26, 1957 (released document).

Gardner, D. P. (1967). *The California oath controversy.* Berkeley, CA: University of California Press.

Gundlach, R. H., & Riess, B. F. (1954). Criticism of Melby and Smith's "Academic Freedom in a climate of insecurity" (letter to the editor). *Journal of Social Issues, 10*(1), 45–47.

Hellman, L. (1976). *Scoundrel time.* Boston: Little, Brown.

Jahoda, M. (1956a). Psychological issues in civil liberties. *American Psychologist, 11*, 234–240.

Jahoda, M. (1956b). Anti-Communism and employment policies in radio and television. In J. Cogley (Ed.), *Blacklisting* (Vol. 2, pp. 221–281). New York: Fund for the Republic.

Jahoda, M., & Cook, S. W. (1952). Security measures and freedom of thought: An exploratory study of the impact of loyalty and security programs. *Yale Law Journal, 61*, 295–333.

Jahoda, M., & Cook, S. W. (1954). Ideological compliance as a social-psychological process. In C. J. Friedrich (Ed.), *Totalitarianism* (pp. 203–222). Cambridge, MA: Harvard University Press.

Melby, E. O., & Smith, M. B. (Eds.) (1953). Academic freedom in a climate of insecurity. *Journal of Social Issues, 9*(3), 2–55.

Nelson, B. (1969, June 27). Scientists increasingly protest HEW investigation of advisers. *Science, 164*, 1499–1504.

Sanford, N. (1953). Individual and social change in a community under pressure: The oath controversy. *Journal of Social Issues, 9*(3), 25–42.

Sargent, S. S., & Harris, B. (1986). Academic freedom, civil liberties, and SPSSI. *Journal of Social Issues, 42*(1), 43–67.

Stewart, G. (1950). *The year of the oath.* New York: Doubleday.

Subcommittee to Investigate the Administration of the Internal Security Act and Other Internal Security Laws, Committee on the Judiciary, United States Senate. (1953). Stenographic transcript of hearings, March 2, 1953 (Vol. 20, pp. 48–61). (Released under Freedom of Information Act.)

U.S. abandons attempt to deport L. I. Japanese doctoral candidate. (1986, August 21). *New York Times*, p. 1.

Why fear foreigners' free speech? Editorial, (1986, November 13). *New York Times*, I-30:1.

Chapter Twelve

Value Dilemmas and Public Health
A Psychologist's Perspective

We are gathered in memory of our valued colleague Andie Knutson, and I feel particularly honored to have been chosen to speak on this occasion. Andie was a few years older than I, but our lives shared many links. We both had had Social Science Research Council Demobilization Awards following World War II experience, and we had both been involved in the early days of public opinion research. After the war, Andie took his Ph.D. at Princeton with Hadley Cantril, whose holistic and phenomenological orientation in psychology was much influenced by his own doctoral mentor, Gordon Allport, who was also mine. (Our common intellectual heritage made me find Andie's research concerns especially congenial.) After directing research and evaluation and behavioral studies in the U.S. Public Health Service with distinction, Andie came to Berkeley in 1957 (just two years before me) to initiate the program in behavioral sciences in the School of Public Health. He joined the Institute of Human Development as Research Associate at the same time that I did. In 1970, a couple of years after I had left Berkeley, he served the Institute as Acting Director.

Andie Knutson's Contribution

Andie represented the behavioral sciences in public health along a broad front (see [1]), but I think he will be remembered most enduringly for his pathbreaking studies carried out in the mid-1960s—studies of the beliefs and values of public health professionals concerning the beginning of a human life, its nature, its value, and the human or spiritual agencies that properly exercise control over it. This was essentially a venture to explore the "assumptive worlds" of public health professionals—

a felicitous term introduced by Hadley Cantril [2] and elaborated upon by Jerome Frank [3]. Each of us takes our own assumptive world for granted: that *is* our reality. So when we find ourselves in irreconcilable disagreement about matters like euthanasia or abortion or capital punishment, we get exasperated, sometimes to the point of violence, by our opponents' inability to listen to reason. Of course, they *do* reason, even if they don't listen, but they reason from unarguably different premises.

Knutson found that people's present religious orientations and those of their childhood homes, not their professional identities or other demographic characteristics, made the big difference as to whether they held a spiritual or a psychosocial conception of human life, and this in turn mainly sorted out the positions that they took on the five test issues about which he inquired: euthanasia, suicide, human experimentation, uses of the body after death, and capital punishment or shooting in self-defense. Of course, the details are more complicated. But it captures a crucial aspect of the abortion controversy to know that Catholics are likely to say that a human life begins with conception or in the first trimester, in contrast with secularly oriented professionals. His findings about when a human life begins, about its definition and value, and about organ transplants were reported in a series of important articles in the late 1960s [4–6]. The full report on his research is available in the manuscript of a book that remains unpublished, perhaps because Andie's doggedly scrupulous, carefully qualified style that so well suited his high standards of science and scholarship did not quite fit publishers' concepts of what is saleable [7].

I said this was pathbreaking research. We have been subjected to such a continuing barrage of debate between "right to life" versus "freedom of choice," we are so continually bombarded by new developments in medical technology that pose ethical problems for which there are no established consensual guidelines, that it is hard for us to realize how very original Andie's research was at the time he conceived it. The problems that his work highlighted are of course still with us, multiplied. It is difficult to cope with the lack of consensus on issues of health care in the public served by medicine; it is disturbing to see the extent that the members of the health community are themselves at odds about fundamental conceptions. But that is news that should be brought back home.

The Agenda of This Article

In what follows, I begin with Andie Knutson's concern with values and existential beliefs that bear on human health and medical practice. I want to consider the frameworks of thought within which we deal with these issues. For a long time I have been actively perplexed about this boundary region that links empirical behavioral science and practical philosophy. Almost a decade ago, I devoted a memorial lecture in honor of Gordon Allport to worrying about the ways in which psychology bears upon value issues, so it feels right for me to return to the difficult problems on this similar occasion [8].

In the interim, the discipline of applied bioethics has become increasingly professionalized and institutionalized. Although I had a hand in developing the human subjects code for the American Psychological Association, I have remained an incorrigible amateur [9]. I am not an "ethicist!" I want, on this occasion, to make an advantage of my amateur standing, to share concerns and perplexities that involve us all *as* amateurs. We may be professionals as scientists, teachers, and practitioners; the difficult value issues are those that concern us as interconnected persons. In that capacity we are all amateurs, even the ethicists.

Assumptive Worlds in Collision

A first point that needs to be made explicit can be made very briefly. Since the time of Andie Knutson's research, all the issues that he dealt with remain actively controversial, and new ones continually press for attention: "Baby Doe" cases about surgical intervention with defective infants; "pulling the plug" cases involving the concept of "brain death"; issues of compulsory drug testing or AIDS screening; issues of resource allocation for dialysis and other expensive heroic treatments; China's one-child family policy with its implications for abortion and even female infanticide, its coerciveness, but maybe its social necessity; problems of genetic counseling and decision making, now much complicated by the increasing power of high-tech pre-symptomatic screening of fetuses and adults. Our increasing technical competence complicates our ethical choices rather than simplifying them.

It is also the case that people are in sincere, intense, and often shrill conflict about these and other value issues. Just a week or so ago, I read in my local newspaper an essay by a civil libertarian calling the roll of many issues about which different groups are embattled in righteous mutual intolerance (the health-related issues were only a couple among many others), ending with a statement of his gratitude for the First Amendment guarantees of a free press and the right of peaceful assembly. As he wrote, ". . . if all of these 'good, sincere people' had their way, we would have nothing left of books, magazines, speeches, films and theatrical presentations but Bambi and Bugs Bunny" [10]. That caught my attention since I had just noted how Neil Smelser, speaking for the Academic Senate of the University of California to the Regents of the University at their meeting September 19, 1986, defended the Regents' policy against awarding of honorary degrees by saying wry words to the effect that given the vehement value dissensus on the campuses, who besides Jacques Cousteau would be generally acceptable to receive our honorary doctorate? I guess he didn't consider Bambi and Bugs Bunny.

We are indeed living in a time of value conflicts that seem in principle to be unresolvable. I think it is an appropriate metaphor to speak of *assumptive worlds in collision.* In regard to a great many matters of central human importance, of which Andie Knutson sampled a few, the citizenry, the intellectual and cultural leaders, the political leaders, the health professionals are divided among themselves, starting from different premises and coming to different conclusions; they cannot argue with each other persuasively.

The Collapse of Moral Community

The moral philosopher Alasdair MacIntyre gives essentially the right diagnosis of this situation, I think, in his contribution to a Hastings Center symposium volume and in his modern classic, *After Virtue* [11, 12]. His view of our contemporary crisis is a grim one, which I take seriously without following him to the same conclusions. In his analysis from the history of philosophy, he contends that the terms and claims that pass each other by in our ethical arguments are relics of coherent ethical world views that have lost their meaning for us, so that our ethical controversies become incoherent and close to nonsensical. Linked with his critique from the history of ideas is an essentially Durkheimian sociological assertion: that such coherent world views are the expression of the society as a moral community, something that we have lost. Lacking moral community, the best we can do is *negotiate*.

Thus, to pick an example from an area apart from health, MacIntyre sees the Supreme Court as keeping [12, pp. 235–236]:

> . . . the peace between rival social groups adhering to rival and incompatible principles of justice by displaying a fairness which consists in evenhandedness in its adjudications. So the Supreme Court in *Bakke* both forbade precise ethnic quotas for admission to colleges and universities, but allowed discrimination in favor of previously deprived minority groups. . . . [It] played the role of a peacemaking or trucekeeping body by negotiating its way through an impasse of conflict, not by invoking our shared moral first principles. For our society as a whole has none.

Will the emerging Reagan Supreme Court define its role in the same fashion, or will it attempt to adjudicate in terms of first principles—as *it* conceives of them? To pose that question is both to accept the cogency of MacIntyre's analysis and to raise some glimmerings of doubt about the warrant for his evident regret at our present state of affairs. The tradition of liberal individualism which MacIntyre deplores still has its advantages.

Our contemporary American society does not provide us with the comforts of moral community, but neither does it impose its severer constraints upon us. The modern world that we inhabit has lost the coherence that was universal in the local parochial cultures which were once the common human lot. Increasingly we live in a flux of worldwide communication and confrontation, in which youth crazes spread around the globe little hindered by political or ideological boundaries and barriers. We live in a world in which, for the worldwide cultural elite, we have physical and psychological access to the entire historical and cultural range of art styles that André Malraux evoked for us in his elaborate image of the "museum without walls" [13]—yet also a world in which we find it hard to settle on our own styles, or to enjoy our contemporary artists as much as we still enjoy their predecessors in the museums. Our world is one in which the sacred meanings of traditional religion have substantially eroded, yet also one in which new fundamentalisms, Christian and Moslem, are militantly asserting themselves against the pervasive secularism. From the standpoint of any one of the contending new absolutist views, religious or ideological, the cacaphony of contending voices is evil because it denies the Truth. The trouble is,

the different versions of the Truth—the different assumptive worlds—
contend and collide with one another. Who can be *sure* of having the
truth—or rather, given the dissension, who *ought* to be sure? History is
replete with examples of how sincere representatives of contending assumptive worlds have successfully sought to slay each other.

It was the great virtue of modern liberalism, from the time of Voltaire
and the Enlightenment until just yesterday, to recognize and deplore the
damage done in the name of moral consensus. From the nineteenth
century until quite recently, participant observers seemed confident that
in pluralistic modern societies, democratic institutions would enable people to modulate their claims against one another and to accommodate
them for the most part to the good of all. Perhaps it is our loss of faith
in progress, whether in the metaphysical realms of the Hegelian or
Marxist dialectic or in the crasser materialism of technological advance
and economic growth, that makes us more strident, less willing to accommodate, when our basic assumptions come in conflict. Or am I
neglecting the extent of strident conflict in a past that is too easy to
idealize?

MacIntyre is nostalgic for the dream of moral community that he
identifies with the Aristotelian tradition. Since he cannot expect to turn
the clock or the calendar back, he ends his book by evoking the situation
of citizens of the incipient Dark Ages in the late Roman Empire when
the challenge, as he reconstructs it, was to withdraw from the ruined
shell of the empire to sow the germs of moral community anew. Thus
with us, too, he says [12, p. 245]:

> What matters at this stage is the construction of local forms of community
> within which civility and the intellectual and moral life can be sustained
> through the new dark ages which are already upon us. . . . This time,
> however, the barbarians are not waiting beyond the frontiers; they have
> already been governing us for quite some time. And it is our lack of
> consciousness of this that constitutes part of our predicament. We are
> waiting not for a Godot, but for another—doubtless very different—St.
> Benedict.

I keep quoting MacIntyre because I agree with much of his vision of our
current predicament and find the rest of it tempting. I am quite capable
of being nostalgic too! I doubt, all the same, whether nostalgia is an
adequate response to our situation. In retrospect, the Utopian communes
of the 1960s were more a symptom of our plight than a solution to it.

Nostalgia for Moral Community

Important recent social critics from the social and behavioral sciences share MacIntyre's nostalgia. Seymour Sarason, for example, has been an eloquent critic of the ways in which psychology contributes to what he sees as the pathological individualism of American society [14, 15]. Since, as he says [15, p. 899]:

> One of the laws governing human behavior is that "you always pay a price; there is no free lunch," . . . one must ask what price has been paid in the substitution of the concepts of morals and values for that of sin as a transgression of divine law? I would suggest, as have many others, that the price we paid was in the weakening of the sense of interconnections among the individual, the collectivity, and ultimate purpose and meaning of human existence.

Sarason discusses in these terms the case of Baby Jane Doe in which the parents did not wish to permit a life-sustaining operation for their severely defective daughter [15, p. 902]:

> If *my* seriously defective offspring is *my* responsibility, about whom I make life and death decisions according to *my* morality, it is quite consistent with the increasingly dominant ideology of individual rights, responsibility, choice, and freedom. If I experience the issue as *mine*, it is because there is nothing in my existence to make it *ours*. And by ours I mean a social-cultural network and traditions that engender in members an obligation to be a part of the problem and possible solution. It is *my* offspring, but whatever problems I have in regard to that offspring are not mine alone. I can count on others in predictable ways, I am not alone with problem . . .
>
> Those who were supportive of the parents' decision not to permit the surgery seemed totally unaware of the possibility that they might be reinforcing aspects of our society that contribute to the sense of isolation and loneliness, aspects that work against the sense of community.

Neither the individualistic proponents of the parents' position nor its religious opponents seemed to him to give adequate weight to the complex interconnections between his triad of perspectives—those of the individual, of the collectivity, and of transcendent sources of meaning. At root he sees the human costs of our secular individualistic society as too high.

Here at Berkeley where we are honoring Andie Knutson, Robert

Bellah [16] and his colleagues mainly from sociology take a similarly critical view of the human costs of American secular individualism in their justly acclaimed book, *Habits of the Heart*. They regret how, at least in California, the culture of psychotherapy has provided members of the affluent middle class with a language of individual costs and benefits to replace the old language of morality appropriate to problematic but committed relationships. They too lament the lack of genuine community, and of the essentially religious basis of shared meaning and value which they see as an inherent aspect of community. There is much in common among the perspectives of MacIntyre, Sarason, and Bellah and his colleagues.

The predicament to which they are trying to sensitize us is real. Modern Western society, and America especially, are uncommonly individualistic in comparison with the spectrum of contemporary and historic cultures, and this extreme individualism is at a cost. As many contributors to the classic tradition of sociological theory have noted in different ways, modern society is deficient in the sense of community, deficient in moral consensus. Indeed we lack consensual first principles. But what are we to do about it?

How Can We Live without Moral Community?

Like it or not, we live in a world of pluralistic value perspectives. We cannot regain our traditional innocence, we cannot recreate community by preaching, prayer, or fiat. In ethics, our situation is the same as it is in aesthetics, where the breakdown of value consensus, the corrosion of cultural tradition, is quite parallel. Our unprecedented exposure to the arts of many times and places allows us to appreciate a wider range of artistic expression than ever before. But even though modern consumers of LPs and compact discs may prefer Bach to Bartok; even though modern orchestras can perform both to perfection, modern composers cannot validly write music like Bach's—any more than modern painters can validly paint like Leonardo, or Van Gogh, or Monet, whose works so many of us prefer to what is current. We are willy-nilly creatures of our own anomic time, and we can only create by participating in it authentically.

In this time of pluralism, those of us who are nevertheless convinced that our own assumptive world is or ought to be valid for everybody

else have several options. On MacIntyre's suggestion, they might withdraw with likeminded people to cultivate their shared version of consensual community, awaiting the new St. Benedict. Given the value of
diversity, it is fine that some people choose this option. Alternatively, the
convinced absolutists might try to *impose* their view of the world on the
others whom they cannot convince—and we've seen that others mostly
cannot be convinced about these things. To an unfortunate degree, this
is the strategy of the "right to lifers" who see their definitions of human
life as God-given or, what amounts to the same thing, as written into
Natural Law. But coercive solutions to a clash of assumptive worlds
have their own heavy costs—not only in the sphere of international
conflict. Since rational persuasion mostly does not work, what remains
is negotiation and mutually respectful accommodation, in the light of as
full a sharing as can be attained of what each party understands to be
the relevant facts, including facts about each others' value perspectives.
But this is just the kind of process of negotiation that MacIntyre disparaged in the Supreme Court's handling of the Bakke case. Compared with
the alternatives, liberal democratic institutions are not all that bad! It is
also a process to which empirical information of the sort that the behavioral sciences trade it can make a contribution.

From my own secular humanist perspective (my assumptive framework should be apparent by now), there are simply no definitive answers
to *any* ethical questions available to us except answers that we have
negotiated in the past and can continue to negotiate among one another
[17]. Of course, I am using "negotiation" in a broad and informal sense.
Here I am in full agreement with Norma Haan and her colleagues in
their book, *On Moral Grounds* [18]. In this connection, they challenge
the old conventional barrier between facts and values head on—the
barrier embodied in the charge that in controversies about values, any
appeal to matters of fact exhibits the "naturalistic fallacy." In effect,
they embrace the naturalistic fallacy cheerfully, asserting that if we rule
out revelation, unexamined tradition, and coercion, empirical evidence
of one kind or another is all we have left to help us in our ethical
negotiations. From this view, sensitization to the complexity of ethical
issues (which ethicists can help with) and empirical facts of the sort
behavioral science can provide (including facts about one another's value
perspectives) can contribute to negotiated outcomes that are humanly
more satisfactory. The more nearly we approximate the state of moral
community, the simpler and more satisfying the negotiation, which—

unlike withdrawal or coercion—at least points toward the cultivation of community.

Ethics in Health Decisions: Two Instances

My discussion of the dilemmas of ethical disagreement has strayed from the area of health decisions that Andie Knutson was concerned with. To bring us back, let me pick two examples from my recent reading. One is Elliot Valenstein's remarkable cautionary tale, his recent history of psychosurgery [19]. The other is a recent discussion by Ruth Faden of the ethical implications of the powerful new methods of pre-symptomatic screening in fetuses and adults [20].

In *Great and Desperate Cures*, Valenstein tells the story of lobotomy, the grossly mutilating brain operation performed on the mentally ill around the world between 1935, when the operation was introduced by Egas Moniz, an eminent Portuguese neurologist and statement, and 1960 when the "epidemic" was essentially ended and the procedures discredited [19]. Between 1948 and 1952, at the crest of the wave, tens of thousands of the operations were performed, in the United States with the enthusiastic promotion of Walter Freeman, a leading figure in the neurology and psychiatry establishment. (In 1949, Moniz received the Nobel prize in medicine for his part—just when the utility of the procedure was beginning to be questioned.) Valenstein shows how the disgraceful episode arose from extreme personal ambition, organicist medical ideology, wishful thinking on the part of both the medical community and the public, and uncritical promotion without any check from carefully controlled clinical trials, and goes on to assert that the same conditions that led to the fad of psychosurgery continue to prevail in medicine today.

In our present context, however, I am most interested in his argument that we cannot turn to either scientific or ethical principles for secure guidance in regard to what risks are justifiable when patients suffer severely from conditions for which current therapies are not effective. Treatments work that we do not understand, and knowledgeable people will disagree about the theoretical justification of any innovative therapy. As for ethics [19, p. 295]:

A risk with a successful outcome is usually not questioned. Where no effective therapy exists for desperately ill patients, equally ethical and knowledgeable physicians may disagree about treatment. Some risks have to be taken, and some harm will inevitably ensue along with some benefit.

Firm established procedures are needed to *limit* the harm, as it was not limited in the case of psychosurgery. Obligatory testing procedures or clinical trials that do not depend on professional self-regulation are needed—procedures such as those that have for some time been institutionalized for new drugs, but are used sporadically at best in most experimental medicine.

If I read Valenstein correctly, the ethical issues involved in psychosurgery did *not* primarily involve clashes of assumptive world views. Rather, common sense ethics was being applied by psychiatrist-surgeons and the public alike, and it was not good enough. Consensus conferences, had there been any, would also not have been good enough. What was lacking were controlled data on the actual consequences of the procedures. On the psychosocial side of mental health, the case could be made that the rapid and ill-prepared deinstitutionalization of the mentally ill, for which I take some responsibility as an officer of the Joint Commission on Mental Illness and Health of the 1950s, had unexamined consequences that are socially almost as irreversible as those of psychosurgery. More than a decade ago, Donald Campbell argued for treating reforms as experiments, studying their consequences in pilot trials before putting them into general operation [21]. In a more propitious political climate, perhaps we might get back to his good ideas on that score.

My quotations from Valenstein remind us that empirical research, including behavioral science, can bear on serious ethical issues in a much more direct, less ambiguous way than my earlier discussion may have seemed to imply. From Ruth Faden, a psychologist who is co-author of the recent classic on informed consent, I take another example that returns us to the context initiated by our concern with Andie Knutson's work [20, 22].

At the recent meetings of the American Psychological Association, Faden presented a complex panorama of the ethical issues posed by the human genetic techniques that are becoming available to determine susceptibility to a wide range of diseases before the symptoms appear [20]. Down's syndrome can already be screened for in the fetus, and genetic testing for Huntington's disease was to begin this fall in both fetuses and adults. We are told that a genetic test for cystic fibrosis should be on the market shortly. Screening seems to be in the immediate offing for a number of other diseases in which genetic factors make for selective susceptibility rather than causing them directly. These developments raise a host of ethical problems, including the issue of whether screening is ethical before effective therapies have been made available, and how to avoid injustice—what Faden calls "geneism"—when genetic information about disease susceptibility can be used to deny health insurance or make it unaffordable, or to screen potential employees for the financial advantage of the employer. The equivalent of clinical trials followed through behavioral research seems needed for guidance as the new technology is deployed in practice, but, as Faden notes, such trials have their own substantial moral and pragmatic difficulties.

The issues about the meaning of fetal life that Andie Knutson explored among public health professionals seem likely to be substantially reframed by the new technologies, according to Faden. Until recently, one potentially serious problem was the implicit challenge to the moral and psychological acceptability of "late" (second trimester) abortions posed by gains in early fetal viability resulting from advances in neonatal care. Selective abortions following amniocentesis usually occur at a time that is very close to what is becoming the new boundary of viability. This difficult situation seems about to be remedied by the new technology of chorionic villus sampling, which permits fetal diagnosis and selective abortion cleanly in the first trimester. On the other side of the balance are rapid developments in the field of fetal therapy. As Faden writes, "depending on the circumstances, increasingly the same fetus could be either a 'patient' or an 'abortus' " [20, p. 18].

All of these unsettling developments are complicated by the unknown psychological impact of the now increasingly prevalent use of the fetal sonogram, which, as Faden says [20, p. 18]:

> . . . has the capacity to make compelling the human characteristics of the well developed fetus, emphasizing its reality and individuality. The impact of the visual image on prospective parents and health care providers is as yet unknown.

She cites Daniel Callahan and others as raising the possibility that the developments [20, p. 16]:

> . . . in fetal visualization, fetal therapy, and the intensive care of premature neonates may be altering our communal psychological and moral views about the fetus and abortion. . . . It seems plausible that as the fetal sono-

gram increasingly becomes baby's first picture, and as fetuses increasingly become fully patients of fetal surgeons and the like, the fetus will move more publicly into the human social community.

Andie Knutson's kind of research is needed more than ever to monitor these changes, and to inform our consideration of the complex ethical issues that they raise.

Coda

We are not about to achieve the state of moral consensus, the ideal community, in which ethical solutions to novel dilemmas such as those posed by innovations in medical technology can readily be derived from first principles that are agreed upon consensually. Nor, I think, need we regard ourselves as actually on the brink of another Dark Ages, *if* we can avoid disaster and possible extinction in nuclear holocaust. In our nonconsensual, too individualistic society, negotiated ethical decisions are the best we can do—unless and until the new St. Benedict arrives. Until that millennium, behavioral science in the manner of Andie Knutson can contribute useful, even indispensable information to the negotiation process.

References

1. A. L. Knutson, *The Individual, Society, and Health Behavior*, Russell Sage Foundation, New York, 1965.
2. H. Cantril, *The "Why's" of Man's Experience*, Macmillan, New York, 1950.
3. J. D. Frank, *Persuasion and Healing: A Comparative Study of Psychotherapy* (Revised edition), The Johns Hopkins University Press, Baltimore, 1973.
4. A. L. Knutson, When Does a Human Life Begin? Viewpoints of Public Health Professionals, *American Journal of Public Health*, 57, pp. 2163–2177, 1967.
5. ———, The Definition and Value of a New Human Life, *Social Science and Medicine*, 1, pp. 7–29, 1967.
6. ———, Body Transplants and Ethical Values: Viewpoints of Public Health Professionals, *Social Science and Medicine*, 2, pp. 393–414, 1968.
7. ———, *Beliefs and Values: Conceptualizations about a Human Life and the Value Judgments of Public Health Professionals*, unpublished manuscript, 1979.
8. M. B. Smith, Psychology and Values, *Journal of Social Issues,* 34:4, pp. 181–199, 1978.

9. American Psychological Association, *Ethical Principles in the Conduct of Research with Human Participants*, American Psychological Association, Washington, DC, 1973.

10. J. R. Joelson, Nothing is Left but Bambi or Bugs Bunny, *Sentinel*, Santa Cruz, September 18, 1986.

11. A. MacIntyre, A Crisis in Moral Philosophy: Why Is the Search for the Foundations of Ethics so Frustrating? in *Knowing and Valuing: The Search for Common Roots*, H. T. Englehardt and D. Callahan (eds.), The Hastings Center, Hastings-on-Hudson, New York, 1980.

12. A. MacIntyre, *After Virtue: A Study in Moral Theory*, University of Notre Dame Press, Notre Dame, Indiana, 1981.

13. A. Malraux, *The Voices of Silence*, (S. Gilbert trans.), Doubleday, Garden City, New York, 1953.

14. S. B. Sarason, *Psychology Misdirected*, Free Press, New York, 1981.

15. ———, And What Is the Public Interest? *American Psychologist, 41*, pp. 899–905, 1986.

16. R. N. Bellah, R. Madsen, W. M. Sullivan, A. Swindler, and S. M. Tipton, *Habits of the Heart: Individualism and Commitment in American Life*, University of California Press, Berkeley, 1985.

17. M. B. Smith, Toward a Secular Humanistic Psychology, *Journal of Humanistic Psychology, 26*:1, pp. 7–26, 1986.

18. N. Haan, E. Aerts, and B.A.B. Cooper, *On Moral Grounds: The Search for Practical Morality*, New York University Press, New York, 1985.

19. E. S. Valenstein, *Great and Desperate Cures: The Rise and Decline of Psychosurgery and Other Radical Treatments for Mental Illness*, Basic Books, New York, 1986.

20. R. R. Faden, Presymptomatic Screening in Fetuses and Adults: Moral and Psychological Issues, paper presented to American Psychological Association, Washington, DC, August 1986.

21. D. C. Campbell, Reforms as Experiments, *American Psychologist, 24*, pp. 409–429, 1969.

22. R. R. Faden and T. L. Beauchamp, with H. M. P. King, *A History and Theory of Informed Consent*, Oxford University Press, New York, 1986.

Chapter Thirteen

The Psychology of Prejudice

In the turbulent times since the appearance of two classics in psychology—*The Authoritarian Personality*, by T. W. Adorno, Else Frenkel-Brunswik, Daniel J. Levinson, and R. Nevitt Sanford (New York: Harper, 1950), and *The Nature of Prejudice*, by Gordon W. Allport (Cambridge, Mass.: Addison-Wesley, 1954)—remarkable events have transformed the terms in which we confront issues of justice and democratic relations between racial and other groups in the United States and in the world at large. Both books were written in the shadow of the Holocaust, a horror so unimaginable that neither tried seriously to come to terms with it. (*The Authoritarian Personality* [*TAP*] had it more explicitly in mind: two of the authors were emigrés.) Allport's skillful synthesis came out almost simultaneously with the Supreme Court's *Brown v. Board of Education* decision, the act of "simple justice" (1) that set the stage for our present conflicts about racial policy in American schools. The years since have seen the collapse of the old colonial empires in Africa and the emergence of the Third World as an international presence.

In American social politics an internal "Third World" has since found articulate voice to challenge the tarnishing ideal of the Melting Pot (now still shiny in Israel), which, at least in lip service, has been virtually replaced by cultural pluralism. Negroes have become blacks. The women's movement, meanwhile, has added *sexism* to *racism* in our vocabulary of social criticism. There is now widespread agreement that racism and sexism are bad—a substantial shift in the social norms since the post-war years when the books were written.

The ground has shifted. Black-white relations are now more tense in the urban North, not the old South, with busing and the schools a focus of conflict. Controversy about affirmative action to correct old wrongs has divided blacks and Jews, as controversy about the role of Israel has embroiled Jews with voices of the Third World. The struggle for justice

220 TOWARD AN EMANCIPATORY HUMAN SCIENCE

seems as problematic as ever, although remarkable gains have been made against prejudice. Do our two classics still talk to our present situation, given all these changes?

The Two Books Compared

It is hard to imagine two books on the same general topic that differ so sharply in approach. Allport's book is a readily accessible, scholarly, reasonable synthesis of what was then known about "the nature of prejudice" and discrimination, interdisciplinary in perspective though written by the most respected expositor of personality and social psychology at mid-century. It did not offer *a* theory of prejudice; as befits a concrete social problem that cuts across the boundaries of theories and disciplines, it sought to put existing theories and the evidence for them in perspective and, taking theory and evidence into account, to provide guidelines for social action in the service of democratic values in intergroup relations.

From Allport we learn about actual group differences including traits due to victimization. We consider the familiar in-group, out-group distinction, and ways in which conformity to transmitted culture perpetuates scapegoating. We examine the psychological roots of prejudice in the economies of normal cognitive process (which favor stereotyping), in the psychodynamics of frustration and aggression and projection, and in childhood and adult learning. The data upon which Allport draws have inevitably become dated, but since there have been no real breakthroughs in social psychology and sociology in the intervening years— only new mini-theories, shifts in emphasis, and accretion of information —the perspective that Allport elaborated is still good applied social science. We return later to consider ways in which the changed social context compels us to read it differently.

TAP is a different sort of classic: the kind that is universally respected but rarely read. Really a collection of research monographs between a single pair of covers rather than a "book," it is quite unreadable except by specialists, and it taxes even *their* patience. The large critical literature that it spawned during the fifties almost entirely concerned the "F scale" and its technical deficiencies. (The F scale was a pencil-and-paper measure of fascist ways of thinking that was offered as an indirect measure of prejudice and of anti-democratic attitudes.) Subsequent discussion virtually ignored other solid studies reported in *TAP* that had none of the technical defects of the pencil-and-paper research on the F scale— studies of prejudiced vs. unprejudiced neuropsychiatric patients and San Quentin prisoners—and also bypassed the careful qualitative analysis of antidemocratic ideology provided by Adorno, who is now much more widely known in the social science community as one of the principal figures in the Frankfurt school of Marxist "critical theory" in sociology, together with Horkheimer, Fromm, Marcuse, and, later, Habermas.

In contrast with Allport's text, *TAP* did propose a theory, a broadly psychoanalytic account of the prejudiced personality. In giving definitive statement to this theory, its status as a (still unread) classic is secure, although its account of the phenomena of racial and ethnic prejudice gets increasingly dated. Since few readers of this essay will have read *TAP*, I need first to summarize the point of view that Adorno, Frenkel-Brunswik, Levinson, and Sanford developed in their thousand-page tome, drawing here on a review of the book that I wrote in 1950.

> The California investigators, to put it figuratively, set out to track a jackal and found themselves at grips with a behemoth. Their initial studies indicated that anti-Semitism, far from being an isolated though unrespectable psychological phenomenon, is an integral component of a general "ethnocentric ideology." Ethnocentrism, pursued in turn, is revealed as the expression of a distinctive "authoritarian character structure" whose unadmitted needs and defenses it serves. . . .
>
> [The authoritarian personality] characterizes the basically weak and dependent individual who has sacrificed his capacity for genuine experience of self and others in order to maintain a precarious order and safety. In the type case, he confronts with a facade of spurious strength a world in which rigidly stereotyped categories are substituted for the affectionate and individualized experience of which he is incapable. Such a person, estranged from inner values, lacks self-awareness and shuns intraception [subjective thought]. His judgments are governed by a punitive conventional moralism, reflecting external standards in which he remains insecure since he has failed to make them really his own. His relations with others depend on considerations of power, success, and adjustment, in which people figure as means rather than ends, and achievement is not valued for its own sake. In his world, the good, the powerful, and the in-group stand in fundamental opposition to the immoral, the weak, the out-group. For all that he seeks to align himself with the former, his underlying

feelings of weakness and self-contempt commit him to a constant and embittered struggle to prove to himself and others that he really belongs to the strong and good. Prejudice against outgroups of all kinds and colors is a direct corollary of this personality structure. (2)

This view of prejudice as an aspect of "authoritarianism" is an outgrowth of the psychoanalytic-Marxist interpretation of Nazism as expounded by Erich Fromm—another Frankfurt alumnus—in *Escape from Freedom.* (3) It brings into rational coherence the patent irrationalities of virulent anti-Semitism, McCarthy-ite anti-communism, "paranoid" anti-fluoridation, and other manifestations of a conspiratorial world view that sees life as a Manichean struggle between Good and Evil forces. I believe that it contains powerful insights into one set of components of the social irrationality of our times.

Whereto Authoritarianism?

The stream of social psychological research stimulated by *TAP* fell far short of doing justice to these ideas. Apart from Else Frenkel-Brunswik's own research on the development of ethnocentrism in children (4) and on "intolerance of ambiguity" as a style of thinking (5), and Milton Rokeach's reformulation in terms of "dogmatism" (6), most of this work got stuck on procedural technicalities, as I have already noted. Interest turned elsewhere before the substantive issues raised by *TAP* had been adequately clarified, much less resolved. So my attempt to appraise the present relevance of the theory of authoritarianism has to proceed without the kind of well-focused evidence that the theory deserves.

Even if one grants that authoritarianism was not so tightly cohesive a syndrome as the authors of *TAP* believed, and that some of the ideological features that they ascribed to defensive psychodynamics can be understood more parsimoniously as unsophisticated responses of working-class people (the "hard-hat" mentality), I think *TAP* gives a persuasive account of some ingredients of prejudice and of other forms of social irrationality that resist persuasion by evidence. There *are* bigots whose bigotry serves them as a buffer against recognition of inner weakness and of their own unacceptable impulses. In retrospect, however, Allport seems to have been right in regarding characterological bigotry as only one among many matters to be considered by an eclectic theory of prejudice, and probably not the main story at that.

So far as the role of education and the schools is concerned, this is altogether fortunate. Ever since the publication of *TAP*, its critics have complained about its dismal implications for social action. Although it is not entirely fair to put the argument so baldly, one could conclude from *TAP* that nothing can be done about prejudice except to psycho-analyze the bigots in the present generation, and to rear the next gener-ation more lovingly and democratically. A view of prejudice as rooted more in real-life relationships than in the unfinished business of intrapsy-chic conflict leaves much more room for democratic schooling to play a preventive and corrective role.

I would guess, too, that the theory of authoritarianism was truer of traditional Germany than of America, and true of more Americans at mid-century than today. One of the best documented trends in recent American psychohistory is the declining reliance on arbitary authority in child rearing—a trend that has led to the present virtual extinction of the cardinal sins for which I remember being spanked and closeted in my own childhood; Impudence and Impertinence. Indeed, the collapse of arbitrary authority not only in the family but in school, in business, and in government as well has brought with it new problems with which we are all familiar: it is still difficult for us to identify and accept rational authority based on competence. All in all, the classical account of fami-lially transmitted authoritarianism, with parents idealized and repressed conflict papered over, now looks historically dated. Life in late twenti-eth-century American society is still complicated by typical characterol-ogical problems, but I think they are mainly different ones from those highlighted in *TAP*.

The pleasure-seeking, disillusioned, and uncommitted individualism that, beginning in the 1960s, affected affluent youth (outliving the tide of political protest) seems to be spreading through the blue-collar ranks. (7) This "new narcissism" (if it feels good, do it) seems to me to reflect an historically understandable decline of hopefulness that carries over to lessened aspirations for democratic intergroup relations—and weaker commitment to the struggle to actualize democratic ideals. Many tradi-tional sources of meaning in American life seem in jeopardy, and worri-some substitutes in the cheap thrill and in the irrational occult are appearing.

Allport's Durability

Allport's compendious book still invites reading and defies summary. What seemed wise and judicious in 1954 mostly still seems so today. Problems that Allport regarded as complex and unsettled at mid-century—his treatment of the dynamics of aggression comes to mind—are mostly still not fully resolved. His pervasive fair-mindedness, his democratic values, and his concern for evidence continues to set a model for humane, problem-focused social science. Here I will note only three points among many on which Allport's position seems to me to have been remarkably sound.

In reviewing a research literature that has greatly expanded since (8), Allport concluded that contact between members of majority and minority groups is likely to reduce ethnic prejudice when the members of the respective groups are equal in status and are interdependent, in pursuit of common goals, especially when their cooperative relationship is sanctioned by institutional supports. His conclusion still stands; psychologists and educators continue to draw implications from it for programming in schools.

Although, as a psychologist, Allport gave closest attention to the dispositions and processes of individuals, he accepted the emerging consensus—certainly the prevailing view of sociologists then and now—that "it is wiser to attack segregation and discrimination than to attack prejudice directly. For even if one dents the attitudes of the individual in isolation, he is still confronted by social norms that he cannot surmount. And until segregation is weakened, conditions will not exist that permit equal status contacts in pursuit of common objectives" (p. 509). The intellectual climate of the ensuing years, as I note later, would give even stronger emphasis to this statement of priority.

Throughout, Allport stressed the many-sided nature of the problem of prejudice and discrimination. The complexity of the problem requires an integration of psychological and sociological theories and an orchestrated diversity of strategies. No friend of "simple and sovereign" theories or remedies, Allport remains in this respect a dependable guide through uncertainty and complexity.

Prejudice and Justice

Yet there is a respect in which the shifting ground, landmarks of which were noted at the outset, leaves even Allport's book something of a period piece. It is less a matter of the book's explicit content than of the point of view from which the book was written that is taken for granted. And that is the point of view of the liberal white Gentile, of which species Allport himself was an admirable example, not at all vulnerable to any conventional charges of hypocrisy. The underlying aim was to spread the gospel of liberalism and tolerance among Gentiles and whites. From the perspective of white Gentiles, their inner experiential fact of prejudice remains central after all, more than the objective facts of discrimination and injustice as members of the ethnic minority groups encounter them. And implicitly, Allport treated prejudice and discrimination mainly as problems for whites and Gentiles to deal with—just as Gunnar Myrdal, in *An American Dilemma* (9), called the "Negro problem" really a white problem. There is still a sense in which both were right: whites and Gentiles should not duck their responsibility. But the new, important fact is that blacks, Chicanos, women, and other "minorities" are taking responsibility for getting justice in society. Jews have mainly got it.

The black movement and the women's movement have made a fundamental difference to our thinking about these matters. The nonviolent protest of Martin Luther King, the violent black eruptions in Watts and elsewhere, the demonstration of proud and truculent separatism by Malcolm X and the Black Panthers (a small minority of a minority) all contributed to shifting the initiative to the minorities themselves. Suddenly, *respect* (for one's own group, as well as between groups) seemed much more important and consequential than liking or disliking (which is what prejudice is mainly about). And *racism*, a rhetorical term identified with minority protests—which for all its ambiguities implies consequential effects more than subjective feelings and intentions—began to replace *prejudice* as the target of concern.

The transformed frame of evaluation can be seen in still broader perspective. Both books were written in the postwar period in which the intellectual atmosphere, as we now see in retrospect, was dominated by "consensus theory." Our historians were then reconstructing a benign core American tradition, to which our literary critics also sought to contribute. Our sociological theorists wrote of social equilibrium and the homeostatic mechanisms of societal stability. Our pluralist theorists of political behavior saw our party system as negotiating consensus among competing interest groups. In the same vein, the assumed goal of our psychologists and sociologists of ethnic relations was "the reduction of intergroup tensions." (10) But this was not what Martin Luther King, or Eldridge Cleaver, or Malcolm X was up to!

By now, various versions of "conflict theory" are in increasing ascendancy. If emancipation and justice, not brotherly love or social equilibrium, are the aim, conflict may be essential and unavoidable. From this contemporary perspective, much of the work in intercultural education reviewed by Allport has an air of dated piety. But recently there has been a recession in the morale of the civil rights movement, a resurgence of social conservatism, and perhaps the pendulum is swinging once more.

I should not overdraw the implications of these swings of the cultural pendulum. White Gentile prejudice still does matter, and blacks and Jews can be prejudiced too. That the traditionally oppressed groups are becoming more aware of their oppression ("consciousness raising," another term that is new since our classics) and more capable politically of doing something about it does not make the prejudiced attitudes and discriminatory behaviors of their oppressors irrelevant. Whatever our views of conflict vs. consensus, the interdependence of our ethnic and religious groups is a matter of compelling fact. We are all ethnics, and, except for native Americans (still another significantly new term!), all immigrants. Willy-nilly, we are involved in each other's lives and fates. We can still learn much from Allport and, with more serious qualification, from the authors of *The Authoritarian Personality* about why we continue to have such difficulty living with one another. Especially from Allport, we can still get wise guidance in our attempts to give more human substance to our democratic aspirations.

NOTES

1. Richard Kluger, *Simple Justice*, New York: Knopf, 1976.

2. M. Brewster Smith, "Review of *The Authoritarian Personality*," *Abnormal and Social Psychology* 45, 4 (1950): 775–779.

3. Erich Fromm, *Escape from Freedom*, New York: Farrar and Rinehart, 1941.

4. Else Frenkel-Brunswik, "A Study of Prejudice in Children," *Human Relations* 1 (1948): 295–306.

5. Else Frenkel-Brunswik, "Intolerance of Ambiguity as a Personality Variable," *Personality* 18 (1949): 108–143.

6. Milton Rokeach, *The Open and Closed Mind*, New York: Basic Books, 1960.

7. Daniel Yankelovich, *The New Morality: A Profile of American Youth in the Seventies*, New York: McGraw-Hill, 1974. See also Peter Marin, "The New Narcissism," *Harper's* October 1972, pp. 45–56.

8. Yehuda Amir, "Contact Hypothesis in Ethnic Relations," *Psychological Bulletin* 71 (1969): 319–342.

9. Gunnar Myrdal, *An American Dilemma: The Negro Problem and American Democracy*, New York: Harper, 1944.

10. Robin M. Williams, *The Reduction of Intergroup Tensions*, Bulletin 57, New York: Social Science Research Council, 1947.

Chapter Fourteen

The Social Scientists' Role in *Brown v. Board of Education*
A Non-Revisionist Appraisal

We all agree that the quarter-century anniversary of *Brown v. Board of Education* is an occasion for stock taking in the struggle for racial justice in America. It is also a time for recommitment.

Each of my fellow panel members has a stronger substantive basis for contributing to this symposium than I do, and I want to leave the lion's share of time to them. All the same, I am proud to be part of the panel, and I am even prouder of having played a part in the events leading up to the Supreme Court's momentous decision. But my part was a minor one, offering testimony (along with Is Chein and Ken Clark) in the Richmond case that fed into *Brown v. Board of Education* and signing the Social Scientists' Brief. Kenneth Clark was *the* central figure in developing the social science support for the NAACP case, and, working with Ken, Stuart Cook and Isador Chein did the heavy work on the brief, which I merely signed in good company. In the years since, Stuart has contributed in innumerable ways to our research understanding of prejudice and intergroup relations. So he represents the current forefront of research as appropriately as Norman Miller, who entered the scene more recently.

I agreed to join the panel partly for sentimental reasons. I remain inordinately proud of a paragraph or so in Richard Kluger's (1976) historical account, *Simple Justice*, and I am just as proud of my anonymous presence along with Ken Clark, Is Chein, and the NAACP legal staff in a picture that Kluger prints, taken on the steps of the Federal Courthouse in Richmond in late February, 1952.

There are also less sentimental reasons for my agreement to participate. I want my voice in the APA on record that psychology and psy-

228

chologists still care about the issues that are symbolized by *Brown v. Board of Education*, issues that have yet to be resolved satisfactorily. Much of the early work preparatory to psychologists' contributing to *Brown v. Board of Education* took place under the auspices of SPSSI, the Society for the Psychological Study of Social Issues, which continues today as a strong APA division and as part of a Public Interest Coalition (PIC) in APA politics. From my SPSSI or PIC point of view, the public responsibilities of psychology continue to require the same assiduous attention that we give so readily to our scientific and professional guild concerns.

For persons who care about social justice—the old liberal causes and some new ones—this is *not* a good time. Understandable cynicism about American government—we can all list many historical reasons for such cynicism, however much we deplore it—has fed into a general retreat from the social liberalism that prevailed in my own young adulthood. Some of our colleagues in the social sciences are contributing to this retreat by rewriting the history of the main liberal enterprises from the New Deal on, supposedly to the discredit of these enterprises but I think mainly to that of the neoconservatives themselves. The War on Poverty gets written off in this vein as the folly of misapplied social science, ignoring the fact that the guns of Vietnam took priority over the butter of social programs before most of the social programs had been tried in depth, and also ignoring the actually impressive side-effects of a number of Poverty programs that really could not have succeeded on the terms in which they were overtly proposed. (An establishment cannot be expected to subsidize its own defeat and replacement! Yet the Poverty programs did generate hope, surgency, and new leadership in their constituencies, and while civil rights gains have still not appreciably reduced the basic inequalities, the transformations that they brought about seem substantial all the same to someone who remembers the amiable, white-produced radio show *Amos and Andy*.)

As controversies about busing, white flight, and affirmative action replace the hard old issue of legally imposed segregation in the South and Border states, the revisionist account proposes to undermine the continuing efforts that we must put forth if we are only to stay even in the struggle for justice. It is hinted in various quarters and said openly in others that the social science testimony in the cases culminating in *Brown v. Board of Education* was tendentious and ungrounded, and, naturally, it is also said that the testimony made no difference—or

230 TOWARD AN EMANCIPATORY HUMAN SCIENCE

maybe, it ought not to have made a difference; this sort of argument quickly gets confused in overrefutation. As we look back on the controversies of 25 years ago, I think it is important to our present morale to know and declare that we have no apologies, only pride, about the role of social scientists and psychologists in the courts of the 1950's.

We need to reground our current efforts toward social justice and effective democracy in hopeful realism—or in realistic hopefulness. I don't believe that Utopias are foreordained or attainable around the corner—or that they ever will be. I think the human enterprise is one of continuing struggle, in which we can hope for the reward of the chance to continue the struggle, if we do our part well, and ought to fear the end of human liberty and perhaps of life as potential punishment if we give up on the challenge. To continue the struggle, we cannot afford false readings of our effective struggles in the past.

I am helped in my reappraisal by a paper Stu Cook (1979) has just written with the subtitle, "Did We Mislead the Supreme Court?" With careful scholarship, Stu confirms what I believed: after a quarter century, the Social Scientists' Brief stands up very well indeed.

He reminds us that the legal challenge to which the brief was responsive was not the one we face today, that of *de facto* Northern urban segregation embedded in a complex nexus of institutional racism rather than in statutory law. It was old-style Southern segregation *de jure*, to which the brief—and earlier oral testimony—spoke with evidence and well-grounded good sense. And the tentative predictions that the brief made about the probable effects of desegregation have hardly been tested in the years since; the desegregation processes studied in subsequent research have seldom been well specified, and for the most part they surely don't fit the principles of effective desegregation outlined in the brief and elaborated in Ken Clark's (1953) "appraisal of the evidence" for the benefit of the Court. We have no occasion to be smug: *Brown v. Board of Education* did not settle the problem of segregation and racial injustice, for all the help and good will of social scientists. But neither do we have reason to apologize. The brief was a solid job, both in the light of knowledge then and of what we have learned since. It made a difference, one in which we can take enduring satisfaction.

This historical appraisal is important because, in the APA, we keep hearing voices that condemn those of us who step forward to bring our psychology to bear in the advocacy of stands on particular social issues— of race and justice, peace and survival, women's rights, corporal punishment, or whatever. The same message keeps getting repeated sanctimoniously, especially by some of our respected scientific colleagues (e.g., Atkinson, 1977): we are said to discredit our standing as scientists (and, it is implied, jeopardize the financial support of our science) if we enter the fray of social controversy as advocates. The desegregation testimony of the 1950's was greeted by many with the same kind of righteous condemnation. Because the advocates of value neutrality and a merely technical role in the marshalling of evidence speak with such unqualified inner assurance on behalf of their own conception of the proper role for psychology and social science, those of us who see a different role for psychology need to be clear about our own position. Our present review of the participation of psychologists and other social scientists in *Brown v. Board of Education* should help.

A *sine qua non*, of course, at the heart of what makes our historical instance something to celebrate, is scrupulous fidelity to the evidence available. It is crucial that Stuart Cook (1979) can answer his own question, "No, indeed, we did *not* mislead the Supreme Court." Stuart and those who worked with him in drafting the brief were first of all competent and scrupulous social scientists. They did not misrepresent the evidence. Necessarily, they went beyond the evidence and drew upon their individual and collective judgment. In so doing, they distressed the scientific purists. It is this inherently judgmental context that makes the signatures attached to the brief and similar statements important, that makes relevant the qualification of expert witnesses. And because the issue is controversial, controversy between psychologists is not to be avoided.

It was not avoided in the cases feeding into *Brown v. Board of Education*. For example, Henry Garrett, a former president of the APA, appeared for the State of Virginia in the Richmond case. Where social controversy concerning central human values is involved, there are bound to be psychologists willing to testify on each contending side. Does this discredit psychology and social science? Only from a very unrealistic perspective on what the social sciences are about.

One can point to the prevalence of conflicting scientific testimony on such technical matters that touch key human interests as the SST (supersonic transport), recombinant DNA, the breeder reactor, and so on—a fair response, when Dick Atkinson (1977) chides politically involved psychologists for bringing discredit on their discipline. Yet I don't think the situation in the social sciences is really comparable to that in physical or biological science and technology. Value considerations are involved more intrinsically, less extrinsically.

Looking on the Richmond case retrospectively, we compare Garrett's testimony with Chein's and mine not just in terms of its representation of presumed psychological fact, but also in terms of the human values that are implicit or explicit. That is as it should be, and I am quite ready to live with the comparison. But Garrett's *was* a minority position in the psychology of 1952. Lest we be too smug about our handling of facts and values in psychology and the social sciences, let me remind you of two examples that are much less comfortable for us to contemplate than our role in *Brown v. Board of Education*.

I am thinking of the generally racist posture of the social sciences, psychology included, around the time of World War I and shortly thereafter (Kamin, 1974). Imagine a consensual "social science brief" from those days on problems of immigration or of segregation! I am also thinking of the scatter of our most competent expert testimony on both sides of the Larry P. case (*Larry P. v. Riles* [343 F. Supp. 306, 1972; 495 F. Supp. 926, 1979])—in which Jane Mercer, Lloyd Humphreys, George Albee, Nadine Lambert, and others just recently testified in support of contrary positions in regard to the use of intelligence tests in the educational classification of California schoolchildren. (After my talk, Federal District Judge Robert F. Peckham banned the use of individual IQ tests in placing black children into EMR [Educable Mentally Retarded] classes in California [cf. Elliot, 1987]).

Looking back to the racism of 60 years ago, I think it helps us to make sense of our present if we accept that discredited past as truly our own, if we do not try to disown it. (Here I am speaking as a white psychologist and social scientist; the case is obviously different for those of minority background.) The racist social scientists of 1920 were surely no more stupid, no less competent than we, and by their own lights they certainly did not see themselves as more in league with the Devil. Their psychology, their social science, was in full continuity with ours. They saw themselves as honorably engaged in the same sort of enterprise. Their disciplines were by no means newborn in the academic world. True theirs was a *different* social science, a different psychology from ours, but that is just my point.

Owning up to our racist past does help us, I think, to maintain that minimal belief in progress that can sustain our efforts. We really do know more, and we have much more powerful techniques for developing evidence, than our predecessors of that racist time. And our value perspectives have changed very substantially, in ways that we cannot help believing make our perspective the more humane. Social science is embedded in human history, both reflecting it and contributing to it; it is not something apart. Value controversy is as much part of the development of social science as factual accretion, conceptual clarification, and technical refinement. We are by no means at the end of the road in changes in value perspectives any more than in empirical development.

The possibility of the Social Scientists' Brief, I am suggesting, depended on the emergence of a new value consensus among social scientists as well as on the amassing of evidence. The anti-racist consensus had emerged through historical processes akin to those in which the new legal consensus was being created. Persistent advocacy by organizations like NAACP had contributed. So had research by scholars like Ken Clark, Franklin Frazier, Otto Klineberg, Gunnar Myrdal. The brief is historically important because of its role in the landmark case that defined the new legal situation. It is a rare instance!

Perhaps the dissensus that characterized testimony in the Larry P. case is more typical of the situations that we currently face. In the testimony in this case, I see no angels or devils. I see competent, engaged psychologists tangling with extremely complex issues and finding themselves unable to come to agreement. The issues involve competing values as much as ambiguous facts. Within APA governance, I have heard the call for developing an "APA position" on the issues in the Larry P. case. But wishing for a consensus won't produce one. I think it is nevertheless responsible and desirable for psychologists to involve themselves in the legal process of social decision, even when they don't agree. The social outcome should be better considered for our participation, and psychology may also be educated in and by the process.

The message I would leave, thus, is easily summarized. *Brown v. Board of Education* was a milestone decision that moved the perennial struggle for social justice along to new positions. Psychologists and social scientists played an appropriate, honorable role of which we can continue to be proud. It was a new role, in which we prided ourselves on being taken seriously by our most respected legal institution.

The social scientists' role depended on both facts and values, in intimate connection with each other. Both classes of considerations are inherently involved in our treatment of controversial social issues. The Social Scientists' Brief was as remarkable for the relatively high degree of value consensus that it reflected as for its good judgment in appraisal of the evidence. The related social issues that currently divide us pose for us a challenge equally complex in terms of producing cogent evidence in our research and integrating it for its bearing on public policy. They seem to me considerably more difficult with respect to our attaining value consensus. On this twenty-fifth anniversary, then, let us renew our commitment to using our greater resources in the never-ending struggle for social justice. The record of *Brown v. Board of Education* gives us occasion for pride, but no excuse to rest on our laurels.

NOTE

Presented at a symposium chaired by John Popplestone at the 1979 meetings of the American Psychological Association, entitled "25 Years After Brown v. Board of Education: Perspectives . . . Prospects." The other participants were Kenneth B. Clark, Norman Miller, Isador Chein, and Stuart W. Cook.

References

Atkinson, R. (1977). Reflections on psychology's past and concerns about its future, *American Psychologist, 32*, 205–210.

Clark, K. B. (1953). Desegregation: An appraisal of the evidence. *Journal of Social Issues, 9* (No.3), 1–77.

Cook, S. W. (1979). Social science and school desegregation: Did we mislead the Supreme Court? *Personality and Social Psychology Bulletin, 5*, 429–237.

Elliott, R. (1987). *Litigating intelligence: IQ tests, special education and social science in the courtroom.* Dover, MA: Auburn House.

Kamin, L. J. (1974). *The science and politics of IQ.* Patomac, MD: Erlbaum.

Kluger, R. (1976). *Simple justice: The history of* Brown v. Board of Education *and black America's struggle for equality.* New York: Knopf.

Chapter 15

Racism, Education, and Student Protest

Anyone, even a social psychologist, who has the temerity to leave his own "turf" and offer comments and advice on such a sensitive topic as racism and student protests on a campus other than his own had best begin by qualifying himself as a witness. In my case, there are two partly qualifying facts to mention. One was my discovery, together with that of an entire contingent of Peace Corp teachers in Ghana whose experience I was studying in 1961–63, that Africans are not "Negroes." All of us, liberal or conservative, prejudiced or relatively unprejudiced, found to our surprise that black people in Africa simply do not fit the conceptual category of "Negro," with the tangle of connotations it has acquired for all Americans, black or white. The "Negro" is an American creation, and the concept has meaning only in the historical context of American slavery and its aftermath. Ever since I made this discovery for myself, I have been sympathetic with the efforts of black Americans to shed the label as tied to a negative identity that they are now in a position to outgrow.

My second qualification comes from studies of student protest undertaken while I was at the University of California at Berkeley.[1] The Free Speech Movement that erupted at Berkeley in the fall of 1964 was, of course, the beginning of the wave of confrontations that have swept American campuses ever since, with echoes elsewhere in the world. This was protest mainly on the part of white students addressed to issues unrelated to the black insurgence.

Yet in the present setting, when a new wave of black confrontations is surging across American campuses, it is significant to note the intimate link between black protest and the FSM outburst at Berkeley. It was no accident that the Free Speech Movement followed the "Mississippi summer." Liberal white students had learned the tactics of protest from working with blacks in Mississippi. They had seen how the traditionally powerless can wield power after all. When political exigencies of the

235

Goldwater-Johnson presidential campaign made it expedient for civil rights activists at Berkeley to hold back on such protest activities as the previous year's sit-ins at the Palace Hotel and on "automobile row" in San Francisco, the energies—and the strategies—that had been mobilized in Mississippi became available for direction against inept paternalism and unwise authority on the campus.

The recent wave of black student protest has special features that distinguish it from protest Berkeley-style, but there is much that we can learn from Berkeley and its aftermath that helps us to understand the current unrest on the campus.

I will, therefore, begin with some general remarks about student protests, and then turn to the topic of "racism" and draw some distinctions that seem helpful to me in grasping the meaning of protest particularly directed against racism on the campus. I will conclude by sharing a personal perspective on some of the challenges, opportunities, and dangers in the present turbulence.

Protest, Berkeley Style

Radical student protest as it has emerged since Berkeley is something new under the sun. We hear much about the generation gap, and Lewis Feuer would have us believe that we are merely dealing with a recurring Oedipal conflict between generations.[2] But however we may evaluate the generational conflict, we can be sure that Feuer's explanation is logically inadequate: A particular historical development can't be explained by a purportedly universal psychological fact. And it ought to be obvious that the generation gap of today is larger than and qualitatively different from what we have known heretofore. The present college generation is the first born after the atom bomb. They are a generation separated from their parents by the results of social-cultural change that has proceeded at a faster pace than ever before, and with the atom bomb has crossed a major divide in its effects upon the human condition.

In the United States, moreover, the middle-class students who have been the major contributors to protest have grown up in an unprecedentedly affluent society in which the attainment of material success for themselves is hardly a challenge, and the attainment of human dignity for all is for the first time well within the technical competence and economic capacity of the society. This has been a period in which large social aims have been enunciated—the "Great Society"—yet also one in which accomplishments toward realizing these aims can only be seen as political tokenism. The gap between the ideal and the actual may be smaller than ever before, but what is likely to impress the young is that the gap between the *possible* and the actual has never before been so great. War, poverty, racism, environmental pollution, and urban sprawl continue with business much as usual, in spite of new attention to these problems that are now properly regarded as failures of Man rather than acts of God. Immense resources are poured into the dramatic achievement of placing a man on the moon. This may be fine, but it dramatizes the irresponsibility within which the *human* problems of contemporary society have been dealt with. We expect youth to be idealistic, as the Massachusetts Institute of Technology philosopher Houston Smith has pointed out in an address making essentially these points,[3] but never has youthful idealism had such grounds for impatience. Never has the moral challenge to youth been clearer. Since normal democratic process seems to be failing to come to grips with this novel situation, morally sensitive youths, many of them, are increasingly turning in other directions to express their impatience.

For the white middle-class students who were the main participants in the earlier wave of protest, two sets of issues were paramount: those of the civil rights arena in which they initially found common cause with the blacks (until the imperatives of the new black demand for self-respect made their participation less welcome), and those of the Vietnam War and the draft. Immoral wars are no new thing. Vietnam, however, is a war with unusually suspect credentials that television and the mass media have brought into the households of Americans more vividly and concretely than ever before, and that the draft has brought to the campus.

For the black students of the recent waves of protest, additional considerations are surely relevant. An obvious one is the gap between expectations raised in the early days of legal gains in the civil rights struggle, and subsequent accomplishments in the more difficult sphere of economic and educational discrimination and deficit. But another ingredient in the mounting black protest requires interpretation in a more hopeful vein. By and large, people do not revolt from a sense of desperation: the traditional and inevitable adaptation to desperation is fatalism and passivity. Protest and more violent rebellion require at least a modicum of hope. And hope and emerging self-respect are major and important gains in the Black Power movement. When the starting point is apathy and passivity—or thinking "white" and individually "making it" in white society at the expense of one's black brothers—initial gains in hope and self-respect are likely to have their first visible effects in increasing intransigence, unreasonableness, protest activity, and what looks like compensatory Black Racism.

Kenneth Keniston[4] has recently differentiated black protest from white middle-class protest in somewhat different terms that are nevertheless compatible with the account I have given. For the most part, the black students are fighting, in Keniston's view, in a *first* revolution for more equitable distribution of the material benefits of middle-class society, a revolution that the white working classes have largely won. Many of the white protesting students, on the other hand, are engaged in a *second* revolution, seeking a radical reconstitution of society to provide more meaningful lives for those who can no longer find spiritual satisfaction in the "rat race" for a material success that they take for granted.

Student protest, then, *is* something new. If commentators like Bruno Bettelheim who have experienced the events leading to Nazi repression find disquietingly familiar themes in the young people's disregard for democratic procedure and civil amenities, surely there is much that is potentially constructive in this new version of the generational conflict. As long as the established authorities remain notably unsuccessful in directing social competence to meet our increasingly urgent problems, problems that are mounting to potentially catastrophic dimensions, we ought to be grateful that many of the young are calling for radical change.

Institutional Racism and Black Protest

We know that "white racism" has been one of the major themes of protest for all youth; it is of course the focal concern of the black students. The Kerner Commission Report laid the concept before us all for a public consideration that has still been all too casual and incomplete. But there is much loose usage of the term in brow-beating or breast-beating. We need to be as clear as we can be about our terms of reference. A first step toward clarifying our thinking in this highly charged area, it seems to me, is to distinguish between the *personal* racism of prejudice and bigotry, on the one hand, and *institutional* racism on the other.

We all know what we mean by prejudice, and most of us are likely to give ourselves a relatively clean bill of health. Of course, there are subtle forms of prejudice—such as the school counselor's well-meaning efforts to direct black students toward career options where they would be unlikely to run against existing barriers. These unacknowledged and unconscious forms of racism seem to be particularly exasperating to self-conscious blacks, and I can understand their feeling that honest bigots may be preferable to hypocritical liberals. But I do not at all agree with them on this point, and I do not think that personal racism is the main problem that we must face nationally.

Just what do we mean by institutional racism, which seems to me the main problem? This term labels characteristics and processes of the legitimate on-going institutions of society that tend to perpetuate the second-class status of Negroes, and of other disadvantaged minorities. To be sure, institutional racism finds support in personal bigotry, perhaps especially in its more subtle and unacknowledged forms. But, more importantly, it finds its major support in all of the many honorable values and reasonable justifications for continuing existing institutions much as they have been.

Admissions policies that give high priority to maintaining standards of quality; faculty recruitment policies addressed single-mindedly to the same standards—these aspects and many others of doing business as usual have the consequence of maintaining the status quo with only glacial rates of change. Due democratic process fits comfortably into the existing institutional framework, and it mostly occurs under silent constraints that tend to preserve institutions from radical reconstruction. Thus, what any black student must regard as institutional racism is likely to appear as a desirable and entirely justified practice to the whites who man the present institutional structures. In the competing values that enter into the political processes of society, blacks are now giving absolute priority to remedying their traditional injustices. The faculty and administrators who are responsible for our colleges and universities may want to contribute as liberals to the cause of black equality, but inevitably they will tend to give priority to sustaining what they regard as the core values of their present institutions. This is natural and honorable, but—it is one of the meanings of institutional racism.

This way of analyzing the problem makes it more reasonable than may appear to college faculties at first glance for black students to adopt strategies of disruptive and outrageous action. From the standpoint of individual prejudice and bigotry, such tactics are obviously "counterproductive." You don't make friends and influence people by disruption and violence; you make enemies instead, and individual white prejudice may indeed be on the rise in a "backlash" from the impact of black protest and disruption. But with respect to institutional racism, the story looks different. Democratic process as usual, within the current institutional framework, is not very likely to transform the nature and priorities of the institution within which these normal processes take place. Something is needed to shake the institutional framework. Activist protest is attempting to do precisely that, and, like it or not, we must grant that it often has considerable success. We might find it vastly preferable if those who man the responsible positions in our institutions were to face the problems that give rise to protest before disruption occurs. But, empirically, problems that traditionally have been swept under institutional carpets are most likely to get serious attention in the wake of trouble and confrontation.

The current manifestations of black student protest carry a special message that is especially hard for white liberals to digest and accept: the theme of black separatism. This grates much more harshly on traditional liberal principles than the vague concept of Black Power. Issues of conflicting human values here are sadly tangled. Yet there are some things that can be said, again by way of clarification, that may help us understand and respond constructively.

Black Americans are becoming aware that for integration to work in the ways that are claimed for it, as an ideal, there must also be equality. But equality is precisely what Negroes have never enjoyed. The on-going structure of American society with its congeries of vicious circles has effectively prevented it. Second-classness, to contemporary blacks, is intolerable. And paternalism, leaving the initiative for black betterment to well-meaning whites, implies continued second-classness and is also intolerable. Gains for blacks wrested by black efforts on their own behalf are what count most in counteracting the results of a long history that has, until now, radically undermined the foundation of black self-respect. One can reject black separatism as an ultimate goal—even regard it as a mirror-image racism akin to the doctrine of Apartheid—and at the same time respect the immediate need for separatism as a phase essential to producing the conditions under which more substantial forms of integration can develop. Integration, to be satisfactory in a democratic society, has to be based on the willing participation of equals.

Conflicting Values on the Campus

Having tried thus far to put us in the shoes of protesting students, and to grasp some of the latent reasonableness in apparently unreasonable protest, I must now draw back to remind us of the important values that come in conflict when disruption becomes a recurrent tactic for social action on the academic scene.

The potential value of colleges and universities as foci of social criticism and social renewal depends, as we all know, on a preciously guarded tradition of academic freedom. And academic freedom is a tender thing that, in historical fact, has often been blighted by external pressures and internal adaptations to them. For institutions of higher education to be more than trade schools, more than agencies of socialization to produce conforming citizens, a free arena of inquiry and discourse is essential. One does not need to share all of the liberal faith to regard academic freedom as intrinsically precious. We cannot therefore blame faculties and administrations for seeing in the disruptive, coercive tactics of protesting students a fundamental challenge to the basic tenets of academic life. It is entirely understandable when those who govern our academic institutions take the "hard-line" position that disruptive tactics are simply out of order—ample grounds for expulsion.

But to act from this understandable position is, it seems to me, to take an absolutist stand on the values of academic freedom that is a counterpart to the absolutism of war protestors for whom an end to the Vietnam War takes precedence over all other values, or the absolutism of race protestors that puts the attainment of respect and equality for repressed minorities above all other conceivable social ends. Granted that such absolutist stands have their value in the social process. Particularly for unpopular causes and minority positions it is important to have people who are "specialists" in them, who prevent the rest of us from totally neglecting them. Thus we are generally indebted to the American Civil Liberties Union for specializing in its distinctive perspective, deliberately ignoring the other social values that are always entwined with civil libertarian issues. We should not expect black students to take a balanced perspective on values that compete with their legitimate concerns for equity and respect. To paraphrase the words of Hillel, if they are not for themselves, who will be for them? But, except if one views matters apocalyptically, to attain one's objectives in a field of competing claims requires an accommodation of values. When academics stand pat on the ground of academic freedom, and call upon police power or academic penalties to quell student protest, they may find that the effects they achieve are not the ones they desire. If absolute priority is asserted for academic freedom over the strongly urged counterclaims of students pressing for other preemptive causes, academic freedom itself is bound to suffer.

My point is not that we as professors should abdicate to student protest. It is rather that we must be visibly responsive to claims on behalf of the competing values that motivate it. When protestors act with the enthusiasm and single-mindedness of youth, with its unreasonableness and rejection of adult authority, the demands for maturity on the part of faculty and administration are great. To cleave to our values of intellectual freedom while bending in responsiveness to fervent and provocative pressure—there is no easy formula for this. But that is what is required of us if the essential values of academic freedom are to be preserved and, at the same time, our academic institutions are to be reshaped along lines more responsive to the requirements of our times.

NOTES

Adapted from a talk delivered at the Conference on Racism and Education at Chicago State College, March 26, 1969.

1. M. Brewster Smith, "The Crisis on the Campus," pp. 321–28, and"Morality and Student Protest," pp. 329–43, *Social Psychology and Human Values* (Chicago: Aldine Publishing Company, 1969).

2. *The Conflict of Generations* (New York: Basic Books, 1969).

3. "Like It Is: The University Today," *Phi Beta Kappa Key Reporter*, XXXIV, No. 2 (Winter, 1968–69), 2–4.

4. "You Have to Grow up in Scarsdale to Know How Bad Things Really Are," *New York Times Magazine*, April 27, 1969, p. 27.

Chapter Sixteen

Political Psychology and Peace
A Half-Century Perspective

A long view of my subject, political psychology and peace, seems especially cogent right now when we are reminded incessantly of our participation in the transition not only to a new century but to a new millennium. These all-too-human constructions have already acquired cultural and psychological reality. As Kurt Lewin said, what is real is what has effects. My own involvements with political psychology over more than 50 years touch on some major upheavals in assumptions and preoccupations in our field. I have had plenty of opportunity to mull over them, but as a "senior citizen" in political psychology I cannot aspire to be at the cutting edge of contemporary research. So I will make a virtue out of necessity, and draw on my personal exposure in the hope of contributing a useful perspective on our present historical situation. This perspective will unavoidably be American—probably egregiously so in the international context in which it was presented.

I begin with my own beginnings, first as an undergraduate in the mid 1930s, which linked my early concerns with war and peace with the contributions of one of the honored ancestors of political psychology, the political scientist Harold Lasswell, and with my subsequent work in the field a decade later. Then I attend briefly to the participation of psychologists in World War II, focusing on the Psychologists' Manifesto, a wartime attempt to apply psychological wisdom to the construction of peace. The Cold War in the nuclear age radically changed the issues for peace-oriented psychologists, and I look at some of the major psychological contributions that it stimulated. I take brief account of approaches that arose in the same period in response to the Israeli-Arab conflict, which permitted quite a different involvement of psychology and centered on ethnic/religious issues of a kind that currently preoccupy us. The Seville Statement on Violence, a document not unlike the

Psychologists' Manifesto in its motivation, is examined in relation to the changing climate, which at the end of the Cold War required radical rethinking on the part of psychologists as well as everyone else. I conclude with some thoughts about how psychology—that is, psychologists—might respond to the present challenges.

Beginnings

The Division of Political Psychology of the International Association of Applied Psychology (IAAP), to the Congress of which this address was presented, was founded near the end of the Cold War by psychologists who had a central interest in applying psychology to the pursuit of international peace. Now, a full decade after the end of the Cold War, the former "peace community" in psychology and the social sciences is still groping for a focus in a turbulent world that inspires new hopes and fears. This division of IAAP overlaps in membership with the International Society of Political Psychology, which is also international, but unlike IAAP is interdisciplinary. In founding that society, Jeanne Knutsen was inspired by the work of Lasswell, who was much influenced by psychoanalytic ideas. My own research involvement with political psychology essentially began with a challenge to the conclusions drawn by that legendary ancestor.

As an undergraduate in the 1930s, I had been much interested in two aspects of Lasswell's contributions to political psychology. One was his focus on propaganda as a feature of war making. His book (Lasswell, 1927) on propaganda technique in the World War (not yet labeled World War I) led me to regard propaganda analysis as a relevant social psychological contribution to peace. I took that so seriously that beginning about 1937, I got myself on lists to receive publications from the German, Italian, Soviet, and British embassies in Washington—a collection I eventually gave unanalyzed to a research library. (I later learned that the U.S. Army had me on a suspect list for Nazi associations.) The Institute for Propaganda Analysis (1937–1941; Lee & Lee, 1939) gave prominent expression to this approach to peace psychology, which collapsed with the onset of World War II and looks embarrassingly naive to us in retrospect in regard to its political strategy to avert war, but remains the best single effort to inform citizens about the ways of persuasion. We should note that Lasswell-style concern with propaganda was the forerunner of research on persuasive communication, a major productive field of contemporary social psychology, which has again been giving significant attention to propaganda (Pratkanis & Aronson, 1992).

The other facet of Lasswell's (1930) work that fascinated me was his treatment of the personality basis of political opinion and action in *Psychopathology and Politics.* In a version of popular Freudian conceptualization rather characteristic of the 1920s, he proposed the formula that political opinions and actions are a function of private motives displaced on a public object and rationalized in terms of the public interest. It was that formulation that was challenged by the qualitative research I did with Bruner and White and reported in *Opinions and Personality* (Smith, Bruner, & White, 1956). (See chapter 7.)

Our natural history approach looked closely at how the opinions 10 adult American men held about Soviet Russia at the outset of the Cold War were embedded in their personalities. We concluded that Lasswell's formula dealt with only one of three functional relations of opinions to personality that we observed, what we called *externalization of inner conflict.* We called attention to two others—*object appraisal* (assessment of the attitude object in terms of its bearing on the person's interests and values) and *social adjustment* (which I later reconceived as mediation of self other relationships.) This formulation had later echoes in the experimental work of Dan Katz and his colleagues at the University of Michigan. Such a functional approach has had something of a revival in contemporary social psychology (Pratkanis, Breckler, & Greenwald, 1989). Our three-way classification provided a more inclusive framework than is suggested by any single one of three theories recently contending in political psychology: rational choice theory, social identity theory, and the continuing strains of psychoanalytic theory match up quite well with our three types of functions.

Of course, in developing our individually focused functional approach we merely used the issues of the emerging Cold War as a setting for examining the relations of opinions and personality; we were not trying to understand the dynamics of the Cold War. Another individually focused, psychodynamically oriented approach that appeared at about the same time has shown itself over the past half century still to be very relevant to attitudes that support interethnic and international conflict: the Berkeley studies of *The Authoritarian Personality* (Adorno, Frenkel-Brunswik, Levinson, & Sanford, 1950). This work on authoritarianism was a salient early contribution to political psychology that has survived revivified despite severe early criticism and a long period of latency thereafter. It figures saliently in my personal recollections because I reviewed *The Authoritarian Personality* when the book first came out (Smith, 1950) and have followed the subsequent developments closely (Smith, 1997).

World War II

World War II had intervened, of course, before the particular individually focused approaches just noted had emerged. From an American perspective, it rendered previous psychological thinking about war quite obsolete. After the Vietnam War and its sequellae, it becomes necessary to remind younger psychologists, particularly Americans, that from the standpoint of most participants in the Allied countries, World War II was a completely necessary war, if not a "good war." Unlike World War I, flamboyant patriotism was not expected, but the necessity of deadly struggle toward victory was mostly taken for granted. Both World War I and World War II created a strong national consensus in which most psychologists participated. The various nontrivial contributions of psychologists to the "war effort" should therefore not be attributed to scheming for professional advancement and power, as a revisionist historian (Herman, 1995) recently suggested. (See chapter 2.)

My own exposure to the psychological side of war-making came as an enlisted man in test development for Col. John C. Flanagan's Aviation Psychology Program (Flanagan, 1948) and as an officer in army survey research directed by Sam Stouffer (Stouffer et al., 1949) and in Army research on persuasive communication, directed by Carl Hovland (Hovland, Lumsdaine, & Sheffield, 1949). Having been well launched in graduate study before the war, I really became a psychologist (i.e., found my professional identity) in my wartime experience.

Of course, it was not just American and Allied psychologists who rose to their country's call. Psychologists from each belligerent nation responded to the call to national duty, though Jewish psychologists in Germany were not asked, and were lucky if they had managed to flee. The prepotency of national identity over international science during both world wars should remind us of the extraordinary persisting power of nationalism as a disastrous feature of our century.

The Psychologists' Manifesto

Toward the end of World War II, some leading American psychologists developed and circulated a statement signed by 13 of them (including Gordon Allport, E. R. Hilgard, Otto Klineberg, Rensis Likert, and Edward Tolman) looking ahead to the prospect of peace. Not insignificantly, all of the 13 except Edna Heidbreder were men. Almost 4,000 other American psychologists signed the statement. This document, titled *The Psychologists' Manifesto: Human Nature and the Peace: A Statement by Psychologists* (reprinted in Murphy, 1945; and in Jacobs, 1989), had no discernible impact. It remains of interest, however, as a well-articulated expression of beliefs and attitudes about peacemaking then held by prominent American psychologists. I quote selectively, with brief comments.

1. *War can be avoided: War is not born in men; it is built into men.* We have since come to question the assumed gender neutrality of the word *men*, and our heightened concern with gender differences makes the aggressive tendencies of young men worth some attention, though not as a fundamental cause of war.

3. *Racial, national, and group hatreds can, to a considerable degree, be controlled.* We would still agree, but with less optimistic assurance than half a century ago. I will come back to what we are to make of our disheartening experience.

4. *Condescension toward "inferior" groups destroys our chances for a lasting peace.* The authors explicitly refer to White condescension, and call implicitly for an end to colonialism. It is hard for me to remember that the postwar collapse of the colonial empires was still to come: We have made some real progress!

5. *Liberated and enemy peoples must participate in planning their own destiny.* The drafters of the Statement were understandably preoccupied with the defects of the Versailles Treaty at the end of World War I. The Marshall Plan took this principle to heart.

8. *The root desires of the common people of all lands are the safest guide to framing a peace.* This democratic sentiment is only a little tarnished in the commentary by the somewhat self-serving recommendation that the will of the "man in the street" can be studied "by adaptations of the public opinion poll."

9. *The trend of human relationships is toward ever wider units of*

collective security. The United Nations and the various regional organizations formed in the Cold War and since were still to come. But I don't think, today, that we take much comfort in discerning such a "trend," significant as it has been; the challenge is to make such collective arrangements work.

The manifesto adopted an optimistic view of human nature like that expressed, only a little later, in the song from *South Pacific,* "You've got to be taught to hate." Overall, its recommendations with respect to our enemies (which I've mostly omitted) made psychological sense—and common sense as well. In retrospect, what is striking is its complete silence about relations with our Soviet ally, where the actual threat to peace was very soon to emerge. This was not a matter of unconscious neglect; it rather reflected persisting disagreement among peace-oriented psychologists about the Soviet Union under Stalin, where I was wrong in minimizing and excusing his horrors.

Turning Points in the Psychology of War and Peace

Putting myself back into the frame of mind that prevailed as the war neared its end, I find the manifesto mostly admirable. The optimistic view that it expressed was right for the time. Four turning points since then each reoriented the thinking of American psychologists concerned with peace. First, the use of the atom bomb by the United States as the final act of the war changed the meaning of war and its risks to humankind, introducing a degree of apocalyptic anxiety previously unknown. Then, the emergence of the Cold War as the organizing feature of international relations made the attainment of real peace seem much more chancy and difficult than the psychologists had supposed, although the atomic powers were inhibited from overt aggression against each other. The Cold War took a critical turn with the involvement of the United States in Vietnam, a war that did not produce national consensus in its support. Finally, in the last decade, the end of the Cold War and the collapse of the Soviet Union was an occasion for initial euphoria, but it turned out to inaugurate not a peaceful "New World Order" as President Bush proclaimed at the onset of the Gulf War, but the release of national, ethnic, and religious conflicts that our earlier psychologizing about human nature did not at all anticipate.

Peace Psychology and the Cold War

Jacobs (1989) provided a thorough bibliography and review of psychological publications concerning the avoidance of nuclear war during the Cold War period. The most significant psychological contributions are well represented in White's (1986) collection. For me, the best analysis of war-threatening international conflict integrating psychological ideas that emerged during the Cold War and Vietnam was provided by Deutsch (1983) in his presidential address to the International Society of Political Psychology. He depicted conflicts like those between the United States and the Soviet Union as involving a spiraling, malignant social process that arises in anarchic situations in which "rational" behavior is impossible so long as the conditions for social order or mutual trust do not exist. In such situations, Deutsch noted that for either party to pursue its interests in its own welfare or security without regard for the other is self-defeating. His close analysis of the features of the malignant process has wide application.

Deutsch drew on his earlier research on modes of conflict resolution (Deutsch, 1973), and on the work of Bronfenbrenner, White, and Osgood, which I would also single out as signal contributions of this period. Bronfenbrenner (1961) and White (1970) both called attention to how the parties in such escalating conflicts tend to have views of each other that resemble mirror-images, each diabolizing the enemy and selectively enhancing its own righteousness. As an approach to undercutting the malignant spiral, Osgood (1962) proposed Graduated Reciprocation in Tension Reduction (GRIT), a strategy of carefully planned and vigorously proclaimed unilateral initiatives in tension reduction. Osgood's proposal may have actually had some influence on the Kennedy administration's successful unilateral venture that resulted in the treaty prohibiting atmospheric tests of nuclear weapons—a first step toward nuclear détente.

The ideas touched on thus far were stimulated by the quite possibly apocalyptic conflict of great powers in the Cold War. The Israeli-Palestinian conflict persisting through the same period gave more room for trial of constructive intervention, especially in Kelman's (1982, 1997, 1998) program of problem-solving workshops with middle-level Israeli and Palestinian leaders. Whatever the outcome of the endangered "peace process" that still hangs in the balance, it is amply evident that Kelman's workshops contributed constructively to an atmosphere in which a "peace process" became possible. The constructive intervention of third parties as facilitators and mediators, a key feature that Rubin (1989) helped elucidate, was naturally out of the question in regard to the confrontation of great powers in the Cold War. The Arab-Israeli conflict also foreshadowed the ethnic and religious confrontations that have become increasingly prominent in the years since the end of the Cold War.

The Seville Statement on Violence

The Cold War period also brought forth a statement widely endorsed by organizations of psychologists and other social scientists (including the American Psychological Association and UNESCO) that can be viewed together with the Psychologists' Manifesto as optimistic authoritative pronouncements in the service of peace. The "Seville Statement on Violence" was issued by an international and interdisciplinary group of behavioral scientists called together by the International Society for the Study of Aggression in Seville, Spain, May 1986 (Adams, 1989). Given the persistence of international and intergroup conflict and the recurrent popular supposition that a propensity for war is somehow built into human nature—a supposition encouraged by popularizers of ethology— the group of prominent psychologists, anthropologists, and biologists who issued the statement regarded the unwarranted belief in human-kind's innate programming for violence as an obstacle to the attainment of peace, and sought to counteract such beliefs. I supported its promulgation, but since the end of the Cold War I have had serious reservations about its sufficiency.

Here are key elements of the Seville Statement:

- It is scientifically incorrect to say that we have inherited a tendency to make war from our animal ancestors. . . . Warfare is a peculiarly human phenomenon . . . a product of culture.
- It is scientifically incorrect to say that war or any other violent behavior is genetically programmed into our human nature.
- It is scientifically incorrect to say that in the course of human evolution there has been a selection for aggressive behavior more than for other kinds of behavior. . . .
- It is scientifically incorrect to say that humans have a "violent

brain." There is nothing in our neurophysiology that compels us to act violently.

- It is scientifically incorrect to say that war is caused by "instinct" or any single motivation. . . . We conclude that biology does not condemn humanity to war. . . . The same species who invented war is capable of inventing peace. The responsibility lies with each of us. (Adams, 1991, pp. 20–30)

I can still say a firm personal Amen! Despite pop primatology about territorial imperatives and naked apes, it is indeed wrong to claim a biological basis for war in innate human aggressiveness (see also Groebel & Hinde, 1989, for related scholarly assessments). As a social psychologist, I took satisfaction in supporting the Seville Statement because I saw such an immense gulf separating organized warfare between nation states with its dependence on technology and bureaucracy from the kind of young male fighting illustrated in some (but only some) nonliterate cultures and by modern urban gangs (think of *West Side Story*). I agree that the violence of war is a human potential, not a human necessity, and that its primary roots are in history and culture. All the same, it may turn out to be "scientifically incorrect" to neglect deep-rooted human biases that contribute to making war a persistent historical fact, biases that do not involve genes for aggression. Attending to such biases need not lead us to support preparations for war as "inevitable"; it might actually help us be more realistic in laying the grounds for peace. The resurgence of ethnic and similar conflict since the end of the Cold War seems to call for reconsideration of our former optimism to take such biases into account.

After the Cold War

We have all been surprised by these developments, which have replaced the euphoria that accompanied the fall of the Berlin Wall and the collapse of Soviet Communism with dismay and renewed concern for the human future. President Martin Seligman of the American Psychological Association and President Peter Suedfeld of the Canadian Psychological Association recently launched a Joint Presidential Initiative committing the resources of the two North American organizations to apply the tools of psychology to "Ethnopolitical Warfare: Origins, Intervention, and Prevention." I quote selectively from the document that announced their initiative to identify our present concern. I hope my subsequent discussion may contribute to their objectives, with which I strongly concur.

> With the end of the Cold War, a new, but it also seems, an ancient form of warfare is becoming more common around the world. A series of conflicts have erupted that are rooted in ethnic fear and hatred, historic patterns of privileging, actual and perceived victimization, failed government, economic stress, and ecological disasters. Some major examples are current or recent intra-state wars such as those in Bosnia, Croatia, Northern Ireland, Kashmir [and 19 named other countries]. Not all of these are strictly new conflicts, but the end of the Cold War has spawned many of them, aggravated others, and exposed older ones as essentially ethnic rather than between hostile political ideologies.
>
> These wars are fought by rival ethnic groups with their own cultural identities. They come to believe that a rival group or a state controlled by a rival group threatens their very existence. Each group defines its own identity in part by opposition to the evil other and sees that other as less than human. . . .
>
> The nature of the fighting has also changed. Ethnopolitical wars include atrocities such as mass rape and ethnic cleansing, and they often occur within communities, with former neighbors committing personal violence against each other, sometimes in the name of "race," or "nation," or "religion," or linguistic identity, or some combination of these. . . . (American Psychological Association, 1997)

This old-new kind of conflict seems to call even more insistently on contributions from psychology than older patterns of warfare between nation states, because hatred and murderous personal aggression are more saliently involved. Like the Holocaust, genocidal slaughter in Bosnia, Rwanda, and elsewhere challenges our optimistic views of human nature. It is only natural for our thoughts to turn toward biological predispositions, now more acceptable in psychology than they were only a few years ago. If we don't have genes for war, maybe we do have a biologically-based tendency toward ethnocentrism. People's tendency to organize their social worlds into virtuous "Us" versus evil or despicable "Them" could well have had selective advantage in human prehistory (Ross, 1991). Laboratory research on minimal social groups is at least compatible with a built-in tendency for in-group preference. Tajfel (1981) and other psychologists influenced by him have found that people consistently favor other in-group members, even if the group has just been formed by the assignment of an arbitrary label and there are no interpersonal ties between "members." Maybe our predisposition to re-act in terms of Us vs. Them is hardwired into us, though a societal interpretation is also tenable.

But if such is the case, we must still recognize that neither a biological nor a societal constant can explain a change—the current eruption of ethnopolitical conflict. To understand such a historical change, and to develop ideas about how to cope with it, we need to identify the factors that instigate or release ethnocentric thinking and emotions.

Why the Current Proliferation of Ethnopolitical Conflicts?

I expect that the activities afoot in the joint Presidential Initiative will throw light on why ethnopolitical conflicts are proliferating just now— or at least, sharpen the questions that inquiry needs to pursue. In the meantime, I venture some suggestions, emphasizing respects in which our former assumptions are challenged.

As I just suggested, I am inclined to believe that the emotional steam of sometimes genocidal hatred that can be mobilized by "identity-based conflict" (Rothman, 1997) has a biological basis with evolutionary sources. But both the instigation and the release of potential ethnic hostility surely involve historical and contextual factors that psycholo-gists may have a disciplinary tendency to neglect. The end of the Cold War and the collapse of the Soviet Union removed a set of powerful restraints on interethnic conflict, both in the former Soviet Union and in the former colonial states of Africa, leaving a kind of normative vacuum. As for historical factors, each of the main centers of persistent conflict has a grim history of victimization and grievance, cherished by the contending parties, often kept in check over long periods by superordi-nate authority. History makes a crucial difference, which may be more obvious to others than to psychologists. Neither can we afford to neglect the important role of pernicious leadership, which in case after case can be seen to have capitalized on traditional ethnic pride and grievance for self-serving political purposes.

There may be another, more "psychological" reason for our present vulnerability to identity-based ethnic and "ethnonational" (Kecmano-vic, 1996) conflicts. That has to do with the psychology of hope and hopelessness (Smith, 1983, 1992b). Worldwide, the modern period has seen the attrition of traditional cultures and traditional religion, sources of hope over the reaches of human history and prehistory as people face the inevitable anxieties, disappointments, and tragedies of life (Baumeister, 1986, 1991; Becker, 1973). Marxism as a recent ideology of hope has been discredited. In bourgeois democracies, belief in progress, which had largely supplanted otherworldly expectations as a source of hope, has been shaken by two World Wars; the Holocaust; the still-threatening presence of nuclear armament and other modes of mass destruction; and prospects of planetary overcrowding, pollution, and exhaustion of resources. In the former colonial world, expectations of better life following liberation have remained largely unmet.

So in many respects, people's life prospects and those of their children can look pretty bleak. I see this as a condition that is conducive to unthinking identification with larger entities that promise to restore life's meaning and make hope possible again—religious revival, nationalism, ethnic identification. (Fundamentalism seems to be growing on many fronts—in Christianity, Judaism, Islam, and Hinduism.) When history and contemporary political leadership make ethnic, religious, or national membership salient, people who otherwise would find it difficult to stay hopeful are likely to give that membership priority in their sense of identity. The stage is set for irreconcilable conflict when that identity is threatened.

Some Implications

We know enough about the psychology of war and peace to appreciate how little we know, how shaky is our knowledge. Our consistent inability to anticipate the developments that substantially changed our understanding is itself grounds for modesty. Nevertheless, the dangers of nuclear Armageddon are by no means eliminated, and the current wave of ethnopolitical warfare presents an awesome threat to the future of humankind. There are obviously psychological ingredients in the predicaments that we face. Psychologists are challenged to add to our understanding of the conditions under which peace with justice can be promoted and warfare averted.

Throughout my experience of the Cold War era and since, I have been struck by how psychologists who might have been attracted to work on such humanly important problems have been caught in a kind of Scylla—Charybdis trap. On the one hand is the Scylla of presumption, hubris, chutzpah: taking the problems of war and international conflict as essentially psychological and, therefore, presuming that psychologists—or psychiatrists or psychoanalysts—must have the keys to their solution. Of course the problems cut across all disciplines and specialties; they challenge all the inventiveness and dedication of humankind as they threaten our very survival. We psychologists should not blame ourselves heavily for having contributed rather little to their solution thus far, or set ourselves up for inevitable failure by vulnerable claims that we are about to make crucial contributions.

On the other hand, there is the Charybdis of hopelessness and helplessness, which leads us to withdraw and fail to make even the modest but real contributions that are within our reach. That has always seemed to me the greater peril. At the peak of anxiety about impending nuclear Armageddon during the Cold War, all but a tiny minority of psychologists pursued their profession, their science, their careers in the mode of "business as usual." Our avoidance of the challenge to psychology isn't explained by Lifton's (1967) concept of "psychic numbing"—a concept he developed for the shaken survivors of Hiroshima that was often applied to explain why psychologists and ordinary people tended to avoid thinking about the prospects of nuclear war and doing anything about it. The more appropriate explanatory frame is provided by Frank's (1973) adaptation of the Sullivanian concept of "selective inattention," motivated by our understandable state of "learned helplessness" à la Seligman (Peterson, Maier, & Seligman, 1993) or low "self-efficacy" à la Bandura (Bandura, 1997).

With that preamble, I have the chutzpah to offer a few suggestions. I think it is sensible to regard Us vs. Them thinking and feeling as quite probably a fundamental human propensity, which we have to learn to deal with if we are to reduce and avert identity-based conflicts. We know more about these conflicts than mostly gets acted on by political leadership. Among the things we have recently begun to understand are individual differences in people's vulnerability to initiating and participating in them. Altemeyer (1998) recently linked his classic work on Right-Wing Authoritarianism with the measure of Social Dominance developed by Pratto, Sidanius, Stallworth, and Malle (1994) to give us an empirical grasp on the distinctive personality of leaders as well as follow-ers in vindictive authoritarian movements. This is a valuable elaboration on the Us vs. Them theme.

Practical experience with negotiation and mediation, mainly in indus-trial-organizational contexts, has been extended by Kelman and others to identity-based conflicts on the international scene. Experience here has surely gone beyond theory and firm conclusions, but there are well-articulated schemes to guide practice. The ideas of Burton's (1990) hu-man needs theory enter into Kelman's (1982, 1997, 1998) work in Israel. Also referring to Burton, Rothman (1997) proposed a common frame-work for "Resolving Identity-Based Conflict in Nations, Organizations and Communities." A major research and theoretical issue that has great practical significance is the extent to which conflict and its resolution at interpersonal, organizational, interethnic, and international levels can be conceptualized in parallel terms. The inherently clinical nature of action research in this area makes it difficult to settle such a question, although focusing on identity-based conflicts is clearly a promising first step.

I think psychologists should give more explicit attention to the role of leadership in escalating or reducing these conflicts. As I noted earlier, we have seen in former Yugoslavia, Ireland, Rwanda, and the Congo how ethnic or factional leaders can fan the fire of conflict for their personal political advantage. The role of transformative leadership in recent hope-ful cases is even more impressive. Is the progress in South Africa thus far conceivable without the charismatic leadership of Nelson Mandela? (We hope uneasily that the process of building the nation anew can continue without his hand at the helm.) The progress toward peace in Northern Ireland surely depended on the pressure and blessing from above on the part of Tony Blair and Bill Clinton as well as on Senator Mitchell's commitment and skills. The peace process between Israel and the Pales-tinians got launched through transformative leadership as well as care-ful secret diplomacy; it is stalled for now in good part by leadership problems.

My hunch is that the effective leader, whatever else he or she does, marshals the hope that people need if they are to tolerate and endure the pains and frustrations of mutual accommodation and develop realistic empathy with their erstwhile and continuing antagonists. The kind of hope needed is not rosy optimism; it involves belief in the potential attainability of goals that require great patience and sacrifice and risk taking. Heifetz's (1994) *Leadership Without Easy Answers* suggested some of the features of leadership that are required.

If leadership is as important as I have come to think it is in these matters, there is a limit to the degree to which our social psychological knowledge about conflict resolution can advance the cause of peace directly. So much depends on who gets elected, who succeeds to the helm. This is the stuff of traditional politics and history, not of behavioral science, although behavioral science can and does inform ventures to influence the electorate. Of course, psychologists and behavioral scientists can contribute to the informational and political climate in which leaders emerge and policies get formed, and can give good counsel to leaders well disposed to receive it. As informed activist citizens, they can draw on their psychological insights to support policies that contribute to the resolution rather than the escalation of conflicts. And they can contribute informative research: From a psychological/behavioral science standpoint, the nature of effective leadership in working with identity-based conflict is still not well understood. We have a lot to learn from close study of existing cases, and new ones as they develop.

Concluding Comments

As I wind down this personal perspective on more than a half century of psychology's involvement with war and peace, I see change on all sides. War has changed. World War I was horrible, but the advent of nuclear armament brought new horrors, and the emergence of ethnopolitical warfare continues to raise the costs to noncombatants—or should I say, it eliminates the category of noncombatant? Peace, too, has changed; that is, new mechanisms for peacemaking and peacekeeping are available, although nations have still to learn how to use them effectively. All the same, we can take satisfaction that the United Nations and its agencies are going concerns. And psychology has changed. It is not yet a coherent, paradigmatic science, but its methods of research are more powerful, its experience with the affairs of real life richer, and interdisciplinary political psychology, in particular, is better equipped to contribute to understanding the problems concerning war and peace.

I too have changed. Just getting older probably predisposes me to give less weight to Utopian hopes (having started with a mix of New Deal reformism and Marxist materialist idealism). But I think I share with my younger colleagues an increased awareness of system complexity and of historical and situational contingency that leaves me more cautious than I once was about prescriptions for social action, but no less committed to using psychology and social and behavioral science to promote human welfare according to our best though always imperfect understanding.

During the Cold War, psychologists concerned with peace were pre-occupied with avoiding nuclear catastrophe. In a world that is still armed with nuclear weapons, proliferating to new nations, that crucial challenge remains, and should not be forgotten. New tasks are before us in the present scene—which is not the "New World Order" that President Bush proclaimed at the time of the Gulf War—but a somewhat new world disorder of proliferating ethnopolitical strife, in which the gulf separating "Have" and "Have Not" identity groups and nations is a fundamental causal factor that I have not discussed. I take it as a most fortunate development for psychology that the presidents of our North American psychological associations have taken the initiative to focus psychological attention on this state of affairs. Another hopeful development is the United Nations plan for a Culture of Peace year at the turn of the millenium. I hope psychology can participate constructively in that. Ending my remarks on the word *hope* is appropriate, because we ourselves have to be hopeful if we are to mobilize our resources to meet the challenges and develop the opportunities that we face. At my age, I tend to think of optimism as mostly a mistake, but more than ever I see hope as a necessity. Hope enables constructive involvement, which in turn nourishes hope, in a benign reciprocal process.

References

Adams, D. (1989). The Seville Statement on Violence and why it is important. *Journal of Humanistic Psychology, 29*, 328–337.

Adams, D. (Ed.). (1991). *The Seville Statement on Violence: Preparing the ground for the construction of peace.* Paris: UNESCO.

Adorno, T. W., Frenkel-Brunswik, E., Levinson, D. J., & Sanford, R. N. (1950). *The authoritarian personality.* New York: Harper.

Altemeyer, B. (1998). The other "authoritarian personality." *Advances in Experimental Social Psychology, 30*, 47–92.

American Psychological Association. (1997). *Ethnopolitical warfare: Origins, intervention, and prevention. A joint presidential initiative of the presidents-elect of the American Psychological Association and the Canadian Psychological Association.* (Xeroxed document)

Bandura, A. (1997). *Self efficacy: The exercise of control.* New York: Freeman.

Baumeister, R. F. (1986). *Identity: Culture change and the struggle for self.* New York: Oxford University Press.

Baumeister, R. F. (1991). *Meanings of life.* New York: Guilford.

Becker, E. (1973). *The denial of death.* New York: Free Press.

Bronfenbrenner, U. (1961). The mirror image in Soviet-American relations: A social psychologist's report. *Journal of Social Issues, 17*(3), 45–56.

Burton, J. W. (Ed.). (1990). *Conflict: Resolution and prevention.* New York: St. Martin's.

Deutsch, M. (1973). *The resolution of conflict: Constructive and destructive processes.* New Haven, CT: Yale University Press.

Deutsch, M. (1983). The prevention of World War III: A psychological perspective. *Political Psychology, 4,* 3–32.

Flanagan, J. C. (Ed.). (1948). *The aviation psychology program in the Army Air Forces. Report No. 1.* Washington, DC: Government Printing Office.

Frank, J. D. (1973). *Persuasion and healing* (Rev. ed.). Baltimore, MD: Johns Hopkins University Press.

Groebel, J., & Hinde, R. A. (Eds.). (1989). *Aggression and war: Their biological and social bases.* Cambridge, England: Cambridge University Press.

Heifetz, R. A. (1994). *Leadership without easy answers.* Cambridge, MA: Harvard University Press.

Herman, E. (1995). *The romance of American psychology: Political culture in the age of experts.* Berkeley: University of California Press.

Hovland, C. I., Lumsdaine, A. A., & Sheffield, F. D. (1949). *Experiments in mass communication. Studies in social psychology in World War II* (Vol. 3). Princeton, NJ: Princeton University Press.

Institute for Propaganda Analysis, Inc. (October, 1937–December, 1941). *Propaganda analysis: A monthly letter to help the intelligent citizen detect and analyze propaganda.* New York: Author.

Jacobs, M. S. (1989). *American psychology in the quest for nuclear peace.* New York: Praeger.

Kecmanovic, D. (1996). *The mass psychology of ethno-nationalism.* New York: Plenum.

Kelman, H. C. (1982). Creating the conditions for Israeli-Palestinian negotiations. *Journal of Conflict Resolution, 26,* 39–75.

Kelman, H. C. (1997). Social-psychological dimensions of international conflict. In I. W. Zartman & J. L. Rasmussen (Eds.), *Peacemaking in international conflict: Methods and techniques* (pp. 191–237). Washington, DC: U.S. Institute of Peace.

Kelman, H. C. (1998). Social-psychological contributions to peacemaking and peacebuilding in the Middle East. *Applied Psychology: An International Review, 47,* 5–28.

Lasswell, H. D. (1927). *Propaganda technique in the world war.* New York: Knopf.

Lasswell, H. D. (1930). *Psychpathology and politics.* Chicago: University of Chicago Press.

Lee, A. M., & Lee, E. B. (Eds.). (1939). *The fine art of propaganda.* New York: Harcourt, Brace.

Lifton, R. J. (1967). *Death in life: Survivors of Hiroshima.* New York: Random House.

Murphy, G. (1945). *Human nature and enduring peace.* Cambridge, MA: Houghton-Mifflin.

Osgood, C. E. (1962). *An alternative to war and surrender.* Urbana: University of Illinois Press.

Peterson, A. C., Maier, S. F., & Seligman, M.E.P. (1993). *Learned helplessness: A theory for the age of personal control.* New York: Oxford University Press.

Pratkanis, A. R., & Aronson, E. (1992). *The age of propaganda: The everyday use and abuse of persuasion.* New York: Freeman.

Pratkanis, A. R., Breckler, S. J., & Greenwald, A. G. (Eds.). (1989). *Attitude structure and function.* Hillsdale, NJ: Lawrence Erlbaum Associates, Inc.

Pratto, E., Sidanius, J., Stallworth, L. M., & Malle, B. (1994). Social dominance orientation: A personality variable predicting social and political attitudes. *Journal of Personality and Social Psychology, 67,* 741–763.

Ross, M. H. (1991). The role of evolution in ethnocentric conflict and its management. *Journal of Social Issues, 47*(3), 167–185.

Rothman, J. (1997). *Resolving identity-based conflict: In nations, organizations, and communities.* San Francisco: Jossey-Bass.

Rubin, J. Z. (1989). Some wise and mistaken assumptions about conflict and negotiation. *Journal of Social Issues, 45*(2), 195–209.

Smith, M. B. (1950). Review of *The Authoritarian Personality. Journal of Abnormal and Social Psychology, 45,* 775–779.

Smith, M. B. (1983). Hope and despair: Keys to the sociopsychodynamics of youth. *American Journal of Orthopsychiatry, 53,* 388–399.

Smith, M. B. (1986). War, peace, and psychology. *Journal of Social Issues, 42*(4), 23–28.

Smith, M. B., (1992a). Nationalism, ethnocentrism, and the new world order. *Journal of Humanistic Psychology, 32,* 76–91.

Smith, M. B., (1992b). *Values, self, and society: Toward a humanist social psychology.* New Brunswick, NJ: Transaction Publishers.

Smith, M. B., (1997). *The Authoritarian Personality:* A re-review 46 years later. *Political Psychology, 18,* 159–163.

Smith. M. B., Bruner, J. S., & White, R. W. (1956). *Opinions and personality.* New York: Wiley.

Stouffer, S. A., Lumsdaine, A. A., Lumsdaine, M. H., Williams, R. M., Jr.,

Smith, M. B., Janis, I. L., Star, S., & Cottrell, L. S., Jr. (1949). *The American soldier: Combat and its aftermath. Studies in social psychology in World War II. Vol. 2.* Princeton, NJ: Princeton University Press.

Tajfel, H. (1981). *Human groups and social categories: Studies in social psychology.* Cambridge, England: Cambridge University Press.

White, R. K. (1970). *Nobody wanted war: Misperception in Vietnam and other wars.* Garden City, NY: Doubleday-Anchor.

White, R. K. (Ed.). (1986). *Psychology and the prevention of nuclear war.* New York: New York University Press.

Chapter Seventeen

The Metaphor (and Fact) of War

When the George W. Bush administration announced our "War on Terrorism" in response to the horrific events of September 11, 2001, my immediate gut reaction was that we had taken the wrong tack; that because we had been the victims of an extraordinarily vicious international criminal act, we should have pursued the criminals in full collaboration with the United Nations (UN) and sought their punishment through the agencies of international justice. After the surprising immediate success of our campaign in Afghanistan, I still thought so—but like everyone else, I have had much time to mull over the issues. I have come to regard the War on Terrorism as substantially metaphoric—evoking our thoughts and feelings about traditional wars. Although the metaphor of war has initial appeal as supporting the "mobilization" of patriotic morale in the face of major catastrophe, I see unfortunate consequences of this metaphoric usage, which I develop herewith. As I revise this article in mid-April 2002, and consider current developments, I only hope that our War on Terrorism does not become more actual, less metaphoric than it became even in Afghanistan. Revising the article in the light of rapidly developing events has been a continuing challenge. I do not discuss the implications of the current impasse in the Israel and Palestine conflict, which is crucially relevant.

The astonishing terrorist attack provided us with a legitimizing reason for actual war in Afghanistan. However, our War on Terrorism began as quite unlike the wars between national states that we are used to and that provide the model for the metaphoric use of "war." In traditional wars, we could look forward to one of three outcomes: victory, defeat, or a negotiated peace; not so our metaphorical war. The actual war in Afghanistan sounded like the old wars, but unlike a traditional enemy, Afghanistan was not in itself a threatening rival, and we fought it in a different way. Our War on Terrorism was not advanced very much by military victory in Afghanistan. As of now, many members of al Qaeda seem to have escaped, and Osama bin Laden is probably still at large. The future of Afghanistan and our role in it remain very cloudy. Our continuing War on Terrorism remains conspicuously metaphoric, although it may very well become actual again.

As psychologists and social scientists, we have learned the power of metaphor, which is not just a literary trope, but a major factor in structuring our selves and our views of reality (Lakoff & Johnson, 1980; Smith, 1985/1991). My intent here is to examine ways in which the metaphoric aspects of the War on Terrorism interfere with our dealing effectively with the challenges we face as we wake up to the dangerous world in which we found ourselves on September 11, 2001. I also suggest aspects of a more promising approach to which psychological considerations are relevant.

Other Metaphoric Wars: On Poverty and Drugs

I can best clarify my misgivings about the metaphoric War on Terrorism if we consider two other metaphoric wars with which we are all familiar: the War on Poverty of the Johnson presidency and the War on Drugs, still in progress. Our memory of the War on Poverty has recently been stirred by neo-conservative rhetoric that counts it as a defeat, a failure, claiming that it even aggravated our problems of poverty. The War on Drugs continues, with recurrent American involvement in actual hostilities in Colombia that may be more related to petroleum than to cocaine. What's wrong with this ever-so-natural usage of the war metaphor? Let us examine each of these cases briefly.

The master politician Lyndon B. Johnson (LBJ) proclaimed his War on Poverty as a way of catalyzing legislative enthusiasm for his initiatives to reduce poverty and promote social welfare. From a liberal perspective such as mine, LBJ made considerable headway along those lines before his unfortunate expansion of the Vietnam War preempted national attention and national resources. He did attract public attention to persisting poverty, a source of national shame that had been neglected since Roosevelt's New Deal. He initiated various promising ventures to "empower" the poor, involving them in public attempt to ameliorate their problems. The war metaphor served him well as a device for political *mobilization*—an inevitable term that is another instance of the pervasiveness of martial metaphoric language in our everyday usage.

However, consider essential ways in which the metaphor was a bad fit. In regard to outcomes, all-out victory was essentially inconceivable. In a free-market society, poverty can be reduced, not eliminated. Because the concept of a negotiated outcome made no sense in this metaphoric war, the continued existence of poverty could readily be interpreted as defeat. In a society like ours, recurrent and continued political efforts are required to reduce the otherwise increasing gap between "haves" and "have nots," and to counteract the debilitating effects of "have-not" status. A sustained campaign (I can't escape military metaphors) is called for, with no expectation of "victory."

The metaphor of war is just as bad a fit in the case of the War on Drugs. Again, the term was employed to mobilize national action, this time against the production, sale, and use of addictive drugs. Again, realistic appraisal of the social problem of addictive drugs would have to conclude that we cannot expect victory, and "peace" cannot be negotiated. What are needed are pragmatic efforts to limit the availability of harmful drugs, to decrease their use, and to reduce the harmfulness of their use (much of the harm being entailed by the politically accessible fact of their illegality). In a war, we tend to demonize the Enemy. Our social definition of drug use as Evil makes it harder for us to develop a rational pragmatic drug policy than in the case of even more demonstrably harmful substance abuse—of alcohol and tobacco. In our internal politics, the language of "war" has made it easier for the United States to consider actual military intervention in the attempt to limit drug production and export as in Colombia. In our unchallenged military preeminence, we are all too ready to deploy arms and military "advisors" and interfere in the internal affairs of other countries—some would say, with the ultimate goal of protecting U.S. interests.

In the Wars on Poverty and on Drugs, the metaphor of war was politically appealing as fitting the intended mobilization of national effort. In each case, however, the problems to be dealt with required patient unremitting attention, with little prospect of a victorious end. The "war" metaphor seemed to call for dramatic measures, unlikely to meet with full success and therefore open to interpretation as defeat. And in the case of the War on Drugs, national attention was distracted from pragmatic strategies that might be more appropriate to the long haul.

The War on Terrorism as a Metaphoric War

To return to the War on Terrorism: The sense in which it too is a metaphoric war entails unfortunate consequences. In announcing it (but not "declaring" war by act of Congress), President Bush mobilized the country, evoking patriotic wartime morale as a response to the devastating and unnerving assault and, not incidentally, making criticism of its commander-in-chief unpatriotic. However, from the beginning, this war was defined as different from traditional wars. The al Qaeda terrorists were not from any one country, and when we captured some of them and their Taliban sponsors, we did not regard them as prisoners of war. National states were not the direct enemy, although they could be made enemies by our proclamation that countries that did not show that they were for us by cooperating in our War on Terrorism were to be regarded as against us. All the same, the Bush Administration was scrupulous (and praiseworthy) in stressing that our conflict is not with Islam as such.

As in the cases of the Wars on Poverty and on Drugs, the alternative outcomes implied by the metaphor do not apply. Of course, a negotiated peace with bin Laden or with the suicidal terrorists he trained and coordinated is out of the question, and as of the time this is being written, the focus on bin Laden and al Qaeda has almost been forgotten. Literal defeat is also hard to conceive, except perhaps in the utter worst case of the cataclysmic collapse of modern society; the important point is, so is victory. In a world currently divided between wealthy "haves" and impoverished "have nots," terrorism is a recourse of the hopeless and powerless, a desperate gesture that is facilitated by fundamentalist religion that itself feeds on the hopelessness that it ameliorates. Because the United States is the sole superpower among the "have" countries, we can expect to be the continuing target of terrorism even if bin Laden and most cells of al Qaeda are eliminated. As in the case of the War on Drugs, aiming at victory may be distracting us from seeking to reduce the causes of terrorism. We are not being distracted, fortunately, from intensive efforts to reduce the probable harm produced by terrorist attempts.

I am not saying that our extreme position in the world of "have" and "have-not" nations is "the" cause of terrorism against the United States. Rather, our position as the affluent superpower may breed envy and resentment that provides a sympathetic climate for anti-American terrorist activity. That the United States is the source via movies and TV of cultural trends that challenge time-honored traditional values in other societies, especially Moslem ones, makes its recurrence more probable.

The Turn to Actual War: Afghanistan and After

The metaphoric War on Terrorism led us to real war in Afghanistan. There were cogent justifications for our intervention in view of the gross violation of human rights by the Taliban government as well as its fostering of bin Laden and al Qaeda. However, our air offensive hurt and killed many innocent Afghanis, and bin Laden remains elusive. Especially troublesome, the prospects of constructing a civil society respectful of human rights in Afghanistan are not hopeful, and the dependability of our commitment to participate in the reconstruction is uncertain.

The actual war differed from historically usual wars in one salient respect: it was conducted with remarkably little cost in American lives. With the use of expensive modern technology, heavy bombing, the careful and selective use of special forces, and reliance on the undisciplined forces of local war lords, the United States incurred large monetary costs but small human ones. When a participant in the American attack was killed by enemy action, the American press treated it as worth headlines. Most of our losses were like those in military training, as when a plane crashed into a mountain in Pakistan. From the American viewpoint, the action was indeed more like a realistic training operation than a war.

This great disproportion in human cost, fortunate for us, has less fortunate implications. War that so minimizes our human risk tempts us to rely on brute force when it might be avoided. Although it was bloodier, the Afghan war reminds me of the gun-boat diplomacy we relied on early in the last century, in which we imposed our national will on other, less powerful countries at negligible cost in American lives.

Because we cannot negotiate with bin Laden, if he is still relevant, or with suicidal terrorists like al Qaeda, who will long be with us, where do we turn? Bombing with impunity is a tempting way to go, but the metaphoric war may have prepared us to accept much more costly military involvement. President Bush suggested new steps toward extended real war when he named Iraq, Iran, and North Korea as the "Evil Axis," an egregiously metaphoric reference to the Axis Powers of World War II. The shifting focus from international terrorism to the potentiality for the deployment of means of mass destruction brings the prospect of a major, more traditional war much closer. In the April 1st issue of *The New Yorker* magazine, which I was reading while revising this article, Nicholas Lemann (2002) drew on his extensive insider interviews as well as Bush's addresses to Congress and leaks to the press to support conclusions about our current policy position that I find quite appalling. He wrote the following:

> . . . [A]all indications are that Bush is going to use September 11 as the occasion to launch a new, aggressive foreign policy that would represent a broad change in direction rather than a specific war on terrorism. . . . Inside government, the reason September 11 appears to have been "a transformative moment" . . . is not so much that it revealed the existence of a threat of which officials had previously been unaware as that it drastically reduced the American public's usual resistance to American military involvement overseas, at least for a while. (p. 44)

The prospects of real war without a discernible endpoint, an American war to restructure the power relations in the oil-rich but mostly undemocratic Middle East, seem all too imminent, although the bloody deadlock in the Israeli and Palestinian conflict may have stalled the Bush administration's intended moves against Saddam Hussein for the time being. The policy issues raised by both Hussein and bin Laden are readily framed as black versus white, congenial to the right-wing authoritarian tendency of the Bush administration (Altemeyer, 1996), which has difficulty with the Israeli and Palestinian confrontation in which both sides have strongly warranted justifications and grievances.

Some Costs of Our Metaphoric War

Even if we resist the drift to actual war, a long-term War on Terrorism is dangerous to us as a democratic country, and to our interests in an international world of peace and justice.

It is dangerous to us. A continued war, metaphorical or factual, endangers our democracy. As de Tocqueville wrote

> Those who seek to destroy the liberties of a democratic nation ought to know that war is the surest and the shortest means to accomplish it. (de Tocqueville, 1945, Vol. 2., p. 284, quoted in Sills & Merton, 2000)

The administration of George W. Bush and Attorney General John Ashcroft may not explicitly intend to jeopardize our democratic liberties, but it seems less concerned with protecting them than with sustaining their conservative regnancy. Wartime security provisions and wartime evocation of patriotism do put our constitutional democracy at risk.

Pursuing our War on Terrorism in its current mode is also dangerous to what should be our interests in international peace and justice. I have already suggested that the United States, as the dominant superpower, is bound to be viewed with suspicion by less affluent and powerful nations and people—even by our European allies in the affluent Western World. Our recent conduct of the War on Terrorism shows a serious lack of the realistic empathy that Ralph White called for in his classic analysis of the dynamics of conflictual relations in the Cold War. To quote White

> Empathy is the *great* corrective for all forms of war-promoting mispercep-
> tion. It means simply understanding the thoughts and feelings of others. It
> is distinguished from sympathy, which is defined as feeling with others—
> as being in agreement with them. Empathy with opponents is therefore
> psychologically possible even when a conflict is so intense that sympathy
> is out of the question. We are not talking about warmth or approval, and
> certainly not about agreeing with, or siding with, but only about realistic
> understanding. (White, 1984, p. 160, as slightly modified in McNamara
> & Blight, 2001, p. 65)

I think White's analysis of realistic empathy is the most important con-tribution psychology has made to the understanding and management of the national and international conflicts that imperil our country and the world, so I was pleased to see that Robert McNamara and James Blight (2001) give it top billing in their excellent new book, *Wilson's Ghost: Reducing the Risk of Conflict, Killing, and Catastrophe in the 21st Century*, which was committed to print soon before the events of September, 11, 2001, but is very pertinent to our present situation. Indeed, it is important to consider the War on Terrorism in the broader context of the all-important challenge to avoid the grim prospect that the 21st century may be even bloodier than the bloody 20th century, which is the focus of McNamara and Blight's valuable analysis and advocacy, to which I return shortly.

The Challenge to Realistic Empathy

Just a little exercise in realistic empathy would have stopped President Bush from calling our War on Terrorism a "crusade," evoking an historical episode most offensive to Islam. However, that gaffe is unfortunately typical of our general conduct of our metaphorical and actual war. If we could let ourselves imagine how our claims of righteousness and our continuing and recurrent unilateral initiatives look to our antagonists, to Islamic countries, and to the rest of the world, while we ask for help from the UN and from our European and Asian allies, we should have proceeded quite differently.

It has done no good to demonize bin Laden and al Qaeda, diabolic as their actions have been. They are not excused by the fact that they see the United States as arrogantly prosperous, as a friend of Israel in the bloody stalemate of the Middle East, and as promulgating the evils of modernism that fundamentalist Islam abhors—as the Great Satan. However, if we are to undercut their appeal to the rest of Islam and to the hopeless strata of the "have-not" world, we need to be sensitive to these feelings that are shared very widely. The "mirror image" phenomena highlighted by Urie Bronfenbrenner (1961) in the Cold War recur here. From their own perspective and that of their supporters, terrorists to us are martyrs and freedom fighters to them.

In this context, our attachment to bombing is especially dubious. From our standpoint as bombers, we are at minimal risk, and also feel minimal personal responsibility for the death and destruction that we produce (it is not like hand-to-hand combat). And we expect and "regret" but keep on producing "collateral damage." We see regrettable mistakes as simply to be expected in war. May I try some realistic empathy? "These heartless monsters are destroying our lives and country at little cost to themselves!" Of course, when we bomb weak, "have-not" powers, it doesn't matter to us militarily if the people get angry with us. But it is not a propitious prelude to national reconstruction (which we want in Afghanistan and in Iraq) and to international peace. And people get killed, although not many Americans.

Unilateralism versus Multilateralism in American Practice and Policy

Another important policy recommendation follows from realistic empathy: that we should radically correct our tendency to use our power in unilateral initiatives. In our sense of our own righteousness, we continually act in ways that much of the world views very differently. The

Harvard political scientist, Samuel Huntington (1999), has listed a number of such instances, among them the following:

> Grading countries according to their adherence to American standards on human rights, drugs, terrorism, military issues, and religious freedom.
>
> Applying sanctions to countries that get failing "grades" on these issues.
>
> Promoting American business interests under the slogans of free trade and open markets.
>
> Promoting American arms sales abroad while trying to prevent similar sales by other countries.
>
> Forcing out one UN secretary general and dictating the appointment of his successor.
>
> Categorizing certain countries as "rogue states", excluding them from global institutions because they refuse to kowtow to American wishes. (Quoted in McNamara & Blight, 2001, pp. 50–51)

Huntington goes on to say the following:

> Although the United States regularly denounces various countries as "rogue states", in the eyes of many countries it is becoming the rogue superpower. . . . The United States is unlikely to become an isolationist country, withdrawing from the world. But it could become an isolated country, out of step with most of the world. . . . At a 1997 Harvard conference, scholars reported the elites of countries comprising at least two-thirds of the world's peoples—Chinese, Russians, Indians, Arabs, Muslims, and Africans—see the United States as the single greatest threat to their societies. They do not regard America as a military threat but as a menace to their integrity, autonomy, prosperity, and freedom of action. They view the United States as intrusive, interventionist, exploitative, hegemonic, hypocritical, and applying double standards, engaging in what they label "financial imperialism" and "intellectual colonialism", with a foreign policy driven overwhelmingly by domestic politics. (Huntington, 1999, quoted in McNamara & Blight, 2001, pp. 51–52)

McNamara and Blight (2001) draw from such exercises in international empathy what they call their "multilateral imperative":

> Recognize that although the United States must provide leadership to the world to achieve the objective of reducing the risk of conflict, it will not apply its power—economic, political, or military—other than in a multilateral context, subject to multilateral decision-making processes. (p. 49)

In a variety of contexts, they argue for the desirability of what they call "zero-tolerance multilateralism" (McNamara & Blight, 2001, p. 136), holding that even in the morally extreme case of genocidal communal conflict, unilateral intervention is likely to do more harm than good. Writing before September 11, 2001, they regarded "responding to a direct attack on the American homeland" as the only exception to their multilateral imperative for the 21st century. I believe that in this case the exception is questionable.

In its response to the attack of September, 11, 2001, the United States did seek, and receive, extensive international cooperation. Such cooperation is essential for tracking down the network of al Qaeda, but was limited in the actual war in Afghanistan. As I was revising this in early April 2002, the United States had been invited by the Bush administration to contemplate the prospect of an indefinitely continued metaphorical War on Terrorism with the imminent possibility of new actual wars, with Iraq and possibly with other "evil" possessors or would-be possessors of weapons of mass destruction. Obviously there is no risk-free way of dealing with the international predicament in which we find ourselves, and psychologists lack the expertise in international affairs to be credible advocates of national strategy. However, we have hard-earned distinctive ways of looking at the conditions and consequences of conflict that raise serious questions about the policies that the Bush administration is pursuing. Ralph White's (1984) discussions of realistic empathy are a very important contribution.

Concluding Remarks

My commentary on the War on Terrorism will not be welcomed by psychologists like my old friend Howard Kendler (1999), who would limit our political participation as psychologists to the presentation of research findings. I offer it as a plea by a psychologist-citizen whose long-term affiliation with the Society for the Psychological Study of Social Issues (SPSSI; Division 9 of the American Psychological Association) rests on the conviction that such advocacy, for the most part not directly derived from psychological research but informed by psychological perspectives and analysis, is not only legitimate but is very much needed. I do not segregate my roles as psychologist and as citizen. My role models in social psychology—Gordon Allport, Gardner Murphy, and Muzafer Sherif—saw things that way. The difficult issues of the world since September 11, 2001, call for psychologist-citizens who can resist the mirage of uncritical "patriotism" to speak out.

References

Altemeyer, B. (1996). *The authoritarian spector*. Cambridge, MA: Harvard University Press.

Bronfenbrenner, U. (1961). The mirror-image in Soviet-American relations: A social psychologist's report. *Journal of Social Issues, 17*(3), 45–56.

de Tocqueville, A. (1945). *Democracy in America*. New York: Vintage.

Huntington, S. P. (1999). The lonely superpower. *Foreign Affairs, 78*(2), 35–49.

Kendler, H. H. (1999). The role of value in the world of psychology. *American Psychologist, 54*, 828–835.

Lakoff, G., & Johnson, M. (1980). *Metaphors we live by*. Chicago: University of Chicago Press.

Lemann, N. (2002, April 1). The next world order: The Bush administration men have a brand-new doctrine of power. *The New Yorker*, pp. 42–48.

McNamara, R. S., & Blight, J. G. (2001). *Wilson's ghost: Reducing the risk of conflict, killing, and catastrophe in the 21st century*. New York: Public Affairs.

Sills, D. L., & Merton, R. K. (Eds.). (2000). *Social science quotations*. New Brunswick, NJ: Transaction.

Smith, M. B. (1985). The metaphorical basis of selfhood. In M. B. Smith, (1991), *Values, self, and society*, pp. 73–93. New Brunswick, NJ: Transaction. Reprinted from A. J. Marsella, A. de Vos, & F.L.K.H.S.U. (1985), *Culture and self: Asian and Western perspectives*. London: Tavistock.

Smith, M. B. (2000). Values, politics, and psychology, *American Psychologist, 55*, 1151–1152.

White, R. K. (1984). *Fearful warriors: A psychologist's profile of U.S. — Soviet relations*. New York: Free Press.

Part IV

Reappraising Our Foundations

Commentary

The second half of the twentieth century was a period of substantial change in psychologists' assumptions about the foundations of their discipline. At midcentury, the neobehaviorism of Hull (1943) and Skinner (1938) was still at apogee. Freudian psychoanalysis and neo-Freudianism were gaining in influence in the profession and would-be science of clinical psychology as it burgeoned right after the war. Dollard and Miller (1950) sought to meld psychoanalysis and Hullian neobehaviorism in their *Personality and Psychotherapy*, whereas humanistic psychologists near the fringe of the discipline renounced both of these channels of the mainstream, promoting their own approach as a third force (Bugenthal, 1978).

Mainstream psychologists tended to look to Viennese logical positivism (e.g., Reichenbach, 1961) or to the operationism of Percy Bridgman (1927) for their philosophical underpinnings. I had swallowed and partly digested a heavy helping of that in a Harvard methodology seminar with S. Smith ("Smitty") Stevens in 1941.

But I had also imbibed the Jamesian relish for theoretical openness (cf. Smith, 2002) from other Harvard mentors, so I rejoiced in the relaxation of proscriptive restrictions as the reign of behaviorism and logical positivism faded (cf. Smith, 1990). I became increasingly concerned as the revolt against positivism—the misapplication to human affairs of a physicalistic version of natural science—turned in some quarters to rejection of evidential empiricism. Chapters 6 and 9 have already touched on these concerns.

The two chapters in this section, which both involve reappraisal of the philosophical underpinnings of psychology, serve quite different ends. In chapter 18, "Skinner at 75," my review of a collection of his miscellaneous essays, I looked back on the work of the arch behaviorist, and tried to disentangle his philosophical positivism, which I have always regarded as dead wrong, from his important empirical contributions. I had been pleased when Skinner told me that my earlier review (1972) of his polemical *Beyond Freedom and Dignity* (Skinner, 1971) was one of the few he had read that left him feeling that the reviewer had actually read the book. Addressing the interdisciplinary audience of *Political Psychology* encouraged me to assess his overall contributions on the broad scale they deserved. This chapter represents my selective rejection of Skinnerian positivism as inappropriate for a significant social psychology.

Chapter 19, "Psychology and Truth: Human Science and the Postmodern Challenge," draws together my response to the threat from the opposite direction. This is the still proliferating extreme relativism of the postmodernists, who carry their rejection of positivism to the nihilistic abandonment of science as a fallible but corrigible endeavor. I wrote the essay in the conviction that the demoralizing loss of faith in rational inquiry is a symptomatic response to the cultural stresses of our time, and that social psychologists and other social scientists who are trained in such inquiry have the obligation to resist this trend.

In writing this chapter, I had in mind the vulnerability of human science and scholarship to the postmodernist infection. But postmodernism also undermines professional practice if one takes its claims at face value. Educators and therapists make real efforts in a real sociocultural world of human relations, which require assessment in terms of real effects, effects transcending the solipsistic linguistic world of "discourse" in which postmodernist constructionism sees us as immersed. From the standpoint of psychological practice, philosophically inclined spokespersons are rising to the challenge of postmodernism.

Daniel Fishman (1999), for one, advocates a "pragmatic psychology" that goes along with the postmodernist rejection of law-like causal generalizations but seeks systematic empirical evidence for the effectiveness of interventions that "work." His version of pragmatism is closer to Rorty's (1979) antirealism than I prefer but does respect the relevance of "data." He also provides a clearer exposition of postmodernism in its several versions than one can find in the postmodernist sources, which often seem deliberately obscure.

An especially searching critique of postmodern theory in psychotherapy is offered by Barbara Held in her *Back to Reality* (1995), which I had not read when I wrote chapter 19. I take her "modest realism" as essentially equivalent to my own critical accommodation to social constructionism. Therapists like personologists work with persons' "narratives" as partly reflecting, partly creating the life problems that bring them into therapy. But therapists' own therapeutic claims are not just stories. In their reference to consequential realities, we rightly concerned with the validity of their representations.

I am glad to end this book of retrospections and aspirations with chapter 19. It touches on matters that recur throughout the book. A significant social psychology, in the broad sense that I seek to reinstate, has first of all to deal critically and respectfully with empirical evidence, evidence of realities that we cannot know directly but must construct inferentially. "Invention" is indeed involved—but also "discovery": good science and good scholarship design inquiry so that it is constrained by "how things are." The postmodern critics have been effective in sensitizing us to deficiencies in our social science. Culture theorists rightly tell us that we have been ethnocentric and culture-bound, feminist critics that we have been sexist, followers of Foucault (1972) that our doctrines disguise abuses of power. Each of these lines of criticism assumes criteria of truth and justice, according to which the doctrines and practices being criticized are wrong. If we accept this crucial assumption, the criticism arms us with resources to correct and improve social psychology. We are by no means compelled to read their critiques as discrediting the whole social scientific enterprise. If we are foolish enough to agree with that option, we are logically compelled to regard their critiques as equally discredited. Extreme nihilistic relativism undermines the critic's own standpoint. In the family of social sciences, a significant social psychology has a challenging future.

References

Bridgman, P. W. (1927). *The logic of modern physics*. New York: Macmillan.

Bugenthal, J.F.T. (1978). The third force in psychology. In I. D. Welch, G. Tate, & F. Richards (Eds.), *Humanistic psychology: A sourcebook* (pp. 13–21). New York: Prometheus.

Dollard, J., & Miller, N. E. (1950). *Personality and psychotherapy*. New York: McGraw-Hill.

Fishman, D. B. (1999). *The case for pragmatic psychology*. New York: New York University Press.

Foucault, M. (1972). *The archeology of knowledge*. London: Tavistock.

Held, B. S. (1995). *Back to reality: A critique of postmodern theory in psychotherapy.* New York: Norton.

Hull, C. L. (1943). *Principles of behavior.* New York: Appleton-Century-Crofts.

Reichenbach, H. (1961). *Experience and prediction.* Chicago: University of Chicago Press. (Originally published 1938).

Rorty, R. (1979). *Philosophy and the mirror of nature.* Princeton: Princeton University Press.

Skinner B. F. (1938). *The Behavior of organisms.* New York: Appleton-Century.

Skinner, B. F. (1971). *Beyond freedom and dignity.* New York: Knopf.

Smith, M. B. (1972). Review of B. F. Skinner, *Beyond freedom and dignity, American Scientist, 60,* 80–81.

Smith, M. B. (1990). Psychology and the decline of positivism. In R. Jessor (Ed.), *Perspectives on behavioral science: The Colorado lectures.* Boulder, CO: Westview. Reprinted in M. B. Smith (1991), *Values, self, and society* (pp. 149–162). New Brunswick, NJ: Transaction.

Smith, M. B. (2002). William James (1842–1910). *International Encyclopedia of the Behavioral and Social Sciences,* 7949–7954. London: Elsevier.

Chapter Eighteen

Skinner at Seventy-Five

In pondering what I would say in this essay-review of *Reflections on Behaviorism and Society* (Eastwood Cliffs, NJ: Prentice-Hall, 1978), I arrived at the conviction that its author, B. F. Skinner, at a young and vigorous 75, is more than ever a force to be reckoned with. A major figure in American psychology for more than 40 years, he competes with Freud and Piaget for productive longevity. Hull, Spence, Guthrie, and Tolman, his peers of the 1935–1945 decade of grand neobehavioristic systems during which Skinner rose to prominence with *The Behavior of Organisms* (1938) are long gone, and their theories are dead too—of only historical interest.[1] Paradoxically, Skinner asserted that he was not a theorist but only engaging in the "experimental analysis of behavior" in the spirit of radical positivism.

Skinner tells us that *Walden Two* (1948), the utopian novel that he wrote before significant human applications of Skinnerian principles were at all developed, sold only 10,000 copies in its first 14 years but was selling a quarter of a million annually in the early 1970s. Again paradoxically, "behavior modification" based substantially on Skinner's contributions has spread through professional training programs in clinical psychology and, to a lesser extent, in social work and psychiatry, and has emerged conspicuously on the growing edge of practice in the human services, overshadowing the waning psychoanalytic movement— just when the dogmas of positivism on which Skinner grounded his radical behaviorism were generally coming to be regarded as discredited.

Skinner's career has been a resounding success, and the movement that he heads—once a rather narrowly encapsulated band of academic followers—has been absorbed into the mainstream and has come to dominate some of its major currents.

The paradoxes just noted, centering on Skinner's philosophical or metapsychological posture of positivism or radical behaviorism, make it difficult for the thoughtful general public—even for his colleagues in psychology—to form a just appraisal of his contribution and to decide what to make of his polemical claims. These difficulties in digesting and appraising Skinner have become the more troublesome as age and formal academic retirement have drawn Skinner from the laboratory to address himself increasingly to general audiences, and they have their parallel in the perplexities that long attended the still unfinished process by which Freud's radical novelties were assimilated by the intellectual and scientific world. In reacting to Skinner's strong stimulus, people get polarized, into loyal Skinnerians and those like Chomsky who see him as a manipulator and protofascist. An increasing number of unintellectual practitioners merely draw on Skinnerian techniques eclectically along with "humanistic" ones from the California weed-patch, dismissing larger issues of social policy or philosophical consistency. Strong polemics are the enemy of judicious appraisal, especially when the issues are laden with paradox.

Unquestionably, Skinner is an effective polemicist, an unusually good writer—as the occasional essays collected in the present volume, all written since 1972, make amply clear. A miscellany like this is not the best place to come seriously to grips with Skinner's systematic views and claims as they bear upon political psychology: for the general reader, *Walden Two* (1948), *Beyond Freedom and Dignity* (1971), and *About Behaviorism* (1974) remain essential, and they are frequently referred to in *Reflections*. But the quality of these essays is consistently high; they stand on their own two feet; and the newcomer can use them to advantage to get acquainted with Skinner, while the confirmed Skinner-watcher will not want to miss them. Skinner says by way of introduction that "this is not a book to be read straight through," and, to guide the reader to what may be of most interest, he then provides a string of abstracts of all the essays. Your faithful reviewer *has* read them straight through, and has profited enjoyably from the experience. True, there are repetitions, but even these are interesting as displaying the deeper structure of Skinner's polemical armamentarium.

Skinner groups the essays under four rubrics: *society*, the essays most directly relevant to political psychologists; the *science of behavior*, where there is the heaviest dose of metapsychological polemics and also a fascinating, almost telegraphic, historical synopsis of his intellectual development in the creation of his "experimental analysis of behavior"; *education*, where he talks about his innovations in programmed learning and supports Fred S. Keller's increasingly respected "Personalized System of Instruction" based on Skinnerian principles, but mostly devotes himself to a devastating critique of educational laissez-faire on the horticultural model of Rousseau's *Emile* and of latter-day *Summerhill*; and *a miscellany* of brilliant scattered pieces ranging from evolutionary theory through literary criticism to a satirical proposal for socializing the young to become lottery addicts, which is so sound technically that some government might take it at face value. The first set of essays will be of interest to political psychologists regardless of their judgment of Skinner's philosophical predilections, and I will return to them later. My main purpose, however, is to try to disentangle what is brilliant and important and useful in Skinner from what is brilliant but wrong-headed and, in Nixon's memorable term, counterproductive.

Skinner is hard to disentangle. In one sense, he is all of a piece; all of his writings from the early 1930s on cohere. He is still a loyal positivist— yet, unlike his almost forgotten contemporaries of the '30s, he has used positivism (but not, be it noted, its version in the once-prevalent hypothetico-deductive method) to create and promote an ever-expanding salient in psychology that has indeed *worked*. His animal research on schedules of reinforcement is a solid achievement that underlies, for example, the deployment of animal subjects in research on psychopharmacology. His development of programmed learning as an explicit set of strategies and tactics for attaining training objectives, when these can be specified, is an achievement that will surely become even more important than it is today. (All the same, I have to note that training is not identical with education.) The strategies of the "experimental analysis of behavior" and the techniques of "behavioral modification" that follow from them have amply proved their value in restricted domains, and I don't doubt that they will turn out to be even more generally useful. All of these contributions emerge from the same Skinner, who accounts for them in the same behavioristic terms. How *can* one break in?

Yet we must break in. We must, because Skinner uses these acknowledged successes to justify a view of the task of psychology and of the nature of humanness that I am convinced is dehumanizing, and, I believe, can be cleanly dissected from his real and important achievements. The crux of the matter is his dogmatic rejection of human subjectivity and of the reflexivity (self-regardingness, hence potential self-correction, self-investment, and self-development) of minding, and, therefore, his mindless interpretation of contingent "reinforcement" as what thus becomes a mechanistic principle for the explanation and control of behavior.

Skinner is insistent on his rejections:

> Do I mean to say that Plato never discovered the mind? Or that Acquinas, Descartes, Locke, and Kant were preoccupied with incidental, often irrelevant by-products of human behavior? Or that the mental laws of physiological psychologists like Wundt, or the stream of consciousness of William James, or the mental apparatus of Sigmund Freud have no useful place in the understanding of human behavior? Yes, I do. And I put the matter strongly because, if we are to solve the problems that face us in the world today, this concern for mental life must no longer divert our attention from the environmental conditions of which human behavior is a function. (p. 51)

An honorable, deeply felt position, stated with the chutzpah that can be taken as charisma, but why should we forswear our hard-earned humanistic heritage and much of our scientific heritage to boot?

In the passage that immediately precedes the quotation I have extracted, Skinner talks about how people go about answering such questions as "Are you going to go?" "Do you intend to go?" "Do you feel like going?" saying that, in answering such questions, one learns to observe the strength or probability of one's behavior. He goes on to say, "The important fact is that such contingencies, social or nonsocial, involve nothing more than stimuli or responses; *they do not involve mediating processes.*" The italics are Skinner's, and I fear that italics are the last refuge of the beleaguered dogmatist, who lets strength of assertion stand in for convincing argument.

The dogmatism comes from the received doctrines of Vienna-Kreis positivism, the intellectual frontier in Skinner's formative years. Historians and philosophers of science have since moved on, and, looking back, they regard Vienna positivism as a mistaken account even of the work of the physical scientists which the positivists took as their admired model. Psychology too has moved on, with "cognitive behaviorism" (about which I still have doubts) now characterizing the mainstream— except for Skinner and his closest followers. So it is easy, now, for the rest of us to challenge Skinner's unreconstructed behaviorism. But that requires us to tease out the creatively useful from the philosophically dogmatic in the Skinnerian corpus.

Here we must look closely at Skinner's central idea: probabilistic contingent reinforcement as the shaper of behavior. For rats and pigeons it works—so predictably that a mechanistic interpretation is reasonable, though strict mechanism is probably fair neither to pigeon nor to Skinner. For people, it also seems to work by and large, though the clearest successes of behavior modification based on reinforcement principles have been with rather thoughtless people (retardates, schizophrenics, children) or thoughtless problem behaviors. But we need to look more closely at how it works for people.

People are not like pigeons, because they do talk to themselves and each other and, surely not epiphenomenally, they do sometimes think.[2] Thinking people have always been guided by incentives, and psychologists who have tried to give an account of people's behavior have written about incentives and reward and punishment since the earliest days of the science—social philosophers and political economists before them. Because Skinner and his followers have made a particularly incisive analysis of the role of incentive contingencies—the domain of their incontrovertible and important empirical results—they ask us to accept the positivistic metapsychology that happened to inspire their search. There is simply no good reason for us to go along.

In fact, some of the useful things that Skinner has to say in *Reflections on Behaviorism and Society* about the advantages of positive over aversive reinforcement—of reward over punishment—were said before him by other astute psychologists who were not bound by Skinner's behavioristic constraints. I think particularly of Kurt Lewin's classic analysis of reward and punishment—of the "forces" induced by conflicts set up by positive and negative "valences." As Skinner recognizes, the idea that people, as well as animals, guide their behavior at least in part in terms of costs and benefits was far from new with him. Many of the details that Skinner highlights in regard to contingent relationships between behavior and its consequences are new and important. Recognizing them need not commit us to ascribing to people the same unthinking blindness that is a good fit for pigeons. A political psychology that followed Skinner strictly on this point would not only find the very concept of democracy enigmatic, but would contribute to self-fulfilling, antidemocratic trends.

For Skinner, his insistence on a nonmentalistic, positivistic language for talking about incentives, reward and punishment, is no mere philosophic quibble. I think he is wrong in believing that his empirical successes and his conceptual insights hinge on this language, that mentalism is a threat to human survival. But, for me, the issue is also not a quibble.

While I don't think Plato or Descartes or Locke or Kant or James or Freud had a close hold on the permanent truth, I see loss rather than gain in cutting anchor from a metaphorical tradition that, by my metapsychology, is *formative* of mind as well as descriptive of it. Especially in the realm of political psychology, I want to keep the door open, the language available, for imaginary conversations with Isaiah Berlin!

Having cleared the air, I hope, so as to make it possible to appreciate many of the insightful and important things that Skinner has to say without accepting his metapsychology, I turn briefly to the first section of *Reflections on Behaviorism and Society*, which, as I said, has rich offerings for the student of political psychology.

The initial essay, "Human Behavior and Democracy," goes a good way toward meeting objections that the Skinner of *Walden Two* and *Beyond Freedom and Dignity* had no grasp of the political realm.[3] True, he sidesteps the issue of who will control the controllers [*Quis custodiet ipsos custodes?*] rather than dealing with it frontally. But he makes his own priorities clear in this essay and elaborates upon them in a subsequent one, "Walden Two Revisited": big government, bureaucratic organization, and mass society have gotten out of hand, so hope lies not in tinkering with these wrong-scale mechanisms [that accompany a scandalous economic system also out of hand], but in redesigning the culture of face-to-face community life so that people "control" one another's behavior directly and informally. That is, he joins with Schumacher's Small is Beautiful, for which I can only cheer. Skinner's preferences clearly tend toward the anarchical and are far from fascistic. [But Lenin, too, looked forward to the "withering away of the state."] If he still underplays the need for political institutions to formulate social decisions, allocate resources, resolve conflicts, and modulate the exercise of power, he has many provocative things to say about the criteria for workable systems of social incentives. These are important essays.

Even more important—itself a good reason for buying a book—is Skinner's essay "Are We Free to Have a Future?" This is a subtle and powerful treatment of current dilemmas that is illuminated by Skinner's distinctive behavioral analysis and only minimally distorted by his philosophical commitments. How can people be induced to take the future into account?—as they mostly don't, but will have to if our culture and the species are to survive. This is a dramatically important question, and what Skinner has to say should sharpen every reader's thinking about it.

To put part of the argument in a nutshell, both natural selection in biological evolution and behavioral selection in the individual life yield behavior adapted to a future that resembles the past. And operant learning, on Skinner's model, takes only the immediate future into account, unless there are cultural structures that support the linkage of behaviors leading to more remote goals [not Skinner's language, but it covers the same ground]. In the past, societies relied heavily on aversive or coercive controls, and the trend toward replacing these with positive reinforcers is what we mean, Skinner says, by the trend toward freedom. [Some of us mean more, but we surely mean at least that.] Recently we have been dismantling these controls faster than we are replacing them with positive equivalents, and an affluent, welfare-oriented society has also been replacing contingent reinforcers with noncontigent gratifications.[4] We all live in a token economy (the monetary system), but the contingencies of reinforcement that it now provides have become less clear and compelling than they were in leaner times. The result is life oriented to the "here and now," but also fecklessness and apathy—and poor survival prospects. Skinner's conclusion must be quoted directly:

> Are we sufficiently free of the present to have a future? Our extraordinary commitment to immediate gratification has served the species well. The powerful reinforcing effects of drugs like alcohol and heroin are no doubt accidents, but our susceptibilities to reinforcement by food, sexual contact, and signs of aggressive damage have had great survival value. Without them the species would probably not be here today, but under current conditions they are almost as nonfunctional as drugs, leading not to survival but to obesity and waste, to overpopulation, and to war, respectively.
>
> No matter how free we feel, we are never free of our genetic endowment or of the changes which occur in us during our lifetime. But if other aspects of human nature, aspects we sum up in the word intelligence, come into play, we may design a world in which our susceptibilities to reinforcement will be less troublesome and in which we shall be more likely to behave in ways which promise a future. The task can scarcely be overestimated. Happiness is a dangerous value, and the pursuit of happiness has clearly been too successful. Like other affluent nations, we must, to coin a horrid word, "deaffluentize." People have done so in the past when pestilence and famine have deprived them of natural reinforcers, and when revolutions in government and religion have changed their social environment, but the power of immediate reinforcement continues to reassert itself and with ever more threatening consequences. This could happen once too

often. It is possible that the human species will be "consumed by that which it was nourished by." We have it in our power to avoid such an ironic fate. The question is whether our culture will induce us to do so. (p. 32)

Up until the final sentence, I can only applaud the agenda that Skinner sets for us. There he recedes to the extreme and doctrinaire environmentalism that is a final complaint I must make about his metapsychology — a feature of it that, as here, invades his actual psychology and affects its implications for human action and the human future. In spite of a good deal of sensible inconsistency, Skinner says repeatedly that people are under environmental control (via the reinforcement route), and Skinner the metapsychologist really means it. That amounts to a passive view of human nature. If we really "have it in our power to avoid such an ironic fate," why should we wait around for our culture to "induce us to do so"? Of course, Skinner the psychologist and citizen has no such intention.

What his view of human nature lacks, however, is any explicit conceptualization of interaction, in which the developing person, shaped by previous experience, plays an increasing role in selecting and shaping the environments with which he or she interacts. Bandura and, recently, Mischel, among social learning theorists who share much of Skinner's general orientation but are less prone to dogmatic exclusions on philosophical grounds, do considerably better. Even they fall short, it seems to me, of achieving the sort of dialectical formulation that would both do justice to the human facts and provide a better warrant for the human hopes and commitments that will be required if we are to meet the challenge that Skinner has put to us. They fall short of giving a workable account of the citizen for political psychology.

This, you see, is a very good book which demands active, not passive, reading, and which one can enjoy and respect even when one violently disagrees with it.

NOTES

1. Tolman has a different standing from the others: he was a "premature" cognitive behaviorist — now the mainstream in American psychology, apart from Skinner.

2. Skinner regards *Verbal Behavior* (1957) as his most important lifetime

contribution—perhaps because it has the job of adapting his animal-based formulations to the facts of humanness. But its entirely speculative analyses have impressed neither the new linguists, from Chomsky on, nor psychologists actually working on the problems of language competence.

3. Elsewhere I have written that there is no place for either ethics or politics in Skinner's world. I still think he misses much of the point of ethics.

4. Parts of the argument resemble points made by Donald Campbell in his 1975 presidential address to the American Psychological Association.

References

Skinner, B. F. (1938). *The behavior of organisms.* New York: Appleton-Century-Crofts.

Skinner, B. F. (1948). *Walden II.* New York: Macmillan.

Skinner, B. F. (1957). *Verbal behavior.* New York: Appleton-Century-Crofts.

Skinner, B. F. (1971). *Beyond freedom and dignity.* New York: Knopf.

Skinner, B. F. (1974). *About behaviorism.* New York: Knopf.

Chapter Nineteen

Psychology and Truth
Human Science and the Postmodern Challenge

The topic addressed in this essay is one that I care deeply about, as it involves my lifetime investment in psychology. Psychology is in a time of transition, but as I have come to realize after more than half a century in the field, psychology and science generally are *always* in transition. We live in history just as inescapably as we live in culture. But there may be features of our *fin de siècle* time that make it seem more saliently transitional than in earlier times to which many of us have been accustomed. Particularly, some claims going with the term "postmodern" suggest a more radical transition in our self-understanding as psychologists than I think is warranted or desirable. I am worried about the readiness with which some of my colleagues seem eager to discard the ideal of truth as a quaint and perhaps ideologically tainted "enlightenment project." Before I go into these matters, however, I should sketch a bit of my own background in regard to the philosophical underpinnings of psychology with which I will be concerned here. A welcome feature of the current metatheoretical atmosphere is the common agreement that it is a good thing to put one's implicit philosophical cards on the table.

The Development of my Metapsychological Assumptions

The psychology I encountered in the 1930s before World War II reflected a climate dominated by behaviorism and logical positivism. We learned about Percy Bridgeman's (1927) operational definitions and about the Vienna Circle of logical positivists, who promoted the physicalist unity of the sciences on an empiricist and logico-mathematical basis. We were excited by Clark Hull's (1943) attempt to produce a hypothetico-deductive system that could explain apparently purposive behavior mechanistically. All the same, such attempts to model psychology on physics did not produce a monolithic psychology, even in the United States. There was psychoanalysis—naughty, alluring, overambitious, and seemingly requiring initiation by personal analysis to be understood or criticized. At the boundaries of North American psychology were the emigrating German Gestaltists and Kurt Lewin (e.g., 1935). There were also Gordon Allport (1937) and Henry Murray (1938), both of whom became my teachers and mentors, whose visions of a psychology of personality could not be confined by positivistic proscriptions. And there was Marxism, which had a strong appeal to me as an undergraduate at the time of the Spanish Civil War and the Popular Front. There was also the exciting culture-and-personality movement that wedded neo-Freudian psychoanalysis with cultural anthropology, which even gave promise, via Erich Fromm (1941) and Abram Kardiner (1939) of incorporating aspects of Marxist historical materialism. These were inviting vistas, at a time in my graduate studies when the prewar Harvard pro-seminar in psychology created the expectation that its products would become general psychologists besides developing a specialty. We students certainly enjoyed an Eriksonian moratorium in regard to our identities as psychologists. We could only wonder how people like Gordon Allport or Smitty Stevens (S. Smith Stevens, 1935) on our Harvard faculty or Clark Hull at Yale could construct their coherent versions of psychology.

My wartime experience in applied psychological research and research after the war in personality and political psychology left me less in awe of positivistic prescriptions and proscriptions, and ready to rejoice in the successful revolt against positivism, at least in its more proscriptive variants, in recent decades (Smith, 1991a). It was good to have people's thoughts, feelings, and experience back into the picture without apology or double talk about verbal behavior. It was good to recognize that as a biological and human science, psychology did not need to model itself on Newtonian or modern physics. It was good to recognize the inevitable involvement of human values in the agenda of psychology. It was good, also, to recognize that psychology and the social sciences are themselves social constructions that are subject to distortion from the historical and social perspectives of their creators. Bringing in the perspectives of women, oppressed minorities, and non-Euro-American cultures called attention to the fact that what was claimed to be universal general psychology was actually more Eurocentric and androcentric than mainstream psychologists were aware—that some of our supposedly universal generalizations might be mainly true of white middle-class North American undergraduates, maybe also mainly men, at that.

All this seemed to me to be liberating psychology from unwitting self-imposed limitations, to be setting the stage for realizing Sigmund Koch's (1959) optimism when he wrote prematurely:

> For the first time in its history, psychology seems ready — or almost ready — to assess its goals and instrumentalities with primary reference to its own indigenous problems. It seems ready to think contextually, freely, and creatively about its own refractory subject matter, and to work its way free from a dependence on simplistic theories of correct scientific conduct. (p. 783, italics his.)

I agree with Koch that the proscriptive philosophy of science held back the development of psychology in the United States, maybe by a generation. I agree with so much of the recent criticism of establishment psychology—by feminists, minority psychologists, cultural and cross-cultural psychologists, contextualists, social constructionists, and narrativists—that I find it important to draw the line firmly and object as strongly as I can to a central feature of the "postmodern" position that seems to me to be destructive of the potential contribution of both scientific and applied psychology. That is, in Kenneth Gergen's (1994) words, postmodernism's abandonment of "the traditional view that propositions about the world are driven or required by the particular characteristics of the world. . . . Whatever is the case makes no requirements on our descriptions or theories" (p. 412). According to this view, which can be labelled "anti-representationism," the conception of knowledge as a "mirror of Nature" (Rorty, 1979) is a chimera. The claims of science have no special privilege as compared with those of intuition or myth. At the extreme, scientific theories are just "stories that scientists like to tell" (White & Wang, 1995). This radical attack on the ideal of scientific truth has made surprising headway in the humanities and social sciences, and is a present danger in human psychology. My aim here is to try to understand the reasons for the attack and some of its implications, and to help us as psychologists regain a footing from which we can do our scientific and professional jobs.

Psychology and the Two Cultures

Almost four decades ago, the English scientist and novelist C. P. Snow (1959) gave the English-speaking world an evocative account of what he saw as the "two cultures" that his own career spanned—the cultures of the arts and humanities and of the sciences and technology. It now seems to me that the gulf which he saw as impeding communication and mutual understanding between scientists and engineers on the one hand and humanists, participants in high culture, on the other, has become even deeper and less bridgeable. Postmodernism as a phenomenon emerged in the humanities, is spreading to the social sciences, and has had little impact in the natural sciences, except as an external threat (as was becoming recognized in the conference "The Flight from Science and Reason" held by the New York Academy of Science—see "Reason Under Fire," 1995). I interpret it as a natural response from the humanistic culture to demoralizing stresses in our late modern situation (Giddens, 1991). In this respect, the humanities and arts are like the canary in the coal mine—artists and writers are especially sensitive to such stresses, and are followed by humanistic scholars. The principal stress that underlies postmodernism, it seems to me (Smith, 1994), is the prevailing loss of hope. Events of this bloody century have undermined the belief in progress that sustained people who were no longer comforted by the other-worldly hopes of traditional religion. Belief in progress was the hallmark of modernity—in contrast with the static sacred world envisioned in medieval times.

Two world wars and the Holocaust shook previous assumptions about human progress and perfectability; the prolonged imminence of nuclear catastrophe stirred ultimate anxieties; the collapse of Soviet communism laid another version of Utopian hopefulness to rest. Add the recent resurgence of ethnic conflict, the widening gap between "haves" and "have-nots" within and between nations, and the emerging concerns with overpopulation, pollution, and resource exhaustion, and the grounds for increasing hopelessness become obvious. In the United States, there have been other special grounds for political alienation and cynicism in recent decades. The approaching millennium may heighten people's sense of futility.

From the standpoint of the culture of the humanities and arts, moreover, it is easy to blame science. Fear of the results of technology and revulsion at them have long been common responses of humanistic intellectuals. In the United States and Europe, one can probably add in a measure of jealousy about the lavish support previously received by the sciences while the humanities and arts got slim rations at the foot of the table. Little wonder that participants in the culture of the humanities resonate to the anti-scientific aspect of postmodernism, while participants in the physical and biological sciences still enjoy high morale about their continual advances in understanding that invariably lead to new vistas of important problems demanding investigation, though they are frustrated in many technically advanced countries by declining financial support.

We should not forget, too, that philosophy of science is a humanistic, not a scientific specialty. Many of us look back critically on the presumptuous rule-giving by the logical positivists of the Vienna Circle. Current philosophical fashions of "anti-foundationism"—the abandonment of the search for firm ground on which to justify judgments about knowledge or ethics or aesthetics—that feed into postmodernism might be regarded with a similar grain of salt. It has ever been the case that good working scientists have paid little attention to the prescriptions and proscriptions of philosophers, though implicit philosophy may indeed guide and limit their practice.

The social sciences including psychology are intermediate between the humanities and the natural sciences in their vulnerability to postmodernism. Economics with its mathematical mystique is probably least touched, and the popularity of its models of rational choice in the field of political science suggests that this field, too, is minimally touched, though a segment of it is philosophical and humanistic. On the other hand, cultural anthropology has been swept over by a self-critical interpretative wave that often regards traditional ethnography as the tainted accomplice of colonialism, and vigorously rejects the model of natural science. (See American Anthropological Association, 1995, 1996, for thoughtful discussion of the issues.) Sociology is quite split, some sociologists continuing to test causal theory against quantitative models, others pursuing qualitative studies which may or may not be intended as a form of science.

A closer look at two subfields of psychology with which I am well acquainted may be instructive: social psychology and life-span developmental psychology.

The pioneers of North American social psychology—wide-ranging scholars like Gordon Allport, Gardner Murphy, Muzafer Sherif, Theodore Newcomb, and Otto Klineberg, all of whom I was privileged to know—saw their enterprise as interdisciplinary, embedded in historical context, and relevant to pressing social problems. They had no misgivings about its scientific aspirations, though they were typically modest about its achievements. By the time of Leon Festinger (1957) and the subsequent "cognitive social psychology," however, social psychology in the United States had become an artificially narrowed field devoted to establishing supposedly context-free generalizations experimentally. It paid little heed to cross-cultural psychology (Triandis & Lambert, 1980–1981), which required comparative cross-cultural research before regarding any pan-human generalizations as tenable. And it was therefore vulnerable to Gergen's (1973) claim that social psychology should be regarded as history rather than as science. (At that time, I argued [Smith, 1976] that if social psychology were to *become* a good science, it would have to be a historical science to a substantial extent; history and science are not mutually exclusive categories. Consider paleontology and cosmology!) At present, the North American social psychological mainstream goes its traditional way, with creative empirical work at its applied borders of health and gender psychology, and its rebels, such as Gergen and Sampson (1993), joining the postmodern revolt. The situation in England and the European continent is more propitious, with versions of postmodernism that show greater respect for empirical evidence apparent, for example, in the work of Michael Billig (1991) and Helen Haste (1993/1994).

Life-span developmental psychology provides an instructive contrast. Under the leadership of investigator-theorists like Paul Baltes (1987), Glen Elder (1994), Richard Lerner (1984), and Warner Schaie (1965), life-span developmentalists followed their initial attempts to disentangle the age, period, and cohort effects that had been confounded in traditional cross-sectional studies by explicitly conceiving of their field as a historical science. They enter into fruitful collaboration with historians, but show no signs of feeling that they have faltered in the scientific enterprise—quite the contrary. Naturally the extreme postmoderns like Gergen do not come from life-span developmental psychology. Nor do they come from the increasingly strong current in developmental psychology influenced by the historical-cultural approach of Lev Vygotsky (1978)—e.g., J. V. Wertsch (1985) and Barbara Rogoff (1990).

Discussions of how psychology fits in with the postmodern movement are confused by the introduction of the term "human science"

(Polkinghorne, 1983). Mostly, it has been used simply as a translation of the German *Geisteswissenschaften* (Dilthey, 1976), historical-cultural studies infused with meaning and value in contrast with the *Naturwissenschaften*, the natural sciences. Using the term in that way obscures the fundamental difference in aims and methods between the traditional sciences and humanities. The sciences abstract from the richness of experience, and aim at ever more powerful and comprehensive causal formulations. In aim and mostly in result, they are progressive; new science supersedes old science. In contrast, the arts and humanities recreate and interpret visions of concrete human experience in ways that can enrich and sometimes reshape the experience of their audience. They are not progressive: history moves on, but Proust does not supersede Shakespeare, nor Shakespeare replace Homer—or the Bhagavad Gita. I would prefer to reserve the term "human science" for efforts to bring human meaning and value, the stuff of the humanities, in coordination with systematic causal analysis: generalizing, explanatory science—real science—that deals with distinctively human material.

Indeed, it seems to me that the big methodological and theoretical challenge to human psychology is how to coordinate explanatory (scientific)—and interpretive (hermeneutic or humanistic)—approaches. The work of Albert Bandura (1977) on self-efficacy, of Julian Rotter (1966) and his successors on locus of control, and of Martin Seligman and others (Peterson, Maier, & Seligman, 1993) on learned helplessness and optimism illustrates such coordination: these psychologists have explored the casual conditions and consequences of people's self-interpretations and attributions very effectively. A number of postmodern writers have emphasized self-reflexiveness—the implications of the fact that people including psychological investigators are objects to themselves. An adequate treatment of this central human phenomenon has to put people's self-interpretations in a causal/explanatory context, has to conjoin the hermeneutic/interpretative and causal/explanatory approaches. (See Smith, 1991, for fuller discussion.)

The Problem of Truth: Anti-representationalism

I return now to the critical feature of postmodernism's challenge to psychology: its anti-representationalism, its denial of the ideal of scientific truth. I think this claim has disastrous consequences, and reflects a caricatured misunderstanding of the nature of science.

We can grant that the sciences as we know and participate in them in any historical period are social constructions in a historical context, subject to the vagaries of culture and the effects of perspective and of human prejudice and error. Science does not pretend to deal with absolute truth. As a cultural innovation of the seventeenth century, however, modern science has developed a set of strategies for approaching an understanding of the targets of its investigations—strategies that have resulted in *progressive* gains in understanding that meet pragmatic tests. I speak of strategies rather than of the "scientific method": the critics of scientific positivism are right, I think, in regarding the worship of scientific method as having badly hampered the work of psychology. Each science and sub-discipline has its own changing kit bag of methods and techniques. Human psychological studies obviously have little in common with the physical and even the biological sciences in this respect. But common strategies do warrant the honorific label "science." These have to do with the maintenance of an intercommunicating community of investigators, who make their various claims to advancing understanding by presenting *evidence* that meets criteria that are commonly shared in the relevant scientific community. Claims gain general acceptance when they stand up successfully to challenge. The public evidential self-critical basis for claims to increased knowledge is what makes scientific approaches intentionally progressive. They clearly have been progressive in the natural sciences in spite of the "paradigm shifts" emphasized by Thomas Kuhn (1970), and the postmodern challenge is absurd to deny it. The case is shakier in the human and social sciences, but I believe it is strong. The case for postmodern nihilism in psychology does not rest on a detailed analysis of psychology's successes and failures.

To the extent that scientific claims to knowledge are actually corrigible, as they always are in principle, scientific "narratives" have a different standing from the narratives of myth and revelation, of artistic imagination, of therapeutic collusion (Spence, 1982), or of plausible humanistic interpretation. Sciences have their own politics, and the politics and ideologies of the society to which the scientist belongs may also enter to shape and distort scientific activities and conclusions, doubtless more so in the social sciences than in the natural sciences. The kind of progressivist "Whig history" with which I was indoctrinated (Boring,

1929) underplayed these distortions in the history of psychology. The newer critical history, which calls attention to these "external" factors, does not discredit the scientific enterprise but actually improves our ability to identify and reduce ethnocentric, sexist, or other contextual/ perspectival sources of distortion. Just as scientific strategies in the human area help us discount and compensate for the wishful thinking to which all of us are prone in matters that touch our human concerns, the strategies of critical history help us to correct for the biasing effects of the limited perspectives linked to our location in history, culture, and social structure.

My rejoinder to the postmodernist assault on scientific truth is mainly pragmatic. The scientific enterprise, fallible as it is, has worked, even in the human area, and critical awareness of its fallibility can help it work better. But a more abstractly reasoned response to the critique of "foundationism" that comes from recent philosophy of language and science may be required. ("Anti-representationalism" is an aspect of "anti-foundationism," the widely current doctrine asserting the failure of the Enlightenment project to identify foundations apart from religious authority upon which to ground knowledge and value claims.) For my part, I like Donald Campbell's (1991) compromise position, which does not attempt to refute the philosophical critique of foundationism yet justifies belief in the results of scientific inquiry in terms of their coherence with the import of the whole body of accepted beliefs—an admittedly fallible criterion (remember the medieval flat earth) that scientists, like lay persons, can live with. This argument is also essentially pragmatic. It is only when we are so unreasonable as to ask science for reflections of absolute truth about reality that Richard Rorty's (1979) anti-representational challenge to the "mirror of nature" finds a vulnerable target.

The anti-representational position of postmodernism, with its attack on the special privilege of science, raises just as serious problems for enterprises that may be dearer to the hearts of postmodern critics. If judgments of truth are ruled out of order, the case for social and cultural criticism would seem to be undermined just as radically as the case for conformist science. Criticism of capitalist or colonialist or sexist ideology loses its relevance unless it is conceived in the service of ideals of truth or goodness in some sense. If feminist psychologists find North American psychology to be sexist, and Afro-American psychologists find it to be racist, they are calling for correction in the name of truth and justice.

Evidence that this poses a serious problem for postmodernists is provided by a recent book entirely devoted to attempts to cope with it: *After Postmodernism: Reconstructing Ideology Critique* (Simons & Billig, 1994). I don't pretend to evaluate the adequacy of these attempts here; what is relevant to my argument is the elaborate intellectual maneuvering that postmodern critics now find necessary.

The grounds for applied science are also undermined by the postmodern radical relativization of truth. A good while ago, Edelstein (1983) pointed out that the denial of any special privilege to science not only is incompatible with the aspirations for a cumulative generalizing science but also undercuts the justification for basing recommendations for social practice on scientific results. Are the postmodern critics ready to jettison meta-analyses of the effects of therapeutic interventions? (Yes, some of them are!) Do they really believe that program evaluation, which is obviously embedded in political processes, is only or merely a piece of political action? (Again, evidently, some of them do.) I am aware that some advocates of the humanistic position heartily reject all recourse to empirical evidence as part of our contemporary alienation from I-Thou authenticity, but I believe that many psychotherapists and other applied psychologists who have looked with some favor on the postmodern critique of academic scientific psychology have not thought through its bearing on the justification of their own professional practice and on its improvement.

A Response to the Postmodern Challenge

As the foregoing discussion bears witness, I take the postmodernists' challenge very seriously. I agree with much of their case against the previously dominant positivist philosophy of science. In psychology, positivism amounted to a misconception of the methods of the physical sciences misapplied to the study of human experience and behavior. It should be clear to us all by now that people's understanding of themselves, of others, and of society is socially constructed (Berger & Luckmann, 1966), and that our sciences are also human constructions. But our sciences are not freely conceived inventions; our scientific constructions are constrained by "how things are," and good science is the art of probing this constraint, a matter of discovery as well as invention. So the fundamental challenge to the human sciences is to find ways, conceptual and methodological, within our limited historical, cultural, and social context, to formulate processes and relationships in terms that transcend that context. I believe that our heightened awareness of the importance of contextual factors is the first essential step in moving beyond an unwitting state of history- and culture-boundedness. Awareness of the contextual limitations of our would-be generalizations is a step toward improved understanding that we have good grounds to hope will be less context-specific. We need to be able to stretch a little beyond our culturally and historically limited perspectives to have a chance at grappling productively with the enormous problems of our times.

I take the postmodernists' challenge seriously because, as we have seen, their attack on the ideal of truth as approachable if not finally attainable undercuts the basis of both scientific and applied psychology. Both aspects of psychology depend on our continuing commitment to *empiricism* in its sense of concern for *evidence*. We can quite properly debate what we will respect as evidence in the domains of our concern. We can also debate the norms of scientific practice in our areas of specialized competence, the seriousness of our argumentation reflecting our respect for the necessity and importance of such norms. (That is the context in which I interpret the demise of positivism.) In our time of pervasive hopelessness, we have good reason to retain our hope for *progress* in one last realm—the pursuit of understanding. Psychologists who give up this hope risk the loss of their constructive identity as scientists and practitioners, their justification for a role in restoring hope on a larger scale.

I have focused here on the challenge of postmodernism to the ideal of truth. Of course, its radical relativism also undercuts parallel human ideals (and evaluative frameworks of thought) concerning goodness and beauty. An examination of the extreme ethical relativism involved in some versions of multiculturalism—a current movement in the postmodern mode—would be equally relevant to social policy and practice in matters with which psychologists are concerned. (See, for example, Kağitçibasi, 1995.) In regard to truth, psychologists are warranted to act on the belief that good science remains a privileged approach.

References

Allport, G. W. (1937). *Personality: A psychological interpretation.* New York: Holt.

American Anthropological Association (1995). Commentary, by Lee Drummond, Timothy Earle, E. G. Hammel, and Daniel Little, *Anthropology Newsletter*, November, 1, 4, 9, 42–50, 52

American Anthropological Association (1996). Commentary, by Michael Agar and E. L. Cerroni-Long, *Anthropology Newsletter*, January, 15, 52.

Baltes, P. B. (1987). Theoretical propositions of life-span development psychology: On the dynamics between growth and decline. *Developmental Psychology, 23,* 611–626.

Bandura, A. (1977). Self-efficacy: Toward a unifying theory of behavioral change. *Psychological Review, 84,* 191–215.

Berger, P. L., & Luckmann, T. (1966). *The social construction of reality.* Garden City, NY: Doubleday.

Billig, M. (1991). *Ideology and opinions: Studies in rhetorical psychology.* London: Sage.

Boring, E. G. (1929). *A history of experimental psychology.* New York: Appleton-Century.

Bridgeman, P. W. (1927). *The logic of modern physics.* New York: Macmillan.

Campbell, D. C. (1991). Coherentist empiricism, hermeneutics, and the incommensurability of paradigms. *International Journal of Educational Research, 15* (6), 587–597.

Dilthey, W. (1976). *Selected writings.* (H. P. Rickman, Tr. & Ed.) Cambridge: Cambridge University Press.

Edelstein, W. (1983). Cultural constraints on development and the vicissitudes of progress. In F. S. Kessel & G. W. Siegel (Eds.) *Psychology and society: The child and other cultural inventions.* New York: Praeger.

Elder, G. H. (1994). Time, human agency, and social change: Perspectives on the life course. *Social Psychology Quarterly, 57,* 4–15.

Festinger, L. (1957). *A theory of cognitive dissonance.* Stanford, CA: Stanford University Press.

Fromm, E. (1941). *Escape from freedom.* New York: Farrar & Rinehart.

Gergen, K. J. (1973). Social psychology as history. *Journal of Personality and Social Psychology, 26,* 309–320.

Gergen, K. J. (1994). Exploring the post-modern: Perils or potentials? *American Psychologist, 49,* 412–416.

Giddens, A. (1991). *Modernity and identity: Self and society in the late modern age.* Stanford, CA: Stanford University Press.

Haste, H. (1993/1994). *The sexual metaphor.* Hemel Hempstead: Harvester Wheatsheaf/ Cambridge, MA: Harvard University Press.

Hull, C. L. (1943). *Principles of behavior.* New York: Appleton-Century-Crofts.

Kağitçibasi, C. (1995). Is psychology relevant to global human development issues? Experiences from Turkey. *American Psychologist, 50,* 293–300.

Kardiner, A. (1939). *The individual and his society.* New York: Columbia University Press.

Koch, S. (Ed.) (1959). *Psychology: A study of a science*, Vol. 3. New York: McGraw-Hill.

Kuhn, T. S. (1970). *The structure of scientific revolutions* (2nd edition). Chicago: University of Chicago Press.

Lerner, R. M. (1984). *On the nature of human plasticity*. New York: Cambridge University Press.

Lewin, K. (1935). A dynamic theory of personality. New York: McGraw-Hill.

Murray, H. A., et al. (1938). *Explorations in personality*. New York: Oxford University Press.

Peterson, C., Maier, S. F., & Seligman, M. E. (1993). *Learned helplessness: A theory for the age of personal control*. New York: Oxford University Press.

Polkinghorne, D. E. (1983). *Methodology for the human sciences: Systems of inquiry*. Albany, NY: State University of New York Press.

"Reason under fire" (1995). *Science, 268* (30 June), 1853.

Rogoff, B. (1990). *Apprenticeship in thinking: Cognitive development in social context*. New York: Oxford University Press.

Rorty, R. (1979). *Philosophy and the mirror of nature*. Princeton, NJ: Princeton University Press.

Rotter, J. R. (1966). Generalized expectancies for internal versus external control of reinforcement. *Psychological Monographs, 80* (1), Whole Number 609.

Sampson, E. E. (1993). Identity politics: Challenges to psychology's understanding. *American Psychologist, 48,* 1219–1230.

Schaie, K. W. (1965). A general model for the study of developmental problems. *Psychological Bulletin, 64,* 92–107.

Simons, H. W., & Billig, M. (1994). *After postmodernism: Reconstructing ideology critique*. London: Sage.

Smith, M. B. (1976). Social psychology, science, and history: So *what? Personality and Social Psychology Bulletin, 2,* 438–444.

Smith, M. B. (1991a). Psychology and the decline of positivism: The case for a human science. In R. Jessor (Ed.), *Perspectives on behavioral science: The Colorado symposium*. Boulder, CO: Westview. Reprinted in Smith (1991b).

Smith, M. B. (1991b). *Values, self, and society: Toward a humanist social psychology*. New Brunswick, NJ: Transaction.

Smith, M. B. (1994). Selfhood at risk: Postmodern perils and the perils of postmodernism. *American Psychologist, 49,* 405–411.

Snow, C. P. (1959). *The two cultures and the scientific revolution*. New York: Cambridge University Press.

Spence, D. (1982). *Narrative truth and historical truth: Meaning and interpretation in psychoanalysis*. New York: Norton.

Stevens, S. S. (1935). The operational definition of psychological concepts. *Psychological Review, 42,* 517–525.

Triandis, H., & Lambert, W. W. (Eds.). (1980–1981). *Handbook of cross-cultural psychology*. Boston, MA: Allyn & Bacon. 6 vols.

Vygotsky, L. S. (1978). *Mind in society*. Cambridge, MA: Harvard University Press.

Wertsch, J. V. (1985). *Vygotsky and the social formation of mind*. Cambridge, MA: Harvard University Press.

White, D. & Wang, A. (1995). Univeralism, humanism, and postmodernism. *American Psychologist, 50,* 392–393.

Name Index

Adams, D., 250, 251
Adams, H., 142
Adler, N., 14
Adorno, T. W., 21, 33, 188, 219, 221, 245, 287
Allport, G. W., 1, 5, 7, 8, 12, 13, 17, 37, 52, 54, 59–61, 71, 82, 89, 177, 188, 219, 220, 224, 225, 272
Almond, G., 128
Altemeyer, B., 21, 180, 255, 267
Anderson, J. W., 59
Aronson, E., 245
Asch, S. E., 24, 26
Atkinson, J. W., 61
Atkinson, R., 231

Back, K., 18
Bakan, D., 164, 175
Baltes, P. B., 291
Bandura, A., 170, 175, 181, 255, 291
Bateson, G., 53
Baumeister, R. F., 154, 155, 174, 176, 179, 254
Becker, E., 89, 135, 173, 254
Bellah, R. N., 164, 212
Benedict, R., 71
Bentley, A. F., 54, 181
Berger, P. L., 135, 149, 295
Bernstein, R., 41, 48
Billig, M., 291, 295
Blank, T., 26
Blatt, S. J., 164
Blight, J. G., 268, 270, 271
Block, J., 61, 63

Block, J. H., 189
Blumer, H., 15
Boring, E. G., 13, 293
Bourne, E. J., 73
Bray, D., 62
Breckler, S. J., 245
Brehm, S., 26
Brewer, M. B., 180
Bridgeman, P. W., 286
Bronfenbrenner, U., 249, 269
Broughton, J. M., 154
Brown, J. F., 11
Brown, N. O., 145, 146, 150
Bruner, J. S., 18, 19, 63, 87, 91, 151
Bugenthal, J. F. T., 273
Bury, J. B., 138, 149
Bush, V., 35
Butzer, K. W., 132, 149

Campbell, A., 17, 19
Campbell, D. T., 173, 215, 294
Cantril, H., 24, 205, 206
Carlson, R., 62, 88
Cartwright, D. O., 17, 18, 24
Chein, I., 21, 83, 228
Christie, R., 21
Clark, K. E., 21, 36, 228, 230
Clark, M. P., 36
Clark, R. A., 61
Clausen, J., 15
Cole, M., 89, 176
Collins, M. E., 21
Cook, S. W., 14, 21, 22, 202, 228, 230, 231

About the Author

M. Brewster Smith is Emeritus Professor of Psychology, University of California, Santa Cruz, and former president of the American Psychological Association.